# The Beginner's Guide to Launching a Private Label Supplement or Cosmetic Brand

# Forward

*Lorand Fabian, Ingredientsage™*

On and off, for a few decades, my office has been a front-row seat to the global manufacturing line. I have seen it first hand in America, Canada, South East Asia, India, China and Europe.

I've seen thousands of products designed, hundreds of brands launched, and countless entrepreneurs chase a dream. I have witnessed, down to the decimal point, what separates a fleeting idea from a sustainable, scalable brand.

The ugly truth is that the biggest bottleneck to a startup's success isn't manufacturing capacity, supply chain issues, or even a lack of funding.

It's the unprepared entrepreneur.

I have watched too many promising ventures fail or simply stall for months, sometimes years, not from a lack of vision, but from a fundamental lack of systematic preparation and process knowledge.

This book is my answer to that problem.

I wrote this guide to put the power of process back into your hands.

I've witnessed the complete journey of numerous brands that started with nothing and achieved monumental success.

This book is a synthesis of their winning common denominators, the essential prerequisites, strategies, and operational steps honed over two decades inside the contract manufacturing world.

My single greatest objective here is to equip you with the knowledge that makes you the ideal partner for any world-class private label manufacturer. When you walk into a partnership with a clear, documented understanding of your target costs, your compliance needs, and your next three steps, you eliminate the chaos, the constant changes, and the fighting of "bright ideas" that derail projects.

Clarity equals velocity.

This is not a book about marketing trends; it is a foundation builder.

It's the checklist I wish I could hand to every new entrepreneur before they spent their first dollar on inventory.

I ask you to treat this road map as your mandatory preparation course.

If you understand and implement the core requirements laid out in these pages, you won't just launch a product, you'll launch a sustainable business with a trusted manufacturing partner.

The private label journey is rarely a straight line; it is a dense, high-stakes convergence where seemingly disparate aspects must flawlessly intertwine. Successfully taking a product from concept to market demands more than just sequential checklists.

It requires the simultaneous execution of crucial steps, from rigorous **target cost modeling** and the complex navigation of **regulatory**

**compliance** to the parallel development of **packaging specifications** and the establishment of a robust **quality control protocol**.

Within these pages, we deliberately shine a different light on these interwoven elements, combining strategic insight with the tactical actions and activities that must be executed **concurrently**.

This systematic approach is designed to ensure that your attention is sharply focused on these critical, simultaneous tasks, eliminating the costly lag of bottlenecks and guaranteeing that no essential detail is overlooked or left to fall out of the process.

The path to building a successful brand still has its challenges, but it doesn't have to be long. I am excited to share the keys that will unlock your velocity.

Clearwater, Florida – September of 2025

# The Beginner's Guide to Launching a Private Label Supplement or Cosmetic Brand

Lorand Fabian

# CONTENTS

# Chapter I

## Foundations of Private Labeling

### *Section 1.*
### Basic Overview, Introduction to the Private Label Journey

Bringing a cosmetic or supplement product to market is a thrilling adventure, blending a captivating creative vision with unwavering regulatory precision.

This involves meticulously transforming an initial concept into a commercially triumphant product.

Launching a wellness or cosmetic idea into the hands of real customers begins with a simple spark and a clear road map.

In a field where a bottle's feel, a claim's truth, and a brand's story all matter, the craft is as vital as the spirit behind the product. The designer must create a look that protects the product, communicates the story, and supports the brand throughout the journey from conception to market-ready launch.

Think of a line of skincare whose elegant visuals are complemented by transparent labeling and easy-to-understand instructions. Real-world brands like Glossier show how a strong identity can drive demand.

The best packaging keeps safety and clarity front and center.

The regulatory arena is tight, but a clear structure lets the product stand out in a crowded market.

Bold wellness claims may be tempting, yet they must be scrutinized to meet regulatory standards. This balanced approach ensures every bottle not only looks good and delivers on its promise but also stands out in the competitive market.

Start by taking a practical look at your methods: map the rules, confirm what tests or substantiations are required, and document every step so your team can defend decisions if needed.

Follow this step-by-step guide to compliant product development, balancing imagination with restraint:

- Identify market gaps and opportunities.
- Develop a distinctive brand identity and framework.
- Ensure all regulatory requirements are met.
- Trademark your brand and protect your intellectual property.

While intellectual property is a critical first step, the distinct regulatory frameworks governing products like cosmetics and supplements also present unique challenges and considerations.

The wellness and cosmetics space are a veritable jungle. It encompasses skincare, makeup, and dietary aids, each governed by its own regulations, claims, and requirements.

These include those enforced by the FDA and FTC, and standards like Good Manufacturing Practices (GMP). Understanding and complying with these foundational concepts—crucial concepts you'll master in Chapter V—is paramount.

Applying these steps enables you to navigate this complexity, delivering a product that looks good, performs well, and meets every cosmetic standard from conception to launch.

The more you understand these differences, the more you avoid costly missteps and strike the right balance between your strategy and your action. To set realistic expectations for success, validate ideas through market research, craft a unique value proposition and brand identity, and develop a product that aligns with regulatory requirements.

Protect what you create through trademarking and other IP measures.

## 2. The private label mentality

The line is razor-sharp, and the only thing that separates a compliant company from a branding triumph is the decision that sparks its own metamorphosis: will this product stand the test of time or achieve rapid, but short-lived, success?

The opening of my private-label approach to wellness is the realization that we must navigate the realities of regulation while meeting the aspirations of consumers in a rational, coherent fashion. True signs confirm this: 73% of consumers see wellness as essential for a brand, and 75% feel brands could do more to make wellness worthwhile.

These numbers are not soft preferences; they set the baseline for trust and loyalty. Integrating compliance into every stage of product development is essential— it cannot be a shelf-stand for later.

Build a pre-approval checklist at the outset, covering every ingredient, claim, and label statement. Clarify roles and objectives so that the regulator, or your internal compliance team, is seen as the guardian of the brand's integrity.

By embedding compliance from the start, you avoid costly turnovers and product removals, and you demonstrate that the rightness of your product is clear in every way.

This clarity keeps the teams working together while meeting consumer standards.

Embrace consumer-centric thinking: make the user central to every choice, from ingredients to packaging to messaging. The product ideals must always stay at the center of analysis, ensuring they do not overrun the needs, pains, and pain points of the market while still meeting regulatory expectations.

The brand builds rapport on transparency, perceived trust, and stated values.

To earn trust, be explicit about ingredients, manufacturing steps, and compliance, and lay out everything buyers must know in a clear, consistent manner.

Publish a simple, verifiable ingredient and process page for each product.

Regulatory-aligned launches reduce risk, delays, and post-release removals.

Prepare validation documents, ensure label accuracy, and align claims with evidence from the outset, balancing speed to market with rigorous checks.

Build a timeline that prioritizes rapid iteration while maintaining safety, and test early to catch issues before major investment.

Developing successful private label wellness products necessitates a comprehensive strategy that meticulously integrates regulatory discipline with profound consumer insight.

This approach ensures the creation of high-quality, enduring products that genuinely serve diverse consumer needs.

### Key Takeaways:

- **Foundational Planning:** Integrate rigorous regulatory compliance and robust financial planning from the earliest stages of product development.
- **Strategic Alignment:** Clearly define the roles of regulatory bodies, branding objectives, and sourcing strategies, ensuring product concepts align with market demands and operational realities.
- **Controlled Execution:** Balance efficient development processes with diligent caution and continuous quality control to deliver superior products.

## 3. Entrepreneurs embrace supplements and cosmetics

In the crowded aisles of health, wellness and beauty, a quiet shift is reshaping the world, bringing new products to market—and for whom.

The private-labeling industry offers a fast, brand-led way, giving control over how a product looks, feels, and resonates with a particular audience.

It isn't a shortcut for everyone, but for the right entrepreneur it can grow into a potent force and propel the brand to the stratosphere.

Clarity, the compass for the venture, thrives only when the entrant is genuinely passionate about health, wellness, and branding, and has a clear vision for the brand story.

They truly understand their target buyers—their wants, motivations, and the moments of truth that shape purchase decisions.

This deep customer insight, coupled with a relentless commitment to partnership in production and compliance, makes them ideal candidates for private labeling.

Whether as a sales manager, a chief compliance officer, or a product manager, the right person must blend a customer-first mindset with practical tolerance for ambiguity. They should be ready to learn, adapt quickly to market shifts, test ideas, and adjust based on data—all while maintaining a clear vision for the brand story.

It lets the entrepreneur build a brand on their own terms, gaining the freedom to shape product, messaging, and packaging from the outset.

By launching quickly—before heavy overheads take hold—one can test the market, capture early interest, and refine the offering with real customer feedback.

This approach delivers immediate control over quality and fit, while unlocking cost discipline and the ability to scale as the product-market fit solidifies.

In short, it gives founders the luxury of creating a brand that truly resonates with their audience, all while keeping production and compliance in the hands of trusted partners.

With these examples, the practical rhythm is clear: define your audience as precisely as possible, test your products with compelling formulations, and refine the offering based on real responses.

**Actionable take-away**: first, identify a precise target segment and the benefit your private-labeled product will deliver. Second, map regulatory milestones early and partner with a reliable manufacturer and a knowledgeable advisor. Third, establish a rapid-iteration plan: short cycles, measurable feedback, and clear decision criteria.

With this clarity, the right founder turns the private-labeled concept into a brand with purpose, credibility, and momentum.

## 4. What you shall learn and expected practical outcomes

The greatest products start with a clear sense of purpose and a solid plan for how customers will discover them.

For a maker building a private-label brand, the journey from idea to market is a concrete series of decisions, tests, and refinements.

The focus is on practical action, real-world constraints, and measurable outcomes. Identifying market gaps and viable product opportunities is the first step in this rigorous market-sensing process, guiding you to the needs your product can fill.

To succeed, use data, observe consumer behavior, and act quickly on what you learn.

Start by following these key steps:

- Conduct thorough market research to identify trends, patterns, and gaps in the market.
- Assess the competition and saturation level, then evaluate the potential for profit.

- From this analysis, define a clear category that meets a real need—such as a clean-label cosmetic line for sensitive skin that offers genuine purity and value.
- Test the concept with pilot launches, refining or even redefining and reinventing the product until it resonates with the target segment.

Adherence to regulatory requirements, including accurate claims and proper labeling, is essential from the outset to build trust and ensure compliance.

By grounding every decision in measurable outcomes and staying focused on practical action, you'll turn insights into a viable, profitable product.

Be bold enough to define your brand:

- Develop a unique value proposition that sets your brand apart.
- Create a consistent visual identity—logos, packaging, and labeling—that reflects that proposition.
- Establish a tone of voice and brand messaging that resonates with your target audience.

**Tip:** study brands that already connect deeply with their customers—clean, purpose-driven cosmetics or wellness labels—and translate those lessons into your own distinctive voice.

Defining your brand extends beyond a mission statement; it encompasses its tangible representation.

Packaging, labeling, and trademark considerations are not afterthoughts; they are strategic assets and regulatory touch points.

A smart package supports safety, usability, and shelf presence while protecting your brand's intellectual property.

**Key considerations:**

- Ensure compliance with regulatory requirements for packaging and labeling.
- Protect your intellectual property through trademark registration.
- The ideal packaging strategy should align with your brand identity and meet regulatory requirements.
- Start with concrete market validation and a clear definition of your target audience.
- Match sustainable packaging with compliant, green labels to avoid misdirection.
- Safeguarding intellectual property via trademark registration is vital to protect your brand from imitators.
- Keep the design simple yet distinctive, ensuring it preserves your brand's market identity while meeting industry standards.

## 5. The credibility factor

The crowded shelves of private-label supplements tell a story.

In a market saturated with many brands and bold claims, low consumer trust makes transparency the real competitive advantage.

My own perspective anchors credibility in clear, actionable steps.

To truly build trust, brands must show exactly where ingredients are sourced, how purity is measured, and how their own production compares to what they buy.

For instance, imagine "PureForm Supplements" clearly detailing their ashwagandha comes from organic farms in Rajasthan, validated by third-party testing for heavy metals and active compounds, with a QR code linking to their Certificate of Analysis (COA).

This level of detail builds immediate confidence and establishes undeniable proof of quality.

By consistently sharing these critical details, you give customers confidence that what they take is pure, potent, and produced with disciplined control.

When a label clearly explains each ingredient's essential role and includes a reputable sourcing certificate, it becomes more than a marketing line, it becomes irrefutable evidence of quality.

Achieving this level of transparency requires a systematic approach.

Start early with thorough research and trend forecasting, define the precise product claims you want to support, and keep your calculations and formulas free of jargon.

Follow a clean, fair checklist that meets FDA and FTC guidelines, and you'll demonstrate that your marketing is grounded in real, verifiable facts rather than empty hype.

### Ensuring Product Compliance and Consumer Trust

A typical label contains a statement of identity, an ingredient list, a nutrition-like panel, and any required allergen and caution statements.

- **Integrate Compliance Checks:** Build a compliance check into your development sprints. Verify each claim against evidence, confirm that only permissible language is used, and keep thorough documentation for audits.
- **Leverage Third-Party Validation:** Third-party testing adds credibility. Seek lab results and certifications from reputable bodies such as NSF International or ConsumerLab.com and publish them.
- **Prioritize Transparency:** Clear ingredient disclosure, transparent manufacturing, and rigorous testing demonstrate that your marketing is grounded in verifiable facts and builds trust with consumers. Accessible, verifiable data for every claim, published transparently, is essential.

- **Certify Information:** Certify ingredient information as sound, complete, and correct, and obtain independent certifications to substantiate your claims and results.

## 6. The Tally System and SMART goals

Establish SMART goals (Specific, Measurable, Achievable, Relevant, Time-bound) for product success, focusing on actionable metrics like quarterly revenue targets, new SKU introduction quotas (e.g., 1-2 new SKUs per season), and repeat-buyer percentages (e.g., 20%).

Crucially, secure the intellectual property and exclusivity for your unique product formulations or designs to prevent market dilution and maintain competitive advantage.

Actively analyze market trends, consumer preferences, and pain points to identify specific gaps your products can fill.

Focus on under served niches or demographics to sharpen your product development strategy.

Proactively integrate compliance planning, intellectual property protection, and liability avoidance from the outset, asking:

What unmet needs exist?

How can my product uniquely address them?

Which market segments have significant demand exceeding current supply?

To effectively establish a private-label brand and translate its foundational concepts into a compelling, compliant offering that meets real consumer needs, one must build upon crisp concepts, precise execution, and a firm grasp of the rules governing product claims and labeling.

This practical application commences by utilizing basic templates and checklists for Product Concept, Positioning, and Storytelling, which articulate the brand's essence and communication strategy.

Subsequently, these adaptable templates should be tailored to fit specific product categories and target markets, ensuring core brand consistency is maintained.

Regulatory checklists must be thoroughly reviewed and validated by their outcomes. Products, labels, and branding require examination to confirm their authenticity and reliability.

This comprehensive evaluation process, referred to as the 'Tally System', includes critical tests such as intellectual property protection checks (e.g., trademark clearance) and product freshness assessments (e.g., shelf-life studies), alongside structured templates for developing the product concept, market positioning, and brand narrative—the foundational elements of a brand story.

The launch strategy should be developed in alignment with these findings.

The Tally System offers flexibility and adaptability.

- Branding, Packaging, and Claims: Tools to align branding with trademark considerations and to ensure product claims are legally supportable.
- Regulatory Checklists: Step-by-step guidance to meet FDA/FTC requirements and reduce compliance risk.
- Workflows for Supplier Vetting and Contracts: Standardized evaluations to safeguard intellectual property and assure product quality.
- Launch Plan Templates and KPI Trackers: Structures for milestones, funnels, and ROI, keeping your launch efforts on a measurable path.

**Using the Concepts:**

1. Start with the basics and become familiar in the concept, positioning, and storytelling templates and checklist
2. Adapt the templates and checklists to your brand and use it as your canvas.
3. Ensure compliance by walking through the regulatory checklists before any external commitments to make sure that nothing has been skipped or overlooked
4. Have in your processes clear, reliable workflows that also build strong partnerships as you may need to rely on external help and consultants too. Assign responsibilities and timelines.
5. Prepare a launch plan using the ready-made templates, tracking KPIs and refining tactics as you go.

Practical application steps come from real-brand case studies of cosmetics and supplements, show how teams shape concepts, position products, and enter markets.

Use specific product features, consumer insights, and brand identity clues in your templates, stay flexible to market signals, and monitor progress regularly to keep your course on track.

## 7. Sequence of events: moving from idea to product

Developing a shelf-ready product sets a strict timeline, with clear decision gates that keep momentum strong.

### Milestones and Gates

- **Idea Generation** – Spot a market gap your product can fill.
- **Market Research** – Uncover consumer needs, trends, and preferences to validate the concept.
- **Product Definition** – Pin down features, benefits, specifications, and regulatory requirements.

- **Regulatory Compliance** – Confirm that all applicable rules and standards are met.
- **Supplier Selection** – Find a reliable maker who can deliver to your specifications.
- **Product Testing** – Verify quality and safety across all relevant tests.
- **Launch Preparation** – Plan marketing, packaging, and distribution so you can launch confidently.

Private label and white label offer several key benefits:

*Cost Savings: the manufacturer handles R&D and upfront development (see Chapter VI. Finding and Vetting Manufacturers), as the product is already perfected.*

*Speed to Market: Products that face consumer resistance are quickly removed from shelves in today's market.*

*Reality: your offering should align with the brand identity providing what the market is asking for*

*Assess the readiness of your product before proceeding:*

- *Brand Identity: is your brand clearly defined?*
- *Market Demand: is there a tangible need for your product?*
- *Financial Resources: do you have the funds for its development and marketing?*

To effectively identify consumer trends and behavior, it's important to consider several key aspects: understanding consumer demand in health and wellness, specifically for healthy and sustainable alternatives.

- **Sustainability**: the packaging, sourcing, and life-cycle impact matter.
- **Personalization**: your products reflect personal taste.

- **Using market information**: obtain credible signals on trends and buyer behavior.
- **Sales Data Analysis**: Analyze data to reveal patterns that inform strategic prioritization.
- **Product Definition and Sourcing**: Define product criteria, assess feasibility, and evaluate supplier capabilities.
- **Regulatory Compliance**: Align with all relevant regulations and understand critical distinctions.
- **Product Safety**: Prioritize safe usage and materials, ensuring product integrity.
- **Labeling Requirements**: Ensure labels meet applicable standards, including understanding distinctions between cosmetic and supplement regulations (e.g., FDA's Center for Food Safety and Applied Nutrition, DSHEA).
- **Minimum Order Quantities (MOQs):** Understand their impact on cost and operational efficiency.
- **Lead Times:** Anticipate and manage production and delivery timelines.
- **Testing and Quality Control:** Implement and confirm robust testing and quality control protocols.
- **Brand Identity Foundations:** Articulate your unique value proposition and market stance.
- **Brand Messaging and Communication:** Define a clear brand voice, proposition, and factual safeguards, especially for private label offerings.

## 8. Glossary of words you shall meet in this long journey

For a comprehensive glossary of key private-label terms, including detailed explanations of COA, GMP, and regulatory frameworks, please refer to the Glossary of Terms.

## *Section 2.*

## *Foundations: private label, white label; consumer trends; regulations differences*

Bringing a unique product to market quickly and efficiently often hinges on the right partnerships.

The first step is to distinguish between private-label and white-label models, each offering different levels of brand control, speed to market, and capital investment.

Building a compelling brand narrative and visual identity is essential to earn consumer confidence and make the product stand out.

Preparing for launch means staying attuned to market trends, securing reliable suppliers, safeguarding intellectual property, and committing to sustainability for long-term success.

## *1. What does private label mean in wellness and cosmetics*

When bringing a product to market, a team faces two main routes: private label and white label.

Both involve working closely with a third-party manufacturer, yet they differ significantly in control, timing, and brand ownership.

Private label gives you the greatest control over every detail, from formulation and packaging to naming and marketing claims, so the finished product feels unmistakably yours.

This route allows you to retain full ownership of your brand and existing formulas, but it also requires a longer development cycle and more hands-on involvement.

White label, on the other hand, offers a quicker path to market.

With pre-made products ready to be branded with minimal changes, it allows you to focus on positioning and branding while the manufacturer handles the core product formulation.

The trade-off is that you have less control over the final formula, packaging, and messaging, and any tweaks require coordination, testing, and validation.

Choosing between the two depends on your desired level of brand control, the time you can commit to the launch, and your tolerance for risk.

By partnering with manufacturers, you gain access to proven, tested bases that you can package, brand, and market under your own name.

This approach provides the advantage of a reliable platform while saving you the expense and time of starting from scratch.

You can focus your marketing resources on entering new markets, and the speed of market entry is a key benefit.

For instance, 'Honeyskin' a well-known brand in the skincare and hair care industry, particularly focused on products made with natural and organic ingredients, with manuka honey as a signature component, leveraged a manufacturer's per-formulated, regulatory-compliant formulas to quickly introduce its premium line, rapidly capturing a segment of the competitive wellness cosmetics market.

Regulatory readiness, ingredient transparency, compliance with claims, and packaging standards is essential, especially in wellness cosmetics.

By building on a solid foundation, you can concentrate on brand strategy and avoid costly missteps.

While these strategic partnerships provide a strong operational foundation, success ultimately hinges on meticulously building trust and ensuring rigorous compliance.

A brand that delivers clear, reliable safety signals to regulators and consumers earns trust and keeps costly corrections to a minimum.

Establishing and adhering to Good Manufacturing Practices (GMP) through robust contracts, manufacturer audits, and third-party testing is fundamental for product quality and regulatory compliance.

This disciplined approach not only satisfies regulatory requirements but also sharpens the messaging and packaging, effectively differentiating private-label brands in the marketplace through consistent quality and enforcement.

A compelling brand story, effective visuals, and precise claims build consumer trust and loyalty. The narrative should be engaging, the imagery impactful, and the assertions accurate.

Start by mapping goals: control and timeline versus speed and scalability. Assess regulatory readiness early, plan for audits, and integrate quality assurance processes like GMP testing and transparent records. Use a real-world example, such as Kirkland Signature at Costco to demonstrate how strong branding and rigorous quality can drive success.

This level of integrity will differentiate the brand in the marketplace.

The framework defines a clear methodology for the product line, outlining concrete steps, operational modes, and practical checklists to facilitate its strategic development.

## 2. What I find most attractive about the private label

A founder with a sharp idea and a shoestring budget can prove that a low capital barrier to entry is a real advantage.

In the world of physical goods, private-label programs shorten the time from idea to shelf, allowing you to get your product to market quickly, learn from early feedback, and move faster than competitors who rely on larger investments.

They amplify this speed by providing an established manufacturing framework, ready-made certificates of authenticity (COAs), quality documentation, agreed minimum orders (MOQs), and scalable production options.

This approach lets you start with a small batch to learn what customers really want before committing to full-scale production, keeping capital flowing and risk low.

With the right supplier network, you can pilot prototypes, test packaging concepts, and refine specs without tying up inventory.

The result is a strategy that lets you test the market, refine your offering, capture market attention quickly, and grow cash flow—all without the heavy upfront costs that often stall new ventures.

The system allows for rapid adjustments in product shape and form, eliminating the need for large sample stockpiles.

Quick iterations become standard practice, enabling comprehensive testing and idea validation with minimal waste.

This enables a shift from generic messaging to specific value propositions that resonate with the target audience, ensuring brand stories are highly relevant.

This approach offers clear benefits: reduced inventory costs and faster, more precise product development.

Improved agility: limited runs and ready-made supplier templates enable rapid response to feedback.

Improved product-market fit: validation with minimal investment and repetitive refinement.

Enhanced brand positioning: testing messages and packaging, then refining based on data.

Real-world example: Amazon Basics demonstrates how a disciplined private-label approach can test and scale across categories by starting with essential products, validating the line quickly, and expanding in response to customer signals.

This strategy enables a shift from generic messaging to specific value propositions that resonate with the target audience, ensuring brand stories are highly relevant.

To effectively prepare for product launch and market assessment, ensure the following steps are completed:

Define the product concept, detailing:

- Required Certificates of Analysis (COAs)
- Minimum Order Quantities (MOQs)
- Lead times
- Two distinct packaging concepts
- Two primary messages
- Two market angles for testing
- Two projected cash flow lines

## 3. Market trends: wellness, beauty, personalization, and science-backed claims

On the surface the wellness and beauty aisles promise a simple equation: feel better, look better.

Yet a closer look reveals a market in motion, driven by new tools, smarter sourcing, and a richer understanding of what people want from the products they use every day.

For anyone building a private-label brand this is not a static snapshot but a set of moving parts that must be counted, aligned with, and responded to with speed and clarity.

To succeed, a private-label effort must begin with an unshakable grasp of the forces shaping demand.

Consumers are not just buying products; they are selecting solutions that fit their evolving routines, preoccupations, and values.

The market is growing at the speed of life, and the wellness sector is expanding as people return to holistic ways of living.

In beauty, consumers seek personalized solutions that fit their unique routines and values, not a one-size-fits-all approach.

This demand is relentless, and brands must deliver science-backed claims and clear, credible descriptions to meet it.

By understanding these forces, a private-label effort can identify gaps, craft fast-fit offerings, and keep every promise true.

In fact, 73 per cent of consumers say they trust brands more when they know about ingredients and processes and can see clearly the ultimate result of a single product.

Practical implication: build modular formulations, offer adaptable packaging, and present measurable data for claims.

Track wellness rituals and beauty routines, helping customers achieve targeted goals such as stress relief, better sleep, and healthy aging.

Growing interest in self-care drives demand for products that promote relaxation, reset, and rejuvenation.

Consumers now expect clear, science-backed claims and transparent ingredient sourcing.

A coherent value proposition backed by certified ingredients and supplier reports, helps win trust and scale responsibly.

By pairing complementary items into cohesive routines, designers can meet these expectations.

- Ensure labeling, sourcing, and efficacy data are fully transparent.
- Align product development with sustainability, self-care, and performance goals.
- Address regulatory considerations early to avoid costly rework.


## 4. Understanding consumer behavior and trust signals

On a crowded shelf a label can speak before you touch it; the first impulse is often an instinct that steers you toward a choice.

When you launch a private-label brand, establishing buyer confidence is what nudges that decision, not a cold calculation but a strong relationship with the buyer.

Positive emotions—comfort, pride, relief—drive purchases and build loyalty, while negative ones seize attention.

Brands that project calm, light, and dependability win steadily, because the emotion behind the purchase is the real driver of choice.

A simple, consistent presentation across packaging and marketing signals that a brand is steady in its promise.

When the design is clear and truthful, consumers feel the care and material intent of the product at first glance, reducing doubt and risk.

Trust signals—quality and transparency, accurate product claims, and social proof through ratings and reviews—are the main cues that guide a purchase decision.

Brand Storytelling: Meaningful narratives that align with customer values foster stronger customer connection and shared purpose.

When a brand demonstrates these qualities, credibility increases, leading to a greater willingness to buy.

Packaging, often the first tangible touchpoint, signals the brand's values and quality before a single feature claim is read.

It is not merely about containment; it is a communication tool that reflects the brand's standards.

For example, Apple's minimalist, well-finished packaging instantly conveys premium engineering and careful curation, establishing trust.

Well-designed packaging and a cohesive design language communicate a brand's commitment to product quality and the buyer's experience, reaffirming credibility and elevating value.

This is further enhanced by accurate product claims and precise labels, which create a consistent and dependable signal.

The ultimate effect is a unified message of confidence, ensuring product integrity and reliability, and establishing true credibility when the product consistently reflects the brand's promise across all channels.

Encouraging praise from satisfied buyers expands the pool of positive signals that others can trust.

High-quality reviews and transparent replies sharpen the legitimacy of the brand, while compelling stories, rooted in clear origins, ethical values, and real impact, serve as powerful symbols of credibility.

When these narratives resonate across every channel, product pages, ads, and information sites, they create a unified brand image that reassures customers and displaces anxiety.

By tapping into this emotional pulse, we can craft packaging and copy that deliver the key results this category deserves, all while maintaining a consistent, reliable voice that feels both confident and authentic.

Invest in honest labeling and verify that all performance aligns with your brand's standards.

Engage customers transparently, respond to their comments, and weave a compelling brand story that shines through every envelope, page, and letter. Ensure consistency across all channels, correcting misalignment swiftly and subtly.

Study proven examples: Patagonia's environmental transparency, Dove's inclusive storytelling, Warby Parker's social proof and value-led positioning, and Apple's packaging as a quality signal.

### 5. Cosmetics against supplements: the regulatory realities and market conditions

The worlds of cosmetics and dietary supplements are governed by specific regulatory frameworks.

The FDA ensures product safety, labeling, and claims, while the FTC protects consumers from deceptive advertising. These foundational regulations are critical for brand success.

Good Manufacturing Practices (GMP) provide a rigorous framework for product manufacturing, testing, and shipping, ensuring purity, consistency, and safety.

Label claims for beneficial effects must be scientifically supported.

Such claims must also include disclaimers clarifying that products are not intended to diagnose, treat, cure, or prevent any disease.

These standards protect consumers and safeguard brand reputation.

Transparent packaging and marketing, coupled with clear, evidence-based labeling and honest communication, are crucial for building consumer trust and ensuring long-term success.

Brands that disclose product ingredients and back claims with evidence foster credibility and protect their reputation in a competitive marketplace.

Winning consumer trust involves establishing a strong rapport with regulators through clear, evidence-based practices like GMP compliance and third-party testing.

These certifications enhance brand credibility and signal proven quality.

Robust intellectual property (IP) protection further safeguards the brand against counterfeits, preserving long-term value and fostering buyer confidence across all sales channels.

Regulatory readiness is paramount for market success and brand credibility.

## 6. Quality expectations, certifications, and third-party credibility

In markets where choices are marked "privately-labeled," the only common thread between you and your competitors becomes the brand you can rely on.

The system that delivers quality begins to define what counts, so the first question a market must ask is:

What are our standards of safety, efficacy, and consistency?

We begin by defining the initial product concept, set clear acceptance criteria, and then move into product development.

Here, ingredient criteria are specified, performance targets are fixed, and the quality of the product is measured at every stage from design through production to validation, so that no one is left untouched by this principle of quality.

Manufacturing requires robust process controls, batch traceability, and clean-room practices.

Quality control must set testing frequencies, sampling plans, and acceptance criteria for every SKU.

Partners should meet or exceed these expectations through regular reviews and corrective-action plans.

Certifications prove what a brand can achieve; where such standards are absent, the public remains unaware of the true quality.

Demonstrating a serious stance builds internal confidence and earns external trust, making certification the engine of success in public relations.

In a market where transparency is paramount, brands align their development and manufacturing with recognized standards like GMP and ISO 9001.

They then earn retailer or independent trademark seals, which signify the highest quality.

This approach involves an ingredient transparency and honesty that sets new industry benchmarks.

To substantiate product safety and composition, and to separate claims from marketing, the following are crucial:

- Rely on independent tests and lab results for validation.
- Include third-party testing for key claims and ingredients.
- Maintain easy access to all documentation necessary for audits and customer queries.

Additionally, establishing a clear, concise Quality Charter, covering all phases of development, manufacturing, and QC, provides a significant advantage.

To demonstrate quality, adopt standards such as GMP for manufacturing hygiene or ISO 9001 for quality management, and keep open copies of validation results.

Achieving third-party certifications like GMP and ISO independently validates product quality, providing a strong signal of reliability and prestige to shoppers and retailers.

Further enhance credibility by using independent tests to verify ingredient safety and label claims, leveraging third-party seals to drive performance on every shelf.

## 7. To Brand Storytelling vs Commodity Products: Lessons from Ritual and The Ordinary

On crowded shelves, a brand that communicates with clarity and consistency establishes a deeper connection with consumers, evolving beyond a mere product to a trusted presence.

This fosters a sense of assurance and transforms the buying experience into a consistent engagement that justifies price and builds loyalty.

Brand storytelling shapes values, mission, and personality into a cohesive narrative that integrates across every touchpoint, guiding the consumer subtly.

This narrative can be significantly amplified by incorporating archetypes, particularly those related to personal rituals, which establish a deeper, more resonant connection with consumers and further guide their purchasing decisions.

The result is a natural premium perception, positioning the brand as an essential, integrated component of daily life.

Consumers are willing to pay a premium for a superior experience.

This willingness to pay a premium, in turn, allows certain brands or retailers to establish their offering such that the premium becomes a prerequisite for accessing their distinct, superior experience.

Therefore, a product's value extends beyond its basic function to how effectively it performs that function, offering transparency in its proposition.

Brands can demonstrate their value through a clear, vivid, lucid, and personal story, or by justifying a premium price through perceived quality.

A compelling narrative makes the brand stand out, justifies its price with clear value, and cultivates lasting loyalty.

It is based on three pillars:

-differentiation: a distinct story that sets the brand apart.

-justification of price: a precise account of the product's worth and benefits.

-loyalty: an engaging narrative that fosters repeat purchases.

By weaving these elements together, the brand can create a memorable, authentic story that resonates with its audience and supports a premium position in a crowded market.

While the brand image is primarily visual, its underlying story remains consistent across all touch points: packaging, typography, color, and other final cues.

Consistent alignment between image and story fosters immediate brand recognition.

This consistency is further enhanced by adherence to rigorous regulatory discipline: clear, verifiable claims protect consumers and ensure the brand image is transparent and truthful.

When visual elements and language are perfectly aligned, the premium perception is strengthened and sustained.

To achieve this, a practical checklist should include:

- Defining the brand's core purpose and mapping it to visual representation.
- Auditing packaging and typography to ensure they convey the brand story clearly, verifiable, and honestly.
- Establish guidelines for tone, language, and consistency across all touch points.

By embracing these elements, brands not only attract attention but also earn trust, enabling a durable premium perception and a loyal customer base.

## 8. Risk factors and potential landmines in private labeling

On Amazon or TikTok or on a crowded shelf, a private-label line faces the same scrutiny as any product requiring sustained consumer engagement.

Product longevity is critical for brand success.

Success relies on a foundation built not on individual successes but on disciplined, repeatable practices that manage risk and maintain quality.

From the outset, it is essential to identify potential risks such as a sudden regulatory recall of a key ingredient or an unexpected quality control failure and recognize the stability that disciplined practices provide.

This establishes that the brand must maintain its trustworthiness and longevity.

The practical guidelines established early will be crucial for brand protection and sustained reputation.

In cosmetics and supplements, the rule books are often complex, covering labeling, claims, and testing requirements across many agencies.

It is essential to stay on top of these details so that compliance errors do not stall growth.

A useful illustration comes from medical product development: reported outcome measures reveal how a product performs in safety and efficacy, providing claims that withstand scrutiny.

**Actionable takeaways:**

- Create a risk map early, covering the product, suppliers, and target markets, and revisit it periodically.
- Track labeling, testing, and permitted claims by region, and schedule regular reviews.
- Consider how outcome measures or data points can inform your claims, even if the product is not medical.

Prioritize supply-chain resilience and quality control, as these remain essential throughout all operations.

A resilient supply chain is the backbone of reliable availability and stable pricing.

Prepare by forecasting potential disruptions, diversifying suppliers, and maintaining safety stock to avoid shortages. Rigorous quality control, starting with a thorough first inspection and a first-in, first-out readiness plan, ensures that every batch meets standards.

Protecting intellectual property and vetting suppliers guard against copycats and brand confusion, giving customers confidence in your products and your dealings.

To protect intellectual property, maintain quality, and build customer confidence in your products and dealings, the following proactive steps are recommended:

1. **Ensure Trademark Compliance:** Verify that every brand name, logo, and packaging design is free from infringement on existing trademarks.

2. **Conduct Thorough Supplier Vetting:** Implement comprehensive checks to avoid counterfeit or shoddy manufacturers.

3. **Require Partner Verification:** Demand audits, certifications, and traceable documentation to confirm partners are bona fide.

4. **Proactively Monitor IP:** Routinely monitor for changes and potential problems in names and marks before they arise.

5. **Establish Clear Contract Controls:** Set clear contract controls and define delivery terms with partners.

6. **Prepare Emergency Procedures:** Develop emergency recall procedures.

7. **Implement Financial Safeguards:** Set price and duty safeguards.

8. **Create Crisis Communication Plans:** Develop crisis communication plans to minimize disruption.

Draft a concise supplier agreement that includes:

- Explicit Minimum Order Quantities (MOQs)
- Clear change-control processes
- Defined delivery expectations
- A comprehensive recall plan with assigned roles
- Provisions for insuring against and adapting to the impact of new regulations
- Safeguards for intellectual property
- Commitments to product quality

Regularly review the agreement and stay abreast of all vital developments so nothing catches you by surprise.

This proactive approach safeguards your brand, keeps customers confident, and minimizes disruption during crises.

## 9. *Sustainability as a competitive angle in private label*

Look carefully at the items on the shelf and you will see more than just ingredients and packaging.

You'll notice a set of choices that hint at the brand's values, signaling the ethical standards that will guide every step from design to delivery.

Start with a clear strategy that integrates sustainability as a core brand value.

Ensure these ethical standards are applied throughout every policy, in the selection of materials, and in the sourcing and formulation of products, so that the brand's responsibility is evident from the factory to the customer's home.

Efforts to elevate supplier and brand standards, alongside advancing environmental performance, demand genuine commitment.

Without it, brands risk undermining their credibility and ethical integrity.

While strategies and product formulations are developed to meet anticipated standards of ecological purity, the practical reality is often different.

Brands, despite publishing supply chains, frequently grant themselves considerable latitude in outsourcing environmentally detrimental activities.

For example, a cosmetics brand might promote its 'natural' and 'sustainable' ingredients while quietly contracting with a supplier that uses highly polluting processing methods or unsustainable harvesting practices for its raw materials.

This enables them to secure rewards from official agencies for their declared 'responsibility,' even when their actions contradict these claims.

This raises a critical question: what authentic message can a brand genuinely uphold when its professed values are presented through a superficial facade of transparency?

Clear labeling of recyclability, compostability, and waste reduction empowers consumers to act on what they learn.

Transparency also gives regulators the data they need.

When brands publish such labels and support them with independent validation standards, they become credible at every point in the chain, and trust is built in both the supplier standards and the traceability of the product.

These data-driven standards raise confidence for regulators and customers alike, fostering a healthier, more responsible supply chain.

Educating consumers is essential.

To foster the adoption of sustainable lifestyles, organizations must apply the same rigor in providing data, evidence, audits, and certifications for their internal practices and claims as they do for their products, campaigns, and branding.

Validating sustainability claims necessitates verifiable documentation, including comprehensive data, audits, and independent third-party certification.

When an organization acts as a "private label" or communicates standards related to its supply chain, it must implement concrete supplier standards, ensure transparent packaging, and secure independent certification for these elements.

Organizations should implement transparent packaging and clearly identify the responsible parties for its implementation.

They must establish clear, auditable rules to ensure compliance and build consumer confidence, providing a tangible guarantee for purchasing decisions.

Consumer education should extend beyond merely informing about sustainable actions, also highlighting the beneficiaries of these efforts and ensuring that everyone benefits from improved environmental practices.

The integrity of private label products and claims must be safeguarded with such certainty that consumers are protected from any potential deception.

## *10. Actionable foundations for success*

Integrate voice-of-customer research, competitive benchmarking, and regulatory checklists *early in development* to shape product specifications, labels, and safety claims.

Proactively clarify the project scope, expected outcomes, and implications, defining what aspects are critical, the degree of customization permitted, and the compliance standards to be met.

This ensures every decision aligns with both consumer demand and regulatory mandates.

Proactively define and protect all intellectual property (IP) rights including trademarks, trade-dress, and proprietary formulations through clearly drafted agreements.

These agreements are crucial for preventing scope creep, clarifying ownership, and avoiding costly revisions.

By carefully mapping legal pathways, you can identify strategic opportunities and mitigate risks while maintaining compliance.

Leverage trend reports, rapid feedback loops, and competitive analysis to proactively identify market gaps.

Ensure robust quality control by verifying label accuracy, backing all claims with solid sources, and vetting every supplier.

Crucially, define project scope, roles, and intellectual property protections *early* in a written agreement, maintaining clear and current regulatory pathways.

This integrated approach builds credibility, fosters customer trust, and enables agile adaptation to new opportunities.

Actively monitor emerging market trends, shifting consumer preferences, and technological advancements to pinpoint genuine gaps or unmet needs within your target audience.

Once these opportunities are identified, adopt a lean and agile approach to rapidly test potential solutions or concepts through methods like small-scale pilot programs, A/B testing, or quick prototyping, minimizing resource expenditure while maximizing learning.

Simultaneously, build and maintain strong customer trust by ensuring absolute transparency in all aspects, particularly through clear and comprehensive labeling that details product ingredients, sourcing, production processes, or data origins and usage.

Reinforce this commitment with rigorous, well-documented quality checks and controls implemented at every stage of development and delivery, guaranteeing consistent excellence, safety, and reliability.

# Chapter II

## Choosing the Right Product

### *Section 1.*
### *The gaps and viability scores; the product categories; the form factors; the shelf-life...and more*

Successful products emerge from rigorous market inquiry, not just novel concepts.

This disciplined approach immediately clarifies genuine demand, assesses viability, and profiles your target audience by uncovering their true needs and willingness to pay.

Combining a concise viability study with deep consumer and competitive insights, market inquiry provides the essential evidence to confidently transform a concept into a truly innovative and differentiated solution, ensuring strategic positioning and profitability from the outset.

### *1. Market gap identification, where opportunity lives*

Before prototype development, a private-label team can identify crucial insights: the essence of a successful launch lies not in pursuing dominant trends, but in identifying and addressing genuine market gaps.

By pinpointing a real customer need and supporting it with a credible supply path, the team ensures the product meets demand from the outset.

When a market gap is identified, a well-crafted solution demonstrates inherent viability, confirming that genuine needs represent reliable opportunities.

Effective teams combine thorough market research with user feedback, alongside monitoring fundamental industry developments.

The objective is to identify unmet needs or deficiencies that can be addressed at various scales, prioritizing opportunities with substantial market potential.

Identifying unfulfilled needs, market trends, and regulatory opportunities is a critical aspect of discovery.

To begin, look for unmet needs: what customers truly want and what existing options fail to deliver.

Then examine the market trends—those currents that shape demand and create opportunities for new products.

Finally, consider regulatory shifts and emerging standards that open space for differentiated offerings.

For instance, the rise of electric vehicles, driven by both consumer demand for sustainability and stricter emissions regulations, created an entirely new market for charging infrastructure and battery technology.

By weaving together these three strands customer gaps, market dynamics, and regulatory possibilities, you can pinpoint the shape, size, and features that will best satisfy the gap and align with future merchandising requirements.

This integrated view guides any growing business toward a product that fits the market, meets compliance, and thrives in the evolving landscape.

With a product concept defined to meet market needs and regulatory standards, its practical execution and long-term success depend on various operational factors.

A practical product viability framework illustrates how its four key elements, demand, competition, margins, and risks, interact to determine a product's overall viability.

By understanding these forces, a company can define appropriate branding, prioritize clear consumer intent, and balance cost against benefit.

A well-defined consumer profile is essential for market success. It ensures:

- Concise messaging
- Optimized packaging
- Effective channel alignment
- An appropriate tone and strategic audience focus

Sustaining demand beyond a single season requires a company to validate trends, gather early data, and test hypotheses.

This process helps identify unmet needs and regulatory shifts.

The objective is to align product attributes and form with market realities.

This ensures the consumer profile remains relevant and market opportunities persist.

This disciplined approach enables a brand to:

- Establish an appropriate tone
- Prioritize clear consumer intent
- Balance cost against benefit

Ultimately, this delivers convenience, cost savings, and stronger market share.

Use a simple scoring rubric to prioritize opportunities with real potential, and define the target buyer, their motive, and their readiness to pay to guide every design decision.

## 2. Defining customer personas for supplements and cosmetics

In the crowded world of wellness brands, you win by buying what you sell, by knowing who will buy it and why.

The real key is to understand the core motivations and psychology of your customer, not just the price or performance of the product.

Start with a clear, research-backed portrait of your ideal customer, a customer persona that cuts across demographics, psychographics, and behaviors.

This persona guides every decision, from formulation and packaging to advertising and distribution, ensuring that what you sell truly resonates with the people who will buy it.

By aligning your product with the needs and desires of that persona, you create a win-win: you sell more, you build loyalty, and you keep your profits high.

In wellness, these portraits help you anticipate safety concerns, preferred communication styles, and the aspects of a product that matter most to your audience.

By creating detailed profiles, you guide every stage of the design process from formulation and packaging to advertising and distribution, ensuring that the product not only meets real needs but also surprises and delights the consumer.

A well-crafted persona grounds your strategy in the realities of your target, revealing distinct safety requirements, ingredient preferences, and convenience considerations.

Expand on your archetypes by including Health-Eater, Fitness-Conscious, Busy-Professional, Cosmetic-User, Beauty-Seeker, Health-Conscious Consumer, and Skincare Enthusiast.

Each highlights different priorities, longevity, performance, efficiency, appearance, natural ingredients, and ingredient knowledge.

Gather data through surveys, interviews, and analytics, then translate it into expert personas.

Understand how you made your buying choices and why, so you can build realistic, accurate representations of your target audience.

To effectively engage customers, you must weave together several key elements.

These include the pain points and goals your product addresses, how customers research and evaluate options, and the safety and efficacy concerns that drive their purchasing decisions.

Start by gathering data through surveys, interviews, and analytics.

Then, translate this data into expert personas that capture the real motivations behind buying choices.

Use clear, reassuring language for important disclosures.

These include:

- Safety statements
- Ingredient sourcing
- Third-party testing

Present these disclosures consistently across all channels, such as social media, advertising, influencer reviews, and your website.

By laying out the information in the exact language your audience understands, you build trust and guide them smoothly from curiosity to purchase.

When a team effectively communicates a unified, evidence-based understanding of their audience and its marketing (provided the organizational culture is supportive and open), the business gains credibility, customer satisfaction improves, and performance becomes more action-able.

To achieve this, we recommend the following process for developing a comprehensive brief:

- **Define Personality Archetypes:** Create a brief outlining 3 to 5 personality archetypes, including at least one primary and several secondary archetypes.
- **Gather and Validate Data:** Collect data through at least two methods (e.g., surveys and interviews), validate each data point, and then synthesize this information into your summary brief.
- **Refine Message:** Eliminate any content that is not essential or immediately relevant to the message's purpose.

### 3. Competitive landscape analysis

The shelves of retail reveal stories in real time: they show who is in business, how customers think and decide, and where opportunities hide in plain sight.

Competitive Market Mapping is about creating a practical map that lets you position your private-label brand with clarity, speed, and confidence.

By understanding market dynamics, you can see where rivals stand, why they fail to cross the line, and where gaps exist.

This insight gives you actionable openings to fill those gaps with value, quality, and experience, helping you stand out in a crowded marketplace and achieve market success.

The people you need to know are those with the most obvious competitors and the groups they serve. Your products, strengths, weaknesses, and strategies should guide how you act.

Consider Trader Joe's, where a private label becomes a compelling proposition, and the home-goods examples of Costco's Kirkland Signature and Walmart's Great Value, which illustrate different routes to value in large volumes.

From these cases you learn the real issue: the choice of which first-class segment to pursue and which segments to focus on must be determined by you.

In premium-goods setting, the brand must carve out a distinct niche for a specific audience, using value, quality, or storytelling as the core differentiators.

A sharp analysis looks beyond the product itself to packaging, usability, and the real contexts in which customers operate.

By examining features, fit within the market, and practical use cases, you can identify how your line can surpass competitors, whether through simpler, more resealable packaging, a deeper use case, or a more compelling story.

Pricing and promotion strategies should mirror this insight, aligning your price points with rivals while highlighting the added value your private label delivers to the target segment.

Look for discount patterns, bundle offers, and the sweet timing of promotions.

This insight will point you to opportunities for competitive pricing bands and promotions that strike the pulse of your audience while protecting your margins.

By recognizing Strengths, Weaknesses, and Gaps, examine potential entry points for your brand, and by knowing how regulatory and other rules are handled in the interest of uniformity, you will have a compliant strategy in line with industry practice, while avoiding the risk of falling behind or losing competitive advantage.

**Buying and Selling Signals** require you to understand what your suppliers and potential competitors are doing, where they are, and why, so that you can secure a reliable source of margins and a strong foothold in the field.

How many brands depend on the same manufacturers?

Examine supply-chain resilience and the potential for differentiation through buying or sourcing. Capture rivals' tone, packaging, and storytelling to understand how competitors present themselves, then adapt and subvert those cues to build a distinctive identity.

Start by listing the top competitors and the segments they serve, grouping players by product type and audience.

Look for gaps, measure form factors, usage contexts, and packaging details, and map pricing and promotions to uncover value opportunities.

Ensure your regulatory language aligns with industry standards while you forge a compliant, differentiated strategy.

Examine supplier operations to understand their business practices, profit strategies, and core identity. This detailed analysis should inform and shape your own professional approach and style.

## 4. Shelf life and stability considerations

The first impression a product leaves goes beyond its visual appeal and scent; it signals safety, reliability, and the promise of lasting performance.

A well-documented shelf-life record shows that the maker has taken care to preserve the product's integrity under heat, light, and everyday use.

This assurance guides consumer expectations and builds trust, ensuring that the item remains safe and effective for as long as it is needed.

Prioritizing shelf-life is crucial for brand safety and consumer confidence.

This program adapts standard guidelines to suit the product's particular conditions of storage.

You should begin by establishing optimal storage conditions tailored to the product's specific requirements.

This involves evaluating its tolerance to temperature ranges, humidity, light exposure, and handling, ensuring the storage environment protects the product's integrity against chemical or physical degradation, and determining its shelf life on shelves and in homes.

Protection for packaging is essential.

Optimal selection of polymers, closures, and sachets is critical, as these components can significantly influence product stability (e.g., causing subtle shifts in stability).

To prevent unforeseen issues at the point of sale, it is crucial to understand the substance's properties, select appropriate stabilizers, and mitigate unstable interactions. These steps ensure product efficacy from inception.

Achieving product stability is fundamental to overall success.

Accurate stability testing is essential to validate product development and application. Our stability tests adhere to Good Manufacturing Practice (GMP) standards.

Clear identification of product stability parameters clarifies potential issues and indicates that the product remains firmly within its defined stability range.

The manufacturing date, which accurately reflects product quality at the time of production, serves as an initial indicator of safety, establishing the product's quality baseline.

In contrast, the 'best-by' date, signifying peak taste and optimal sensory quality, is a distinct concept that informs consumers about the period of highest quality for enjoyment, rather than signaling a safety concern.

These terms relate to product assurance, with the 'best-by' date providing the clearest indication of sensory quality.

From a safety perspective, it is imperative to ensure these parameters accurately reflect the actual product being manufactured.

**Key Principle:** Continuously improve product stability by leveraging existing foundational data and processes.

Choose stabilizers that support the declared claims and document the rationale for every stability claim. Use GMP-approved plans for accelerated and real-time testing to demonstrate safety and efficacy over time.

Define and align the expiration and best-by labels with regulatory definitions to avoid confusion.

Ensure all claims are supported by third-party testing and supplier documentation.

## 5. Forms: capsules, serums, powders, liquids, ...

On a crowded shelf, a private-label brand battles not only price and promise but also the choice of format.

The format serves as a compass for product development and a set of guardrails for shelf strategy, shaping user experience, logistics, and appeal.

This opening section offers a panorama of formats, their strengths and weaknesses, and the protective barriers that keep a new product from slipping off the shelf.

Think of supplement brands, which anchor its nutraceuticals in capsule formats for a constant dose, or skincare lines that rely on serums for targeted delivery.

Choose formats that meet consumer needs while maintaining stability and appeal.

Given the diverse needs for precise dosing, convenient use, and ingredient stability, various product formats are employed, each presenting distinct advantages and considerations:

— Capsules: precision dosing and convenience, ideal for nutraceuticals with regulated dosages.

— Serums: targeted delivery, perfect for skincare products.

— Powders: scale well for blends, with careful attention to texture and mixability; popular for functional beverages and supplements.

— Bars: convenient meal-replacement options that balance nutrition and texture for the health aisle.

— Flavorless and fast-absorbing options cater to consumers seeking easy-to-use products, with labeling considerations varying by format and claim.

The following are key considerations for product development:

– Count ingredients: ensure accurate counting and filling to prevent errors.

– Texture and shelf stability: maintain product feel and stability over time.

Labeling nuances must be strictly followed, ensuring compliance with regulations while clearly communicating benefits and claims.

By understanding the spectrum of formats and their trade-offs, manufacturers can create products that meet consumer preferences and perform well on the shelf.

Success depends on steady attention to stability, humidity control, and precise labeling.

For instance, maintaining the stability of a liquid supplement ensures its potency throughout its shelf life, while meticulous humidity control is vital to prevent caking in powdered ingredients or stickiness in softgels.

Additionally, precise labeling not only guides consumers on accurate dosage for different forms like tablets or drops but also provides crucial storage instructions to preserve product integrity and efficacy.

## 6. Margin potential and pricing scaffolds

Margin is central to a private-label launch.

By measuring the true cost of every unit and comparing it with the price you set, you gain a compass that shows which products to pursue, how to price them, and how to grow over time.

This chapter introduces a practical framework, the Margin-Focused Lens that lets you assess viability and set the right price.

**Viability:** Can the product cover its costs and deliver a healthy return under guardrails you can defend with data?

**Pricing:** What price maximizes value for customers while keeping margins within real-world constraints?

**Long-term growth:** How do you price to weather shifts in cost, demand, and competition while still reinvesting in the brand?

- Materials, packaging, labeling, compliance, shipping, duties, platform and transaction fees (where applicable).
- Regulatory and testing costs: budget for third-party labs, GMP audits, and claims substantiation to ensure compliance and protect margins.
- Product development and design, tooling and manufacturing, inventory management and storage, returns and customer service.

There is no single answer; the right pricing scaffold depends on the product and the market.

- Cost-plus pricing: add a markup to the total cost to secure a desired margin.
- Value-based pricing: set the price according to the customer's perceived value.
- Tiered pricing: offer multiple versions or quantities at different price points.
- Matching pricing: align the price with customer value while considering competitive pressures.

When applying these pricing scaffolds, consider that:

1. Unique features or benefits can justify a value-based approach without heavy marketing.
2. In a crowded market, a disciplined cost-plus strategy often yields better results than a purely mass-market model.
3. Regulatory uncertainty or risk can make tiered pricing a useful buffer.
4. Channel-specific margins matter: direct-to-consumer (D2C) channels, such as a brand's own web store, typically deliver higher margins than wholesale but require greater investment in marketing and customer acquisition.

Remember how each channel reflects your brand, cost structure, and growth plan.

Break down margins into platform fees, traffic costs, and distributor splits, and build these into your pricing model from the start.

Consider how each channel aligns with your brand identity and margin goals, and plan for resilience when regulatory uncertainty or market upheaval hits.

A value-based pricing strategy works well for premium lines, think unique ingredients and ethical sourcing, while a commodity product may rely on a simple price-plus approach to stay competitive.

With just a D2C launch, the margins will indeed rise, as the marketing and the service business will see a healthy boost.

Consequently, with wisely directed investment, the enterprise's profitability can be significantly enhanced.

## 7. Case study: AG1 and Onnit's product trajectories

Case Study Framing: AG1 and Onnit Trajectories Illustrate Real-World Product Evolution and Decision Points. Two brands, AG1 and

Onnit, stand as tangible illustrations of how ideas become products, products become brands, and brands signal what customers value.

This opening framing shows their paths not as isolated wins, but as practical lessons in product evolution, pivotal choices, and the constraints that shape every move from concept to market presence.

Onnit's trajectory echoes these choices, illustrating how branding and broader product portfolios shape growth as much as a single flagship. AG1 Initial Concept and Market Need

AG1, valued at about 1.2 billion dollars and generating roughly 600 million in annual revenue, built a powerhouse around a single daily supplement. It solved a clear consumer need with a simple, convenient all-in-one system that fits busy lives.

The powder form and single-serve packaging make daily use straightforward, while the design reinforces a strong brand identity and shelf appeal.

These choices lower friction, helping AG1 become a staple in everyday routines.

From the outset, regulatory alignment shaped label claims and testing requirements, ensuring compliance and building trust.

Brands pursue validation of efficacy and safety so that claims stand up to scrutiny and match the demands of competition.

Third-party testing and rigorous quality standards underpin their credibility, showing a commitment to a product customers can trust.

Clinical evidence informs their messaging, turning scientific data into a compelling narrative that regulators accept.

Supply-chain and manufacturing constraints are carefully planned: lead times, capacity and quality control are aligned to meet demand without compromising standards.

Pricing is positioned to balance perceived value with profitability, ensuring the product remains accessible while supporting sustainable margins.

A refined SKU strategy allows for tier options and stable margins as growth progresses. Utilize Long-Term Breakeven and Growth Trajectory Forecasts to monitor resources and make informed decisions on new launches and capacity expansions, always looking beyond the immediate horizon.

**Takeaways:**

- Understand real market needs and test assumptions early.
- Establish credibility and validate all assumptions, ideally with third-party verification.
- Balance presentation and packaging, maintaining freshness and relevance across supply and pricing strategies to sustain growth.

## 8. Viability Scoring Framework: A Practical Rubric

The success of a private label brand hinges on a single idea: will the product find its audience and remain a profitable long-term asset?

To answer this, we need a framework that considers market size, target audience, competition, demand, and profit margin.

This realistic view of opportunity illuminates where chances lie, helping you predict not with certainty, but with a clear sense of scope, timing, and positioning that will let the product survive and sustain you for the long term.

By translating insights into a cohesive score, teams can compare options, test assumptions, and set clear go/no-go criteria before committing resources.

To build a robust framework, first define the market signals and the scoring dimensions you will track.

A simple diagram or visual can effectively illustrate this framework, which comprises:

**1. Market Signals:** These fall into three classes:

- **Megatrends:** Large-scale, enduring shifts in consumer behavior or technology that shape demand over years.
- **Demand Signals:** Current levels of interest, expression of intent, and observable purchase activity.
- **Competition:** Intensity and landscape of rivals, potential gaps, and differentiators.

**2. Scoring Dimensions:** These scores are then divided into the following categories:

- **Market:** Size, growth, and accessibility of the target market.
- **Product:** Desirability, viability, feasibility, and regulatory constraints.

By combining these factors into a single, coherent score, you can measure the various options, test assumptions, and set the right criteria before you are ready to commit your resources.

The company's ability to maintain operational efficiency, manage its supply chain, and strategically align resources, when clearly defined with a robust scale, weighting, and calculation, constitutes an effective rubric.

This rubric should be practical and quantitative, designed for straightforward application rather than excessive complexity.

Its fundamental components are *Data*, *Intuition*, and *Risk*.

'Data' specifically encompasses market research signals, sales forecasts, profit margins, and competitive benchmarking.

"Risk tolerance: the level of risk the business is prepared to take before going in pursuit of growth."

This balance keeps a business in the grasp of overdependence on an imperfect supply of information while avoiding over-analysis paralysis.

The *Scorecard* Rubric:

Consider your streamlined grid of criteria:

Low (1-3) Medium (4-6) High (7-9)

Market Size < $1 million $1-5 million > $5 million
Demand Signals: Low Moderate High
Competition: High Moderate
Example: a product with a $3 million market size, moderate demand signals, moderate competition will yield this result, indicating medium viability.

This is like a plan of business which only one step should be taken, and which is not led by haste and desperation.

The team *uses* this method of organizing to ensure a disciplined approach to product evaluation, allowing them to thoroughly assess results and collectively determine the most effective way forward.

## 9. All-important actionable recap

In today's marketplace, a private-label brand begins by asking a single, stubborn question:

What real need am I solving for a particular shopper, in a specific category, and how does my price shape that need?

That question becomes the guardrail that keeps the brand from scope creep, guiding every decision about design, sourcing, and claims.

By defining the target consumer need, the category, and the differentiating promise, the brand translates that promise into concrete product choices, clear, crisp, and focused on what truly matters to the customer.

Private-label leaders like Costco's Kirkland Signature and Trader Joe's provide the most reliable examples, demonstrating what a focused, one-page thesis can achieve: it answers who the shopper is, what problem we solve, and what makes us distinct.

- To build a credible thesis, study real consumer needs, spot market gaps, and design a brand that fills those gaps.

- Map the customer's pain points, quantify how often they occur, and prioritize the needs that offer the strongest appeal.
- Use that insight to accelerate awareness and trial through targeted channels, advertising, in-store promotion, and new distribution, so the brand's power grows at every level, from strategy to shelf.
- Practical note: build your thesis with a realistic pathway to product-market fit, not merely a clever idea.
- Draft three candidate needs and pick the one with the strongest, defendable rationale.
- Assess Market Gaps with Real Data: after naming the need, back it with verifiable signals.
- Gather trends, behavior shifts, and competitor activity to gauge viability.
- Use a viability-scoring framework to rate market need, competition, margins, and feasibility, then translate scores into go/no-go decisions.
- *Data sources*: market reports, category sales trajectories, and retailer performance indicators.
- Actionable checklist: score each gap on a scale, then select the top contender with room to win.
- Validating Gaps with Consumer Surveys and Insights: validity comes from voices outside the spreadsheet.

To verify actual demand and ensure alignment with preferences, gather consumer surveys, retailer insights, and trend reports.

An integrative approach, bridging marketing management and new-product design, strengthens confidence in decision-making.

For validation, use:

- Short surveys
- Supplier feedback
- Prototype feedback loops

Assemble these insights into a clear one-page validation brief.

When planning for the product, consider:

- Shelf life
- Stability
- Preservatives
- Storage (based on product type)

Choose packaging that supports the intended use and delivery mode, and define packaging and shelf-life expectations before prototypes are built.

To make a Rapid Prototype and Test Plan, begin by establishing a clear thesis and constraints.

The process involves rapid iterations and testing with consumers, retailers, and stakeholders, gathering all available data and feedback, tightening up the design, and validating feasibility before scaling production.

A robust thesis should:

- Outline prototype specifications
- Define test panels
- Plan for a retailer pilot or e-com pilot
- Establish clear decision gates

Ultimately, a disciplined loop of feedback and refinement is essential for accelerating the development of a trustworthy, market-ready product.

## Section 2.

## Choose, then, between supplements, cosmetics, and wellness hybrids; product viability tests

The earliest decision in bringing a wellness product to market is the one that defines its core identity: is it a dietary supplement, a cosmetic item, or a thoughtful blend of both?

This initial classification is more than a label, it sets the entire framework for development and commercialization.

From the exacting regulatory requirements that must be met, to the speed at which the product can reach customers, to the way it builds trust and the costs of packaging and operation, every aspect hinges on that first choice.

Making this decision with clarity and confidence pays the greatest dividends, ensuring the product's success from day one.

## 1. Supplements vs cosmetics vs hybrids: which path suits your brand

Choosing Your Brand Lane: Supplements, Cosmetics, or Hybrids (Nutricosmetics – beauty from within)

Picture this: you're at a crossroads with three lanes, each promising a different way to help people look and feel their best.

One lane runs on science-backed nutrition, another focuses on appearance and care, and the third blends these two worlds into a holistic experience.

The decision isn't just about what sells; it's about your true value proposition, the regulatory framework you're willing to embrace, and the trust you're prepared to build with your customers.

Understanding the regulatory map is essential, but it's not a one-size-fits-all solution.

Supplements are governed by DSHEA, and cosmetics fall under the Federal Food, Drug, and Cosmetic Act (FD&C Act).

Hybrid products, combining elements of both, must satisfy the requirements of both regulatory regimes.

This dual compliance demands careful planning to navigate the regulatory landscape efficiently and responsibly.

Regulatory frameworks significantly influence product timelines and consumer expectations.

### Product Timelines:

- **Supplements:** Typically require extensive testing and stability data, which can potentially delay production.
- **Cosmetics:** Often reach shelves faster due to different regulatory pathways.
- **Hybrids:** Face the most intricate timelines, demanding dual compliance.

### Consumer Expectations:

- **Supplements:** Buyers prioritize scientific backing and health benefits.
- **Cosmetics:** Consumers focus on aesthetics, sensory experience (feel), and explicit safety guarantees.
- **Hybrids:** Require a balance of persuasive benefits, attractive design, and a reliable safety record to build trust.

### Margins and Packaging Constraints:

Packaging is crucial for compliance and communication.

Supplement packaging must include a Supplement Facts panel and other mandatory details, while cosmetic packaging prioritizes user experience and safety information.

Hybrids must satisfy both sets of requirements, impacting margins, shelf life, and production costs.

To effectively manage margins and navigate packaging constraints, consider the following actionable steps:

**Plan for packaging early:** This is crucial for saving money and maintaining product line profitability.

**Utilize a small pilot line to:**
-Test demand, costs, and regulatory compliance without overextending resources.
-Identify and resolve formulation, sourcing, and design issues before a full rollout.
-Refine your value proposition—whether it's supplements, cosmetics, or hybrids.
-Map your product to the appropriate regulatory scope and labeling requirements.

**Act fast and iterate:** This approach builds confidence and helps protect margins, shelf life, and production costs, while ensuring a clear, realistic path to market.

## 2. Regulatory burden, and go-to-market timetables

In the world of physical products, a great idea can stall at the threshold of regulation if the plan to bring it to market isn't concrete from the start.

The clock is ticking at every step, and the regulatory burden grows as you approach launch.

A phased-plan principle serves as a practical blueprint: it sets clear milestones that must be met before the product can reach shelves.

When a private-label brand enters the market, the regulatory story becomes even more critical—how the phases unfold and what obligations lie ahead can make or break the launch.

Ultimately, the goal is to navigate these hurdles efficiently, ensuring the product not only reaches customers but does so with compliance and confidence.

When launching a private-label product, the regulatory path is a critical determinant of success. To ensure a compliant and confident launch, consider these essential steps:

- **Formula and Label Review:** Thoroughly review and approve the product formula and label, ensuring compliance with all safety and labeling requirements before marketing.
- **Licensing and Permits:** Secure all necessary licenses, certificates, and permits. While time-consuming, these are vital for compliance.
- **Category-Specific Approach:** Understand that different product categories (e.g., cosmetics, supplements, other consumables) follow distinct regulatory tracks, requiring a tailored approach.

Addressing these steps proactively in an organized schedule avoids costly delays and and positions your brand for success.

Hybrid products, blending cosmetic and supplement elements, require navigating distinct regulatory frameworks, each with specific requirements for ingredients, claims, and manufacturing practices (GMPs).

Realistic launch plans require acknowledging necessary timelines for processes like ingredient validation, batch testing, label approvals, and certifications.

Engaging in third-party testing and audits can significantly reduce delays and build confidence with regulators and retailers by providing concrete evidence for approvals.

A clear regulatory roadmap should include milestones, risk flags, and budget buffers for potential delays.

The best way to bring your product to market is to avoid last-minute scrambles and instead follow a well-thought-out plan.

A phased regulatory strategy that ties each milestone to the product's development steps speeds the process and provides concrete evidence when approvals are sought.

**Actionable Takeaways:**

- Start with a phased regulatory plan that links milestones to development steps.
- Distinguish clearly between cosmetics, supplements, and hybrid products, and assign the appropriate testing, labeling, and approval tasks to each category.
- Build time buffers for ingredient validation, testing, label review, and certification, and plan for potential multi-agency coordination.
- Initiate third-party testing early to provide robust evidence for regulators and expedite approvals.

Real-world note: successful private-label brands treat regulatory work as a strategic asset, not a checkbox, using early planning, precise timelines, and disciplined testing to bring high-quality products into the marketplace with confidence.

## 3. Supply-ecosystems, the market-based supply-chain

For private-label nutritional supplements, establishing a robust and scientifically grounded foundation is paramount, with the groundwork laid long before a product ever leaves the factory.

The focus is on building a robust supplier network and grounding every formulation in science-backed evidence.

First, the sources must meet stringent GMP standards—clean, controlled, and disciplined procedures are non-negotiable. From there, the process moves to rigorous testing and reliable data, ensuring safety, efficacy, and honest labeling.

The laboratories that test products, generate data on efficacy and safety, and publish validated results should carry credible accreditation and use proven methods. Their work provides the data that defends claims and satisfies audits.

Key to this process is GMP compliance and rigorous traceability—from raw materials through manufacturing to the finished container—so that any recall or quality issue can be traced back and addressed quickly.

This safety net protects the public, and the market, while audits, certifications, and detailed batch records reinforce confidence in the product's integrity.

To ensure product integrity and reinforce confidence, a comprehensive approach is taken, encompassing:

- **Factory Oversight:** Audits, quality-control checks, and third-party certifications provide a clear view to monitor manufacturing conditions and regulatory compliance. These third-party endorsements demonstrate a sustained commitment to quality and identify potential issues early.
- **Detailed Documentation:** Reviewing batch records reveals production consistency, testing results, and any deviations that could jeopardize product integrity. Together, audits, certifications, and detailed batch documentation create a transparent, accountable foundation.
- **Scientific Substantiation:** Science-backed formulations and efficacy data are essential for delivering real-world results. Peer-re-

viewed or third-party studies add credibility to claims, proving them beyond conjecture and hearsay.

This integrated approach protects the public, and the market, reinforcing confidence in the product's integrity.

These independent assessments furnish a balanced view of a formulation's performance, reducing the risk of overstated gains and building trust with customers and regulators alike.

The FDA's standards clarify what evidence is required and how it should be presented, keeping claims accurate and keeping the brand intact.

By avoiding regulatory friction and maintaining a rules-based approach, a responsible brand can tell its story without excess information.

Sustainability and packaging are also key: recyclable containers, sustainable materials, and a clear environmental impact appeal to conscientious consumers and reinforce corporate responsibility to the planet.

For instance, a leading beauty brand might utilize sugarcane-derived packaging and partner with a certified fair-trade supplier for its active ingredients, clearly demonstrating its commitment.

The best eco-friendly materials and compliant suppliers complete the picture.

Choose materials from suppliers who are ethical and meet your regulatory standards, ensuring the eco-friendly options you select are as clean as possible and traceable from source to shelf.

Build a network that prioritizes scientific rigor—leveraging GMP-accredited laboratories, peer-reviewed data, and third-party validation—to support every claim.

Maintain a practical checklist that guides continuous evaluation and development of your supply chain, reinforcing both regulatory compliance and environmental responsibility.

## 4. Formulation considerations for safety and efficacy

The launch of a private-label health and wellness brand begins with a single, powerful promise: it must be safe, effective, and worthy of the consumer's trust.

In this opening section we lay the foundations for delivering that promise in every choice, from formula to packaging.

Safety and efficacy become the first objectives, and the credibility of the product rests on reliable protection and on claims that are fully supported by data.

By establishing clear safety and efficacy goals and tracking them through adverse-event monitoring, defined performance endpoints, and verifiable evidence, we ensure that the brand earns and maintains consumer confidence.

**Practical takeaways:**

- Before any formulation work commences, write a short objective brief for the product team and QA.
- Regulatory and consumer-needs focus must guide the formulation. It must satisfy FDA guidelines, GMPs, and labeling standards while also meeting what consumers actually want.
- Align your testing plans with the most relevant regulatory expectations so the product delivers the promised benefits.
- Safety across all user groups is essential. Consider children, pregnancy status, and pre-existing conditions.
- Some ingredients or dosages may need to be adjusted for different ages or health states to ensure safe and effective use.

**Practical note:**

First identify at-risk groups and tailor labels, dosing, and safety information accordingly.

Be aware of foods and substances with allergenic potential and keep a master allergenic matrix updated with current COAs.

Having concrete data on active ingredients helps demonstrate safety and efficacy, reducing criticism and ensuring compliance.

Always review the danger zone in advance and flag any possible allergens immediately.

This approach keeps the formulary practical and responsive to new information while protecting vulnerable populations.

Decide your dose ranges from maximum to minimum and document the rationale for each level.

Create a dose-matrix that links the ranges to the product claims while considering safety, stability, and bioavailability.

Build the formulation, conduct a small-scale stability study early, and evaluate how each dosage form—tablets, capsules, liquids—affects absorption and shelf life.

Choose packaging that protects against light, moisture, and oxygen, and that keeps the product intact.

Quickly assemble a claims matrix and an evidence folder before finalizing the label.

This approach keeps the formulary practical, responsive to new information, and protective of vulnerable populations.

A robust quality-data system and stringent supplier-assurance are the only essentials. COAs and purity audits must be rigorous, and we must rigorously test and verify every batch before release.

Packaging is the final seal of protection, so it must be designed to preserve safety and efficacy for the product's entire shelf life.

We should maintain adequate and secure stock levels and map regulatory requirements to ensure each item meets user demands.

## 5. Consumer expectations for claims and efficacy

A cosmetic claim pertains to aesthetic enhancement and external appearance, whereas a supplement claim is exclusively defined by its focus on internal health, nutritional support, or the body's structure and function.

To establish a reputable presence and ensure long-term viability within the health and beauty industry, it is essential that all claims made for products are rigorously substantiated and ethically presented.

This commitment to solid and fair practices builds a strong foundation, enabling businesses to operate confidently without concern for external scrutiny.

FDA regulation demands that claims be truthful and backed by robust, reproducible evidence.

The more specific or potent a claim, the greater the burden of proof, requiring solid, well-documented data rather than isolated studies or anecdotal testimony.

Building a test plan to produce desired proof, making concrete statements, and avoiding overstatement are crucial for credibility and regulatory compliance.

Adhering to scientific integrity builds customer trust.

## 6. Packaging and labeling impacts by category

Building on consumer expectations for clear claims and proven efficacy, product labeling is equally critical.

Effective labeling serves as a brand's first handshake with the market, demanding clarity, compliance, and compelling communication.

A product's primary purpose dictates its classification, which in turn defines its regulatory and marketing considerations. Different product categories have specific labeling requirements:

- **Dietary Supplements:** Require a crystal-clear Supplement Facts panel.

- **Cosmetics:** Necessitate full ingredient disclosure and category-specific cautions.
- **Hybrid Products:** Involve dual considerations: functional benefits and aesthetic presentation. These products require careful distinction and adherence to both sets of rules, strictly avoiding any health claims that exceed their category.

This foundational accuracy in labeling is key to long-term success.

## 7. Assessing private label feasibility with existing suppliers

Launching a private label is more than choosing a product; it is about building a system that protects and scales your vision.

The first step is to select partners who can carry that vision forward—whether they are established names like Kirkland Signature and AmazonBasics or emerging suppliers.

Think of this as the gate-keeping phase that separates the possible from the probable.

A disciplined partnership will keep you abreast of market changes, maintain rapid production, and handle the minutest details of manufacture, ensuring that the launch stays on track and the brand grows reliably.

A good partner will demonstrate the capacity to scale output as demand rises, offering supply flexibility and the ability to introduce new SKUs without delay.

The supplier should be an asset that runs the entire production process smoothly, maintains consistent quality, and has a proven track record of meeting every deadline.

Look for a steady, high-quality operation with the energy to keep launch schedules on track, ensuring that the brand grows reliably and the product reaches the market on time.

The best partners can meet your particular product specifications while accommodating branding, reducing friction during launch and sustaining momentum afterward.

## 8. Intellectual property considerations of every category

Regulatory readiness and certifications are non-negotiable.

Confirm GMP compliance, facility registrations where required, and labeling standards that match your category. Certifications—cosmetic, supplement, safety—signal a supplier's familiarity with the obligations your product must meet.

A strong QA framework, supplier audits, and access to certificates of analysis are essential. A willingness to work with independent labs adds an extra layer of confidence in product safety and consistency.

Defining QA processes to meet regulatory standards ensures a logical, compliant workflow that protects quality and keeps launch schedules on track.

The backbone of compliance lies in the supplier's documented SOPs, batch records, recall procedures, traceability, and controlled documentation.

These elements ensure that intellectual property is protected, that terms remain fair, and that the cost of production aligns with profit expectations.

By maintaining rigorous documentation and forecasting viability against launch dates and budgets, a company can secure exclusive rights, negotiate favorable terms, and keep product safety and consistency on track.

To ensure a confident launch, consider these key actions:

**Forecast and Plan:**

-Forecast demand, plan buffer stock, and align these with launch milestones and cash flow.

**Select the Right Partners:**

-Choose suppliers who match your timetable and budget.

-Map your private-label objectives to partners with proven QA frameworks and third-party testing options.

**Ensure Readiness and Compliance:**

-Require thorough documentation, including SOPs, batch records, and recall procedures.

-Ensure regulatory readiness early to avoid last-minute delays.

**Implement Checkpoints:**

-Build in practical checkpoints before making final decisions, enabling decisive action to keep the launch on track.


### 9. Mitigating risk in new product concepts


When a whiteboard fills with bold product ideas, the moment of truth is not just a flash of inspiration but a disciplined check that guards against early missteps.

Think of it as the operating system of private-label development, the foundational structure that provides clear guardrails, drives data-driven decisions, and fosters a portfolio approach to reduce reliance on any single idea.

Crucially, this disciplined approach begins with a strategic map for intellectual property (IP).

In a crowded market, a disciplined approach to IP is essential for differentiation, protection, and creating long-term value across supplements, cosmetics, and wellness hybrids.

Ignoring IP considerations at the outset poses a significant risk, potentially leading to costly legal challenges, market rejection, or the inability to secure your unique offerings.

Therefore, before you sketch the first formulation, establish a risk-mitigation mindset that proactively integrates IP. This strategic map for intellectual property includes:

- Defining acceptable risk levels related to potential infringement or brand protection.
- Setting constraints for uniqueness.
- Outlining realistic timelines for IP due diligence alongside each stage of development.

This comprehensive framework keeps the process focused and ensures that every idea is evaluated against the same rigorous standards, with IP as a foundational guardrail.

While understanding IP's overarching importance is key, detailed strategies for safeguarding your brand's unique elements are thoroughly explored in Chapter V.

This frame helps you narrow out ideas early and preserve capital for the best paths, not for its own sake but for deliberate prudence that frees you to pursue proven opportunities with confidence.

Framing Risk Tolerance, Budget, and Timelines: define your tolerance for uncertainty, establish a hard budget, and publish a timeline for ideation, prototyping, testing, and launch.

For example, a lean private-label program might allocate a modest contingency, a 12–16-week window for first prototypes, and a go/no-go decision at Week 8.

These guardrails prevent over-investment in ideas that fail to meet the basic feasibility bar.

In private-label programs like Amazon Basics and Kirkland Signature, teams invest in cost controls, supplier vetting, and disciplined schedules to keep momentum intact.

They set clear go/no-go criteria early, defining Key Performance Indicators (KPIs) such as market interest, unit economics, and regulatory readiness.

When a good idea falls short, lacking sufficient market space, supplier power, brand loyalty, or compliance, the project simply doesn't work.

Use a simple scoring scale to push ideas toward a green light and pause if they miss the mark.

This objective check keeps you from relying solely on gut feeling and ensures early alignment with regulatory paths.

Treat each idea as part of a diversified pool, spreading risk across the hazards already covered.

By marking thresholds early, you avoid costly revisions later and keep the project on a clear, feasible track.

In practice, the branded players, like Kirkland and Trader Joe's, rely on their brand managers to sell and manage risk, to develop a portfolio of risk-reducing concepts, and to distribute them efficiently through a multi-product network of suppliers.

A structured screen reveals the strongest candidates and directs every resource to action. The initial prototype is an early model of the good and is quickly tested for fit, improving its form, use, and packaging.

This approach, early in the field, matches the rapid initial tests of well-run firms.

By testing feasibility, keeping costs low, and iterating quickly, they use rapid cycles of prototype-testing, user feedback, and iteration to refine the product.

## 10. Partner selection criteria for product types

In launching a private-label brand, the journey begins not on the shelf but in the minds of the partners you choose.

The right collaborators translate your product vision into a safe, consistent formulation and a compliant label that stands on par with your own.

Because each product type carries its own regulatory footprint, your criteria must be uniform across partners while preserving a common standard of excellence.

For dietary supplements, regulatory competence is the foundation:

– FDA Compliance: accurate labeling and ingredient lists that match the product reality.

– GMP/CGMP Compliance: manufacturing controls that protect potency, purity, and batch-to-batch consistency.

– Third-Party Testing: independent verification of potency and purity.

These elements ensure that every product you offer meets the highest standards of quality and safety.

Certifications from trusted scientific bodies such as NSF International or ConsumerLab.com are essential for validating a product's purity, safety, and efficiency.

Brands that demonstrate such rigorous certification, like Ritual, often build significant consumer trust.

Cosmetics, however, operate under a distinctly different regulatory regime. Compliance in this sector typically requires adherence to:

- High standards of sanitation, quality control, and safety.
- Strict FDA compliance for product certification.
- Comprehensive safety validations, including reliable assessments to substantiate product claims.
- Recognized certifications such as ISO 9001 or Good Manufacturing Practices (GMPs).

Wellness hybrids, products that blend ingredients from both wellness and cosmetic categories, necessitate their own specific regulatory frameworks.

Unique Formulation:

- Capacity to craft formulations that deliver on all levels of stability and safety for your brand, leveraging expertise across product types.
- Capacity and lead times are verified to avoid stockouts and ensure realistic timelines.

- Scalability is guaranteed, allowing the partner to grow with you without compromising quality.
- Intellectual Property Protection is secured through NDAs, IP clauses, and clear deliverables.
- Audits and quality control are planned regularly to maintain compliance and performance.
- A crystal-clear Contract Development and Manufacturing Organization (CDMO) partner rubric aligns product type, regulatory, quality, and logistics criteria, with routine audits and scores to keep everything on track.

A real-world example shows how a successful supplement line (e.g., Ritual), a cosmetic brand (e.g., The Ordinary), and a wellness hybrid (e.g., Goop) all work together, each choosing the right partner and maintaining continuous checks to preserve trust and consistency.

The result is not just a product; it is a reliable, protected foundation that supports secure and dependable growth.

## 11. Takeaway

Choosing the right category is the first and most critical step in building a private-label brand.

It sets the tone for your mission, values, and product portfolio, and it determines whether your brand can win through word-of-mouth and repeat purchases.

Start by testing the category early and repeatedly: does it meet the needs and pains of your target market?

Does it allow you to craft a clear, compelling, and cohesive story?

By establishing a solid fit, you create a living framework that can be reused and refined as your brand grows.

Test early with viability studies, including margin analysis, production costs, and distribution pathways.

Concentrate first on market research, surveys, and social-media signals to confirm demand before committing to large production plans.

Understand critical operational requirements like packaging and fulfillment logistics so you can weigh benefits against potential hurdles and keep your brand agile.

If you pursue a hybrid, keep it true to your brand values. Record a clear go/no-go rubric that covers packaging, pricing, and supply factors:

- **For packaging:** Is the packaging visually aligned with your brand and appealing?
- **For pricing:** Is the price point competitive, profitable, and aligned with your strategy?
- **For supply:** Is the supply chain reliable, scalable, and compliant with your standards?

Learn from real-world examples, Ritual and The Ordinary show how focused packaging, disciplined claims, and a solid supply chain can bring a product to market successfully. This disciplined approach lets you confirm demand, weigh benefits against hurdles, and keep your brand agile.

Analyze their strategies, strengths, and weaknesses, and bring them to bear on your own method.

Actionable takeaways:

-Map your category against the brand mission and the needs of your audience.

-Run quick demand tests and rough margin analyses before committing to a full-scale launch.

-Consider hybrids only if they clearly enhance value.

-Create a go/no-go rubric with defined thresholds for packaging, pricing, and supply.

-Review real-world examples to extract practical lessons.

With this disciplined approach you establish a solid footing for a private-label brand that can grow confidently.

# Chapter III

## Branding & Positioning

### Section 1.
### *Brand identity and purpose; brand guide creation*

In a competitive environment, the true power of a brand lies in its distinct identity and the way it captures attention and builds emotional connections.

Every product is born of a single purpose and a single voice, and that purpose must be reflected in every claim, value, and promise the brand makes.

The brand's unique voice, positioning, and visual language—logos, colors, and design—create a cohesive image that speaks to its prospects.

By carefully documenting these elements in a brand guide, you preserve the brand's essence and ensure that every interaction, from product packaging to customer communication, remains true to its core identity.

The critical steps in trademark protection and regulatory compliance, helping to build your credibility by transparency, third-party validation, and authentic storytelling, and thereby demonstrating integrity, are also treated.

## 1. Defining the purpose of a wellness and cosmetics brand

On a crowded shelf, a private label brand operates with a clear purpose.

This purpose provides direction for every purchase, every claim, and every interaction with customers.

It defines what the brand stands for, why it exists, and the impact it seeks to create in the world of wellness and cosmetics. It establishes the mission, values, and product lineup, and serves as the foundation for a brand designed for longevity.

A well-defined purpose enhances the brand's resilience, ensures its offerings resonate with customer needs, and fosters a positive influence within its community.

A real-world example shows that brands which openly link their products to well-defined values such as safety, sustainability, or transparency, earn lasting loyalty.

Clarifying the brand's existence beyond profit is essential: ask why the brand exists and what core values and customer problems it addresses.

This purpose must be authentic, meaningful, and concise enough to be read aloud in a few seconds, then tested against every decision from formulation to packaging and messaging.

The mission becomes a practical guide, ensuring that every choice reflects the brand's commitment to its values and to the community it serves.

For a wellness private label, align the brand's values with the results your customers seek—health, balance, confidence, and convenience.

Tailor your messaging to each customer's goals and show how your products support those outcomes with honesty and clarity.

Map common customer outcomes to each product category, verify that every claim is factually correct and substantiated, and ensure the label clearly conveys ingredient sourcing standards, regulatory compliance, and truthful promises.

This approach keeps the message simple, credible, and focused on what matters most to the community you serve.

Real-world guardrails: establish clear internal criteria for ingredient inclusion, avoid overpromising, and document the supporting data behind every claim.

Credibility grows from transparent ingredient lists, sound manufacturing practices, and the science that underpins the product.

Share how your products are made, what inputs go into them, and the evidence that backs their benefits.

By keeping the message simple, credible, and focused on what matters most to the community you serve, you build long-term trust and a brand that truly delivers on its promise.

To define purpose and align stakeholders effectively:

- **Start with a clear purpose:** This purpose should inform every product choice and explicitly state why the brand exists beyond profits.
- **Develop truthful and consistent communication:** Create hooks that are truthful and consistent across packaging, marketing, and in-store conversations.
- **Align wellness goals:** Match wellness goals with customer desires and communication, prioritizing safety, quality, and regulatory honesty.
- **Balance stakeholder interests:** Map the needs of customers, regulators, suppliers, and investors to your product roadmap.
- **Build credibility:** Achieve this through transparency and evidence, ensuring your mission is concrete, realistic, and believable.

By balancing the interests of all key stakeholders, you translate purpose into a concrete product plan that supports responsible growth and reduces risk.

## 2. Brand voice, personality, and positioning

A logo is more than a simple symbol; it tells us what a brand stands for, how it behaves, and why we should choose it.

When a brand speaks with a clear, precise voice and maintains a distinct personality, it cuts through the noise and leaves a lasting impression.

Apple does this with surgical precision, Patagonia with a conscience, and Dyson with an engineering edge that sweeps cleanly across the market. Irrespective of their marketing approaches, these brands attract consumers, prompting alignment with their narratives and adoption of their values.

Your brand voice is the language that embodies your values, while tone is the attitude that gives it personality.

Together they form a unified image that appears across products, ads, and support moments, creating a clear, human presence.

By translating your core traits into tone, style, and customer interactions, you ensure every message feels consistent and resonates with your target audience.

Once you've named yours, translate it into a practical framework:
- Vocabulary: the words and phrases you favor
- Sentence structure: how you build messages
- Rhythm: pace and cadence of communication

Your brand voice guidelines should be a living document for copywriters, designers, and customer-facing teams, ensuring consistency from social posts to customer support.

You need a Cohesive Identity.

A strong identity covers more than language, encompassing every touchpoint:
- Visual identity: logo, color palette, typography, and imagery that echo your personality - Product design: the physical embodiment of your brand values

- Packaging: packaging that reinforces voice and visuals, not just protection Crafting Positioning Statements Positioning statements anchor your brand in the market.

They should:

- Clarify value: the benefits you deliver

–Benchmark against your rivals

-Chose a few reasons to buy

-Compelling incentives that your reader should be ablet to buy in

-Benchmarking Against Competitors Regularly compare yourself to rivals to spot gaps and confirm distinct, compliant positioning.

-Analyze strengths and weaknesses, then adjust your strategy to keep your brand's claim credible and relevant.

**Actionable takeaways:**

- Define 3 core personality traits, plus one-line positioning statement.
- List 5-7 vocabulary choices that reflect your voice and a few concrete guidelines on tone for 3 channels (website, product copy, support).
- Create or update a guidelines document covering vocabulary, sentence structure, and rhythm.
- Assess visual identity, product design, and packaging for alignment with voice.
- Run a quick competitor benchmark and note one thing you do differently.

From a real-world perspective, a brand truly succeeds when its communication, presentation, and packaging are seamlessly aligned to distinctively stand apart.

This fundamental consistency ensures your brand is not just noticed but deeply felt and ultimately trusted by your audience.

## 3. Naming strategy and messaging architecture

Names are a brand's initial impression; in a crowded market they do more than just identify—they promise, clue, and signal.

A strong name can streamline the buyer's decision-making process and build confidence, whereas a weak one can hinder future engagement.

It communicates value to the customer and attracts the target audience.

This underscores the importance of a purpose-driven naming strategy that signals the brand's promise, fosters familiarity, and ensures the engagement of relevant customers.

The name communicates values, personality, and a unique value proposition, helping to separate your brand from the competition.

When developing the strategy, keep these points in mind:

Brand promise: How clearly does the name carry the core value you deliver?

Target audience: Will the name feel authentic and accessible to the people you aim to serve?

Category fit: Does the name sit comfortably within its category, without conflicts?

Trademark-friendly and scalable: Beyond purpose, the name must be practical in the real world, unique, memorable, and flexible enough to cross cultures and oceans.

Aim for a label that is distinct, low risk of conflict, and easy to recall and pronounce.

Flexible: Works across products, sub-lines, and multiple markets.

Checking availability and reserving domain rights protects naming assets from the start.

Practical steps include:

- Trademark searches: Confirm the name is usable within your category and geography.

• Domain rights: Secure relevant domain identifiers to safeguard your online presence and reduce cybersquatting risk.

Think of this phase as laying a foundation that prevents costly re-brands later. A messaging architecture should fit the broader brand framework:

• Core brand narrative: A concise story that communicates purpose and promise.
• Value pillars: Key messages that support the brand's value proposition.
• Tone guidelines: A pure, precise voice that reflects the brand's personality and values.

Building on a robust naming strategy and a well-defined messaging architecture, maintaining distinct and coherent brand naming is essential for aligning communication across all products and experiences.

Implementing audience-specific naming variations helps unify diverse market segments into a cohesive brand identity, ensuring the brand's core essence remains consistent while adapting its expression for various touchpoints.

A brand's objective is to cultivate a distinct and coherent voice, which extends beyond superficial stylistic consistency to encompass its fundamental communication approach.

The strategic development of brand language and visual elements (e.g., words, colors, fonts) serves to define the brand's narrative and guide its messaging to customers.

• Protect the name with trademark checks and early domain registration.
• Build a messaging framework that keeps naming aligned with the broader brand story.

- Create audience-specific naming variations without fragmenting the overall brand.
- Maintain consistent tone and visuals across every touchpoint.

Real-world anchors:

Nike's name and mark echo a sense of achievement within sport, while it's messaging consistently reinforces performance and aspiration.

Patagonia uses its place-based name to signal environmental commitment, shaping product stories and customer expectations.

Warby Parker demonstrates how a founder-inspired name can become a credible platform for value-focused eyewear, supported by a clear brand narrative.

- Write your core narrative as though you were talking to a group of friends.
- Write at least two options for each sub-line.
- Audit your packaging, in-store materials and communications for consistency.

## 4. Logo design, color palette, typography, etc

In a crowded cosmetics scene, your brand's visual identity becomes more than a single symbol; it is the first personal conversation you ever have with a future customer.

It sets expectations, builds trust, and frames every product you create.

To make this conversation effective, design your visual identity with purpose: align your logo, color palette, typography, and brand guide with your core values and the message you want to convey.

A well-crafted logo is the face of your brand's visual identity, the first thing people see, and it should reflect the identity you wish to project.

By carefully choosing each element, logo design, color palette, and typography and documenting them in a clear brand guide, you create a seamless, memorable visual identity that speaks before you even say a word.

For a natural and organic line, choose earthy tones and imagery drawn from nature, while a luxury line should aim for sophistication, restraint, and clean, elegant proportions.

Real-world references help anchor the design: Aveda, for example, uses muted earth tones and simple shapes to reflect its natural ethos, whereas Chanel's iconic black-and-white palette with subtle gold conveys timeless luxury.

The logo must be versatile enough to work on packaging, signage, and digital touchpoints, and it should endure over time.

A thoughtful color-palette strategy does more than look pretty, it communicates trust, credibility, and a brand's distinctiveness, supporting both differentiation and lasting recognition.

Natural brands lean into greens, blues, and earthy neutrals to signal purity and sustainability, while luxury brands turn to black, white, and restrained metallics to convey refinement.

Your palette must pass the cross-channel consistency test: colors should perform equally well on packaging, print, and any display point.

A primary color anchors the logo, with secondary hues supporting graphics and accents, ensuring the brand feels credible and unmistakably yours.

Typography matters too, use a clean sans-serif for body text to guarantee readability and reserve a more decorative font for headings or key phrases so the message lands with impact without competing with the copy.

This balanced approach keeps the logo versatile, the colors trustworthy, and the overall design timeless.

A coherent system means limiting yourself to a small, consistent font family and applying a uniform sizing rule, so the brand's voice stays clear and reliable.

The brand guide is the playbook for every stakeholder, covering essential rules such as logo usage, minimum font sizes, clear space, and unacceptable uses.

It also specifies the color palette, hex codes, Pantone references, and RGB values and outlines approved typefaces, sizes, and typography guidelines for all formats.

By defining these core elements, the guide ensures that every piece of communication, from packaging to digital assets, reflects the brand's values and maintains a timeless, trustworthy look.

To effectively build your brand identity and ensure consistency, choose a primary color and a small set of secondary shades that work together across all print and product visuals.

For typography, pick a readable body font and a distinctive heading font, keeping the family small to maintain uniformity and reinforce your brand's character.

Create a concise brand guide that spells out usage, color specifications, and typography rules to protect your identity and maintain consistency.

Ultimately, your color strategy should translate values into recognizable signals of credibility and differentiation, while typography must be treated with care and practicality to enhance your message.

## 5. Brand guide components and delivery formats

In a crowded marketplace, a brand is more than a logo or slogan; it is a living system that communicates values, promise, and personality wherever it appears.

A brand guide serves as the compass for every expression of that system, ensuring clarity, coherence, and confidence in every impression.

The purpose, scope, and structure of the brand guide are its most important aspects, providing a standard of style and vision that keeps the brand uniform across all channels and touchpoints.

## *Objectives of the Brand Guide*

The primary objective of this guide is to provide a clear, firm, and comprehensive representation of our entire product system. It ensures that all individuals involved with the product, at every level, share a consistent understanding.

This guide is designed for wide circulation to standardize and align all aspects of our work.

Marketing materials and other assets used across channels, and the structure of the brand guide:

1) Brand foundations – purpose, mission, and personality that determine every decision.

2) Visual identity – logos, color palettes, typography, and imagery, with rules for every choice.

3) Tone and message – voice, copy guidelines, and sample language.

4) Applications – packaging, labeling, and communications across products and materials.

5) Governance and maintenance – roles, approval workflows, and processes for updates.

By providing a clear and comprehensive brand guide, all stakeholders can be effective, avoid mistakes, and ensure that every participant can produce consistent, persuasive copy and that the message is delivered uniformly across all channels.

Keep the brand guide brief, clear, and easy to understand.

Use plain language and concrete examples to illustrate key points.

Make the guide easily distributable and regularly update it so it stays fresh and effective.

Treat the guide as a living document that all stakeholders can reference to maintain consistency across every channel.

A company renowned for its environmental stewardship and clear sense of purpose can distill all its packaging, imagery, and visual assets into a single, practical framework.

The brand guide should bring the values, mission, and personality into every asset, ensuring that each piece of communication reflects the company's vision.

By keeping the guide well-drawn, accessible, and regularly updated, it remains fresh and relevant—just like a living document that all stakeholders can reference.

Within this living and accessible framework, real-world examples provide concrete indicators of consistency, helping teams see how the guide translates into everyday practice and keeps every channel aligned with the brand's core principles.

## 6. Trademark considerations: TM versus R and typical pitfalls

In a crowded market, a trademark is more than a logo or a wordmark; it is a promise about the quality, origin, and character of your product.

When a buyer spots the mark, they expect a consistent experience—from packaging to performance—an assurance that the product will live up to its claim.

The TM symbol announces a claim of ownership before formal registration, while the ® symbol signals a registered mark.

Understanding the proper use and protection of these symbols, along with the process for trademark search and registration, is crucial for building trust and avoiding disputes.

### Trademark Registration and Enforcement

The ® symbol indicates a registered trademark, offering robust legal protection and reducing risks when licensing or selling the mark.

To prepare for registration, identify all marks associated with your core brands, including close variants and design elements similar to established brands in your market.

In the United States, the United States Patent and Trademark Office (USPTO) handles registration.

Once registered, you gain exclusive rights to use the mark with your goods or services, the right to display the ® symbol, deter infringers, and add value for investors and partners.

You will also have confidence that your mark will withstand a full search and practical use across all fields of production.

Common pitfalls to avoid include:

- **Generic terms:** These are often refused or canceled at first glance.
- **Improper symbol usage:** This can create confusion or weaken protection. Using the TM without registration can invite legal trouble and confuse partners, so consistent and correct use is essential for maintaining credibility and avoiding disputes.
- **Over-claiming protection:** Claiming protection for goods or services not connected to your mark reduces enforceability.

A proactive enforcement plan is crucial for preserving value:

- Create alert systems for potential infringements.
- Document every case thoroughly.
- Act promptly when issues arise; quick response can prevent damage to reputation and market share.

Embed trademark guidance into your brand playbook, detailing mark-usage rules, the renewal schedule, and licensing terms.

This ensures consistency, cuts risk and helps you effectively manage and protect your intellectual property.

## 7. How branding shapes perceived quality and trust

A unified palette, typography system, and imagery, coupled with a consistent tone of voice, create a reliable standard that shoppers can trust.

Whether on the shelf, in a product insert, or in online ads, the brand presents a crisp, recognizable look that assures consumers of its high level of dependability.

Transparency and regulatory compliance play a crucial role: clear, honest labels about ingredients, manufacturing processes, and brand claims become the stamp of credibility that reinforces the brand's promise.

Compliance with labeling and quality standards is often legally mandated.

In a regulated market, the absence of such verification can undermine credibility.

Certifications, audits, and tests provide essential assurance that products meet specified quality, safety, and ethical criteria.

For example, certifications like ISO 9001, organic labels, Fair Trade designations, or Energy Star ratings signify adherence to rigorous standards, instilling confidence in consumers regarding a product's value and integrity.

A genuine brand story deepens trust and creates a lasting emotional bond. It connects the ingredients to the product's purpose, humanizes the brand, and reveals the honest truth about sourcing, touchpoints, and impact.

By telling a narrative that feels close to the product itself, brands can hold consumers by the hand and build a steady, loyal audience.

Actionable takeaways: audit your visual identity, palette, typeface, imagery, and tone of voice, and build a consistent playbook that defines color, fonts, imagery, and tone for every touchpoint.

This ensures the story remains credible, relatable, and resonant with your audience.

## *8. Lessons from Ritual, The Ordinary, Drunk Elephant branding*

In a crowded beauty aisle, a brand is more than a bottle; it is a promise you can trust at a glance.

This section opens with three industry leaders—Ritual, The Ordinary, and Drunk Elephant—who have crafted repeatable principles that scale product, packaging, and narrative.

Their approach is rooted in purpose-first branding, anchoring every element in a clear mission and values.

Ritual, for example, champions transparency and sustainability, selecting only essential ingredients and environmentally mindful packaging.

These proven strategies inspire first-time buyers and turn them into advocates, giving your own brand a solid foundation for growth.

When you adopt this approach, your brand communicates a purpose that goes beyond merely selling a product, creating a loyal community that aligns with your mission.

**Clear and Simple Positioning** helps a brand define its lineup and improve recall.

The Ordinary demonstrates this with straightforward product names and descriptions. For example, the *Salicylic Acid 2% Solution* uses clear language that instantly conveys the product's purpose and key ingredients.

By following this model, your range becomes easier to navigate, reducing confusion and building trust with customers who value transparent information.

**Consistent Brand Voice** – a single, recognizable voice across packaging, website, and social content – further builds trust and reduces friction.

Drunk Elephant has cultivated a distinctive, playful tone that shines through its packaging, website copy, and community posts, creating a sense of trust and consistency for its audience.

Transparent ingredient stories—clear, honest disclosures about what goes into each product—serve as a powerful signal of integrity, reassuring customers that the brand cares about safety and efficacy.

By studying brands like Ritual and The Ordinary, we see a scalable pattern: a unified voice across all touchpoints, coupled with open ingredient narratives, builds brand recognition and reduces friction.

This approach not only strengthens customer confidence but also makes the brand's value proposition unmistakable and memorable.

- Embrace purpose-first branding: anchor your narrative, packaging and claims in mission and values.
- Adopt clear and simple positioning: define your lineup with memorable language and minimal jargon.
- Maintain a consistent brand voice: ensure your identity reads the same across every channel.
- Tell transparent ingredient stories: provide detailed information about ingredients and safety claims and publish accessible ingredient notes.

Implementation quick checks:
– Define a one-sentence mission and tie product claims to it.
– Name products with clear benefits that avoid excess jargon.
– Review every touchpoint for a uniform voice and clarity.
– Publish ingredient notes and safety information in a single, easy-to-read format.

These steps translate leadership signals into scalable practice, setting your brand up for enduring recognition and trust.

## 9. Brand storytelling framework: rituals and routines

In a crowded shelf, a product can become a daily anchor—an unbroken thread that we weave through mornings, errands, and evenings.

When a private-label brand slips into those moments, it earns more than a one-time purchase; it earns a place in our everyday life.

Brand rituals are the traditions that turn that routine into loyalty, giving the brand a familiar, dependable presence that feels like home.

By making the brand a staple of our daily rituals, we create a lasting bond that boosts margins and keeps customers coming back, not just for the product but for the comfort of the routine itself.

Our goal is to move from a one-off sale to a familiar pattern that customers recognize by name.

Start by mapping the moments in your daily routine when the product naturally fits whether it's the first cup of coffee, the mid-day stretch, or the evening wind-down.

Tie each moment to a concrete benefit the product delivers, and design the touchpoints packaging, point-of-sale cues, and language to reinforce that moment.

**A practical checklist:**

- Identify the top three daily moments that the product supports.
- Link each moment to a clear, tangible benefit.
- Show how packaging, cues, and sales points reinforce the experience.

Craft the ritual by first outlining its steps and timing, then capture the emotions it evokes.

Provide a coherent narrative that lets the customer see the product as a natural, memorable part of their day.

Weave this routine into the brand voice, creating a Signature Routine Narrative that feels real and human.

Rituals give our brand its voice and story.

Use language, imagery, and tone that echo the cadence of everyday routines and the product's role in daily life.

Keep packaging, ads, and copy consistent so customers recognize the brand in familiar moments, both at home and on the go.

Embed sensory cues, sight, sound, smell, touch, and taste, to weave rituals into memory and employ symbolism and metaphors to reinforce our values and personality.

In crowded markets, a well-crafted ritual becomes a powerful differentiator, turning a single purchase into a lasting habit that keeps customers coming back for the comfort of the routine itself.

In crowded markets, distinguish your brand by focusing on the ceremonies most important to customers.

Clearly identify the unique steps, ritual elements, and the product itself within these ceremonies to prevent easy copying. Integrate these distinctive elements into packaging, marketing, and real-life product experiences to make them memorable.

**To implement this:**

1. Map your product's benefits to specific daily moments of usage.
2. Describe these usage moments clearly from the customer's perspective.
3. Make the product synonymous with your brand by consistently linking it to defined actions, tastes, or moods during its use.

## 10. In visual consistency across product, packaging, digital materials

In a crowded market, your brand's visual identity has only a few seconds to speak.

That steady drumbeat is the visual consistency that guides every product, package, and touchpoint, ensuring customers recognize the same visual language and make the purchase with confidence.

By keeping the visual identity system tight, the brand gains resilience and a rise in volume, becoming a standard in its category.

The colors of your brand's visual identity, whether bright or subtle, do more than decorate; they signal category, price, and temperament, anchoring the brand in the minds of consumers.

The luxury label thrives on deep, rich tones that convey sophistication, while a children's line can burst into bright primaries that feel playful and energetic.

The colors of your visual identity, chosen for packaging, typography, and the surrounding atmosphere, do more than decorate, they signal category, price, and temperament, anchoring the brand's visual identity in consumers' minds.

Iconic hues such as Coke red, which evokes prestige and trust, or Tiffany blue, a marker of premium confidence, illustrate how a single shade can become a brand's signature.

By establishing a coordinated color palette that spans every typeface, logo, and surface, you create a natural, real-world feel that keeps the eye engaged and the visual identity intact.

Let no one be too hard on the wordmark or emblem, lest one element dominate the brand.

Consistency is decisive across every touchpoint from packaging inserts to product pages and ads while standardized templates cut waste in paint and ink, keeping the brand cohesive and fresh.

By placing marks correctly and using scalable templates, you streamline approvals, reduce rework, and ensure a smooth flow across vendors.

This clean, efficient system of narrative works seamlessly on Web, Social, and Ads, giving your brand a stable, industry-level presence across all channels.

Your visual identity must tell the same story across every channel.

Use the same typography, color palette, and imagery to reinforce a single message and all the CTAs that feel right to each customer.

No matter what the format, the core elements of your visual identity (the look and feel) should stay the same so that the brand is instantly recognizable whether it appears on a product page, a social post, or an ad.

Regulatory compliance and sustainability cues guide your visual design choices by defining what visuals and claims are permissible.

Ensure labeling meets regulatory requirements and is consistent across products and packaging.

Sustainability messaging, materials, inks, and recycling, should reflect the brand's environmental stance everywhere.

**Best Practices for Visual Consistency**

Build a complete brand style guide that defines the core elements of your visual identity: the color palette, typography, and logo usage.

Establish a central system to govern their consistency across every channel.

Print out all the details for audit purposes and keep refining this visual identity system to protect its integrity and the brand's visual language.

Ensure that the packaging and channel designs scale smoothly and integrate regulatory and sustainability considerations into every creative decision.

This unified approach secures a strong, coherent visual identity that reflects the brand's environmental stance everywhere.

## 11. Takeaway

Anchor your brand to a clear, honest purpose, guiding every decision beyond making money.

Aligning your brand's promise with this purpose creates a trustworthy identity, fostering customer loyalty and growth.

This intentional approach transforms purpose into a practical asset for physical products, compliance, and overall branding discipline, ensuring genuine value delivery.

Translate your brand's clear purpose into a compelling promise—a tangible guarantee that assures customers of its claims.

Ensure this promise is concise, authentic, and aligned with your unique value proposition, highlighting distinct benefits.

Marrying purpose with promise creates a trustworthy brand identity that differentiates you and delivers genuine value to your audience.

Patagonia exemplifies a brand that lives its purpose: 'build the best product, avoid unnecessary harm, and use business as a platform to inspire stewardship of the outdoors.'

Their brand promise clearly reflects this commitment, demonstrating how marrying purpose with promise builds trust, loyalty, and market differentiation through genuine value delivery.


## Section 2.
### Developing a brand guide; registering and using trademarks

But what brand stands out in the face of all your choices?

Simply choose the most consistent one: *to speak with many voices* or *one clear, dependable identity.*

This guidance provides practical methods for creating a singular identity, from its visual foundation to its legal safeguards.

It encompasses developing vivid visual and messaging, protecting intellectual property, upholding consistency across all channels, and integrating elements cohesively across diverse products.

Establishing precise rules of procedure for everything from logo application to brand voice is crucial for securing the rights to name and mark your brand for life.

## 1. Step-by-step brand guide creation

Imagine yourself preparing your newest line of tools, trying to give the brand a clear, faithful identity that cuts through its scattered, disembodied state.

The brand guide is your playbook, a template that ensures every touch-point, every asset, voice, and visual, blossoms with a consistent look, feel, and tone.

By clarifying Purpose, Audience, Channels, and Governance, the guide furnishes a firm foundation of uniformity across all marketing materials, giving the brand immediate recognition and a dependable voice.

The primary users are marketing teams, designers, writers, and stakeholders who create and share brand content.

**Channels:** The guide covers every channel—social media, the website, advertising, email, and offline materials such as brochures and business cards.

**Governance:** A clear governing structure is essential for regular reviews and updates, often handled by a brand manager or a small team that safeguards and maintains the brand.

**Scope:** Include all aspects of the brand's identity—logos, typography, color palette, tone of voice, and key messages—so the guide is complete and actionable.

**Deliverables:** A practical package that contains an up-to-date brand guide, style sheets, and templates for marketing materials, ready for use across all channels.

**Approval Process:** Engage key stakeholders, marketing teams, designers, and senior management, to confirm content and approve changes.

Before building the guide, audit and inventory the current brand assets: logos, typography, color palette, voice, and collateral.

Establish a baseline so you can see what works and what needs updating.

Real-world brands like Nike, Apple, and Patagonia demonstrate how a well-crafted identity guides product design, packaging, and communications, reinforcing trust with customers.

Taken together, these steps let brands create a clear, consistent brand guide that keeps identity cohesive across all channels and builds a recognizable presence.

**Takeaway:** A well-scoped objective frames every decision.

Write an asset inventory before you act, anchoring the guide in real-world facts.

Keep the guide practical, enforceable, and aligned with products and regulatory realities.

Nimble brands appoint a small band of brand owners or a select committee, review changes annually or quarterly, and push updates to the living set of templates so nothing is missed at the last minute.

This governance model keeps the guide relevant and trustworthy.

## 2. Logo usage rules and clear space

In a crowded market, a single mark can start a conversation with a customer before any words are spoken.

A logo is more than artwork; it serves as a doorway to trust, quality, and the story of a brand.

When a logo is used consistently, audiences recognize and remember it, but inconsistent use can instantly damage a brand's credibility.

Think of Apple's clean, versatile mark, Coca-Cola's iconic red, and Nike's simple silhouette as real-world examples of disciplined logo application.

This section provides practical guidelines for creating a consistent identity through standardized logo usage.

## Logo Placement and Sizing

Define minimum and maximum dimensions to maintain legibility across all materials, from business cards to product packaging.

- Establish recommended placements: a steady anchor on collateral such as a card top left, a letterhead header, and a product label, so audiences know where to look for the mark.
- Use a simple rule: the logo should be big enough to read, but not so big that it crowds out other design elements.
- Specify permitted formats, normally vector (AI or EPS) and raster (JPEG or PNG), and ensure a clear space around the logo, or at least an acceptable proportion of the symbol's size.
- Logos Readability and Legibility
- Test the logo against a range of backgrounds and surfaces—signage, packaging, mock-ups, and web pages—to ensure the mark stands out and remains legible from a distance.
- Define primary, secondary, and grayscale color palettes, specifying the purpose of each variant (e.g., primary for core materials, secondary for social assets, grayscale for monochrome uses).
- Set minimum contrast requirements to maximize visibility; avoid busy textures or colors that wash out the mark.
- Use only authorized formats (vector AI or EPS, raster JPEG or PNG) and color variants.
- Follow best practice guidelines: keep the logo's color, weight, and spacing intact, and ensure it remains visible in all approved contexts.

### 3. Color palette and typography usage guidelines

Colors are the first handshake a brand offers its customer, communicating values, shaping expectations, and guiding behavior long before words appear.

A thoughtfully planned color system becomes the backbone of the brand, linking packaging, web presence, and retail touchpoints into a coherent experience.

Coca-Cola's red instantly recognizes its bottles and ads, Tiffany & Co.'s robin-egg blue signals premium quality, and Apple's restrained palette keeps its products and packaging instantly identifiable.

A well-chosen palette starts with clarity: it must be legible, adaptable, and distinctive across all touchpoints, from labels and boxes to signage and merchandising. This foundation ensures that every interaction feels familiar and trustworthy, reinforcing the brand's identity at every moment.

The result is a brand identity that feels deliberate rather than accidental.

The color scheme should be simple, using a single dominant hue as the primary color, applied consistently across marks, packaging, and core materials.

Two or three secondary tones, bright or playful shades, are added sparingly so they do not overpower the primary. An accent color is chosen to catch the eye. For print, note Pantone numbers; for screens, note hex codes.

This framework guides where each color should appear and how the palette should be applied across all touchpoints, ensuring clarity, adaptability, and distinctiveness.

In the storerooms, reflect the brand by making the signs, fixtures, and displays all color-marked.

Well-defined palettes open the teams up consistently, and every touch-point shows the brand in its broad sense at a glance. Start with a five-color system: one primary, two secondary, two accents.

For explicit usage rules, use the specs; for contrast, use the guidelines.

Test each visual at least three times to confirm consistency and run quick checks at every touch-panel.

## 4. Voice, tone, and messaging documentation

In a crowded marketplace, customers judge a product not just by its features but by how the brand speaks.

The Brand Voice Foundation is the compass that guides every word a company uses—from web pages and product descriptions to packaging and support conversations. It is built on purpose, core values, and a disciplined approach to messaging that can be applied across all channels and contexts.

A purposeful brand speaks with confidence, its words crystal-clear about what it stands for, and its voice remains consistent, simple, and indispensable to the brand's identity.

The best voice is authentic, consistent, and directly tied to purpose and values. It speaks with confidence, using clear, concise language that reflects what the brand stands for.

By crafting a one-sentence purpose and three core values, you give your team a simple, memorable framework to test every message against.

Calibrating the voice for each audience segment is essential: know their demographics, needs, and tastes, and adjust tone so it remains engaging and memorable.

In practice, this means writing with transparency, responsibility, and vivid description, and then refining each word against the audience's expectations to ensure clarity and honesty.

This disciplined, purposeful approach keeps the brand's voice consistent across all channels and contexts.

Consider first the distinct groups: first-time buyers and seasoned buyers.

Give each a lightweight "mini-voice" that still reflects the brand's core identity.

List the language traits you prefer, direct, descriptive, practical, aspirational, and pair each trait with a concrete use case that shows how the brand speaks to that group's concerns.

By tying the voice to buyer personas and specific use cases, the brand stays fresh, compelling, and consistently on target, avoiding drift into the twilight zone.

Focusing on practical applications, the cosmetics industry highlights the critical need for regulatory precision.

A cosmetics line requires clear proof points regarding its safety and efficacy.

Achieving regulatory clarity involves establishing consistent boundaries and standards across the entire product line.

This ensures that every product adheres to the same foundational principles, fostering consumer trust.

To ensure consistency in brand voice and tone across all materials, the brand guide defines the appropriate tone and language for product pages, packaging, and marketing materials, supported by practical examples and approved phrases.

This comprehensive guide helps content creators maintain consistency by covering topics such as Content Creators, Channel Design, Culture, Mission, Message, Strategy, Goal, Discipline, and Action.

- Define purpose, three core values, and a concise proof of authenticity.
- Create audience-calibrated voice notes for key segments, linking each to its particular persona and outlining stage-oriented language.
- Build a clear regulatory check for any new claims, whether by letter or printed word.
- Develop a three-pillar framework with simple proofs and a tone guide, refreshed quarterly to keep it vital.
- Set channel-specific adaptations that preserve the core voice and stock a small library of templates and playbooks for everyday use.

- Schedule quarterly governance reviews to refresh and validate the voice.

## 5. Trademark search process and jurisdiction, trademark search strategy

Brand protection is critical from the outset of a product or service's development.

A brand's compliance playbook must clearly define its offerings, target audience, and desired aesthetic.

By laying out these limits, we can guard against all sorts of clashes—whether from consumer confusion or from the hidden threats that lurk in the marketplace.

The first step in a brand's compliance is a thorough trademark search, which opens the door to the potential conflicts that may arise before the brand even reaches its customers.

In this section, we spell out the scope and aim of each search, and we describe how we will truly eliminate the dangers that could erode the brand's unique identity.

To achieve this, first define goods, target markets, and geographical scope to shape the search. Identify the principal jurisdictions to protect and file, such as the USPTO, EUIPO, WIPO, and relevant regional registries.

The boundaries of the Nice Classification define the geographic regions where you can operate your brand.

By treating these boundaries as a solid map, you set a clear standard for searching goods and services.

A precise, well-organized search, focused on the most relevant classes, cuts down wasted effort and reduces the risk of chasing irrelevant marks.

Identifying the primary jurisdictional zones early on lets you protect your brand's identity and avoid costly missteps down the line.

Practical timelines for protection vary by jurisdiction and the complexity of the landscape, but a useful rule of thumb is to conduct a thorough preliminary search before filing a trademark application.

Conduct a pre-filing, multi-database search that considers common-law risk and possible confusion.

Understand each body's criteria for potential conflicts, such as similarity of goods or services, class overlap, and distribution channels.

By mapping out these risks early, you can make informed tactical decisions that reduce the chance of surprise objections later and keep your momentum intact.

To achieve effective search results, identify matches as precisely as possible and mark them clearly, so that any overlap of relevancy will not cause confusion down the line.

Record each risk, the recommended actions, and the timelines in a clear, actionable document, your playbook for trademarking.

This guide will help you decide whether to keep, change, or seek alternatives for each element, ensuring that your expansion strategy remains coherent and effective.

Document the findings in a decision log with concrete acts and dates, plan expansion with local versus global protection in mind, and organize a regional versus global protection scheme.

A diligent search not only protects your brand's identity but also saves time and resources in the long run.

## 6. TM and ® usage guidelines
### Applying Trademark Symbols (TM and ®)

In those cramped aisles of ordinary life, your product may perform well, but it is the careful mark you place on the packaging that signals quality and trust.

This chapter offers a practical guide to using TM and ®, helping you protect your brand's rights and ensure consumers recognize your seal of authenticity when they reach for your bottle of wine.

Understanding the difference between these marks is the first step toward avoiding fraud and building lasting confidence in your product.

The TM symbol indicates a claim to a mark you consider your own, even if it is not yet registered. The ® symbol may be used only after the mark has been officially registered with the appropriate authority.

These symbols are not decorative; they serve as legal notices that the product meets certain trademark criteria and that the claim is enforceable.

### Application of Trademark Symbols

When placing TM or ® on packaging or labeling, follow these steps:

- Use the symbols only for validated trademarks: apply the symbol after the mark has been verified and recognized by the relevant authority.
- Verify registration status: before using ® on packaging, confirm that the trademark is registered and current to avoid misrepresentation.
- Follow the rules of TM and ® by category and jurisdiction, ensuring that each product—whether cosmetics, supplements, or other goods—complies with the applicable laws.
- Keep the marks accurate and legalistic in size and placement and display them in a legible size so they can be read quickly by consumers.
- Only apply marks to SKUs that are authorized and registered; do not add marks to any other items.

By adhering to these practical rules, you preserve the brand's protection and maintain clear, consistent labeling across all packaging.

Ensure every authorized mark is clearly visible to inspectors and consumers, placing it where it can be easily seen without being overused or misused.

Use the 'TM' symbol to indicate a trademark claim you have made, even before official registration, but do not use the '®' symbol until the mark is officially registered. Keep the labeling clean, up-to-date, and compliant with jurisdictional rules, and respect the territorial boundaries that govern the use of these marks.

This approach preserves brand protection and maintains consistent, accurate labeling across all packaging.

## 7. Keeping your brand consistent across all channels

We begin with a simple premise: a brand is the supplier of trust.

The more people can recognize a consistent voice, look, and behavior, the more they know what to expect.

That consistency does not happen by accident; it arises when a single source of truth governs every brand decision, from the logo on the box to the tone in a caption on the product page.

This single reference point serves as the backbone for every team, partner, and contractor who represents the company.

Central to this discipline is centralization: a single repository of brand materials, logos, color palettes, typography, tone of voice, imagery, and messaging, provides the practical foundation for consistent execution.

By placing all brand assets in a single, well-labelled repository, teams gain instant access to the most up-to-date logos, color palettes, typography, tone of voice, imagery and messaging.

This central hub eliminates misinterpretation and misapplication, ensuring that every touchpoint—social media, web, packaging and beyond—reflects the same consistent brand identity.

The result is a solid core that is both abstract enough to travel across channels and concrete enough to stay true to the brand's essence, no matter where it is applied around the world.

Apple, Nike, and LEGO all demonstrate how a shared visual DNA and language can drive consistent brand identity across channels.

The core identity stays true to the brand's essence while flexing to fit each touchpoint.

For example, the social voice is intentionally more conversational, the website emphasizes clarity and credibility, and packaging leans into tactile cues and legibility.

A useful rule of thumb is to avoid rigid tone guidelines and overly prescriptive typographic grids; instead, keep the trademark simple and ensure the logo is used consistently across all channels.

Clear placement rules, line-mark guidelines, color palettes, and co-branding standards provide the structure that lets the core identity adapt without losing coherence.

The guidelines should spell out who can approve co-branding, what to do with protected elements, how to handle variations for partnerships, and what to do with approval workflows and asset management.

**Approval workflow:** The approval process for an asset, from initial creation to final publication, requires a structured approach.

This typically involves multiple stages, including internal review, audit, legal compliance checks, and a final sign-off to ensure all standards are met before an asset is published. Scalable templates for packaging and web speed, which preserve standards, to which should be linked the risk-free reporting of the brand on its own.

Define the core identity with channel-ready adaptations.

Create clear channel-specific style notes and usage rules, and detail trademark guidelines and co-branding procedures.

Implement formal approval workflows and scalable templates and schedule quarterly audits to stay on track.

A disciplined governance of assets and rules gives the brand a uniform identity that remains solid and immune to any identity crises.

## 8. Brand credibility signals: awards, certifications, editorial

Private-label products build trust through verifiable credibility signals, including certifications, awards, and independent testing.

These signals help consumers identify reliable brands.

Showcasing awards, certifications, and third-party testing signals a brand's commitment to quality and builds trust. These endorsements reinforce company values and help consumers make informed choices.

Consistently highlighting these signals strengthens the brand's reputation, builds loyalty, and provides a trustworthy edge.

- Select third-party testing partners carefully: choose labs and certifiers whose standards are recognized in your market.
- Align packaging, online content, and retail communications so that credibility signals appear consistently across product pages, point-of-sale materials, and other touchpoints.
- Credibility signals provide verifiable proof that underpins trust and differentiation; third-party testing and transparent claims demonstrate safety and honesty.
- Awards, editorial features, and proper trademark usage amplify signals and protect brand authenticity.
- A practical approach combines a signal map, credible sources, and consistent messaging across all channels.

Together, these credibility signals form a robust system for private label brands, demonstrating commitment, ensuring clarity, and building trust through verifiable proof across all touchpoints.

## 9. *Case studies of effective branding that increased price parity*

In crowded aisles where price often dominates, a brand that convinces customers its products deliver measurable benefits can let price be the only constant.

By keeping parity close to competitors while maintaining a clear, consistent, and credible identity, a brand can win the purchase.

Ritual, the supplement line, and The Ordinary, the skincare brand, illustrate this strategy: they thrive in markets with fierce differentiation and tight margins by standing out through a solid identity and a compelling bargain that resonates with consumers.

Both brands have maintained a consistent presence across websites, packaging, and retail, which justifies their premium pricing for consumers who value transparency, efficacy, and simplicity.

Ritual conveys quality and scientific rigor through sleek visuals and a credible narrative, while The Ordinary relies on unpretentious, straightforward packaging to communicate the same principles.

The key to their credibility lies in positioning through storytelling and design: linking product benefits to real outcomes, highlighting innovation and scientific backing, and offering a democratized, evidence-driven approach that resonates with shoppers who trust the brand enough to pay a higher price.

Whether it encounters the brand on its official site, in a store, or through third-party traders, the marks must carry a single language and a consistent quality to convey their shared weight.

They should send a clear message: the product delivers on its promises, justifying a premium perception wherever it is found.

**Takeaways:** use your marks to build a uniform image across all channels, advertising, retail, and beyond. Make the same story and tone resonate at every touchpoint, reinforcing parity.

By presenting prices as an exclusive truth and the product story as solid and real, the private label gains enough margin and integrity to compete effectively.

## 10. Branding pitfalls that erode trust

In the private-label arena, success is earned moment by moment through clear claims, reliable performance, and steady experiences.

When shoppers feel misled, the result isn't just a bad review it's a frayed bond that can erode trust, drive sales down, spread negative word-of-mouth, and even invite regulatory scrutiny.

The path to durable success isn't flashy; it's built on honest honesty, proven results, and a resolute commitment to the long run, as long as the customer keeps coming back.

Deceptive product claims, particularly those promising unrealistic cures or rewards, significantly erode consumer trust.

To foster credibility and ensure authenticity, all product claims must be rigorously substantiated by verifiable evidence, demonstrating that the product's performance aligns with its stated benefits.

Reliance on unverified testimonials and fabricated reviews must be avoided, as these practices compromise legitimacy.

The growing proliferation of such falsities poses a substantial risk to consumer confidence and market integrity.

Authentic credibility is built through transparent practices, genuine product experiences, and independent validation.

Consistency in message, visuals, and tone is absolutely vital for credibility.

An unalloyed voice across all touchpoints helps customers recognize quality and intent, strengthening their confidence rather than splitting it.

Today's shoppers care about what goes into products and where it comes from.

Lack of transparency is contagious, so clearly labeled, accessible sourcing details and regulatory compliance are not extras, they are core commitments.

When customers can verify ingredients and provenance, they trust the brand more than they trust advertising agencies. Best practices to mitigate trust-erosion risks: verify every claim, have goods tested by third-party labs, and guarantee transparent sourcing.

Use consistent branding across all channels to reinforce authenticity and reliability.

Ultimately, maintaining trust and a strong brand reputation hinge on the quality and presentation of your private label products.

Be clear and transparent about their quality and how they are handled throughout the supply chain.

Always guarantee that your private label offerings are truly worth the price and are never sold in poor condition; they should consistently represent the best you have ever made, fostering customer loyalty and positive word-of-mouth.

## 11. Takeaway

Develop a strong brand identity that clearly communicates your values and purpose, using core elements like name, logo, slogan, and visual style to tell a consistent story.

Create a comprehensive brand guide as the playbook for consistent messaging and visuals across all touchpoints, detailing logo usage, color palettes (Pantone, Hex, RGB), and visual system specifications.

- Typography: define approved type families, sizes, and styles for different contexts within your brand guide.
- Tone of voice: articulate your brand's personality, typical language, and guidelines for speaking to customers.

Initiate a robust trademark strategy as part of your overall brand protection plan.

Educate employees, partners, and vendors on proper brand and trademark usage to ensure consistency and compliance.

- Regularly review and correct marketing materials, websites, and social media to ensure alignment with current brand standards.
- Periodically revise the brand identity guide to ensure it evolves with company growth, maintaining consistent, true-to-life branding across all products and channels.
- Maintain vigilance in the market, ensuring every product consistently upholds quality and reflects the brand's image, irrespective of name or category.
- Conduct a brand identity audit and develop a comprehensive brand guide covering name, logo, slogan, visual elements, color, typography, and tone of voice. Ensure this guide is succinct and authoritative for practical use across all touchpoints.

# Chapter IV

## Packaging & Label Design

### Section 1.
### *Packaging science, psychology, FDA/FTC label requirements, transparency, sustainability*

More than a protective shell, packaging gives the seal its silent advocate, and its most public promise.

On the instant a product catches the eye, the outer presentation begins a conversation, shaping first impressions and setting expectations.

The seal's narrative, grounded in compliance, balances the demands of regulatory authorities, rules from the FDA and FTC that dictate everything from truthful claims and ingredient disclosures to the critical safety elements of tamper-evident features.

A consistent story across all channels builds credibility, brand recognition, and a lifelong faith in the "seal of honor."

Thoughtful design, grounded in compliance and a firm grasp of public purpose, creates a reputation that sticks and serves as the point to which our moral sensibility may lean.

## 1. Packaging psychology: shelf impact and product narratives

In a crowded aisle, a box arrests a shopper's gaze before the first word is even read.

Packaging psychology is the science that turns a simple vessel into a brief conversation, creating fleeting emotional bonds that build trust and keep a decision on the floor.

The first impression is shaped by color, texture, typography, and the tactile feel of the materials, signals that speak even when the copy is silent.

The shelf impact is not a single element but the totality of design, a clear narrative that tells the customer the product is good, will serve them well, and that they belong to the brand's community.

Let the product's personality shine through its visual language, color, shape, texture, and even scent. Use natural, eco-friendly hues and earthy tones that reflect the ingredients, and pair them with clear, simple icons that hint at use.

A short, benefit-focused line and a distinctive silhouette on the front or back give shoppers an instant sense of value without wading through long labels.

Ensure every claim is compliant with FDA, FTC, and other regulatory bodies, so the design not only tells a story but also meets all legal requirements.

It's not a burden; it's a design constraint that steers messaging toward honesty and clarity.

A health claim must be substantiated, clear, and presented to avoid misinterpretation.

The regulatory environment influences the size and substance of the text, and noncompliance can lead to fines, recalls, and damage to consumer trust.

The design must carefully follow claims and disclosures, ensuring every statement is compliant with FDA, FTC, and other regulatory bodies.

The brand's narrative anchors everything, and packaging must visually echo this story, weaving together color, typography, and imagery into a single, recognizable voice.

By aligning every visual element with the core narrative, the brand speaks consistently and responsibly across all touchpoints, from in-store packaging and shelf placement to social media and websites. This unified approach reinforces trust, highlights sustainability, and ensures an engaging message to the audience.

Practical steps include selecting responsibly sourced materials, using fewer components, and clearly communicating environmental commitments on the package itself.

Material choices and packaging footprint shape perception: the palette and physical size of packaging influence how a product is viewed. Excessive packaging signals wastefulness, while lean packaging suggests efficiency and care for resources.

Brands should weigh the environmental impact of their choices, aim to minimize waste, and optimize design for recyclability or reuse.

Thoughtful material decisions, recycled paper, plant-based plastics, minimal inks, support a positive impression and appeal to environmentally minded consumers.

Design the package to tell the product story quickly, with clear signals about use, benefits, and values.

Build in regulatory checks early to ensure claims and disclosures are as straight as possible, matching all rules.

Keep a consistent narrative across channels so the brand feels solid and trustworthy.

Signal sustainability through materials and packaging and track consumer response to eco-friendly cues.

Favor packaging that minimizes waste while keeping the product protected and convenient.

## 2. Tamper-evident packaging and safety features

Imagine pulling a piece of plastic from the shelf, weighing it by the sight of a seal, and wondering whether it is safe for you to take it.

It isn't about texture or taste, but about that seal that tells a story an entire packet that has not been opened or tampered with since it left the producer.

In a world full of mass-produced chain systems, these signs are the first proof that your product is authentic from factory to consumer, and that it is safe to keep sealed and unopened.

Tamper-evident packaging is essential for protecting consumers and assuring them that a product has remained sealed from factory to store.

Regulations from the FDA and FTC require manufacturers to use clear, reliable indicators that show if a package has been opened.

Common devices include adhesive strips or tapes that break or tear when the seal is broken, and plastic or paper "bands" that wrap around the seal and become visibly damaged upon opening.

These simple yet effective mechanisms give buyers confidence that the contents are safe and authentic, reinforcing trust at the point of purchase.

- Caps: tamper-evident closures that deform or break open.
- Induction foils: foil seals applied via induction heat, creating a tamper-evident barrier.

When selecting mechanisms, designers should consider recyclability and environmental impact so that nothing remains to compromise the packaging's sustainability.

**Consumer Understanding of Tamper Cues, Visual cues matter.**

Consumers rely on clear signals to determine if a product has been accessed.

The most effective designs offer intuitive, unmistakable indicators–such as a broken seal or a distorted cap–so the signal is obvious even at a quick glance, reducing confusion and risk.

### Documentation and Testing for Compliance

To satisfy regulatory expectations, records and validation are essential.

**Recording tests:** keep detailed logs of testing and validation for tamper-evident solutions.

**Third-party verification:** seek independent verification from auditors or testing organizations.

**Audit readiness**: ensure all drawings and testing records are organized and readily available for inspection.

An effective tamper-evident design hinges on collaboration among packaging designers, manufacturers, and regulatory experts, ensuring solutions meet consumer needs and regulatory standards.

Key features must be clear and visually convincing, so that consumers can detect tampering immediately at a glance.

## 3. The FDA/FTC requirement for supplement supplements

For private-label dietary supplements, foundational trust, quality, and repeat business are built on understanding the FDA's authority over product safety and the FTC's mandate for truthfulness and substantiation.

This shared regulatory framework ensures consumers receive accurate, reliable information.

For new launches, all label statements and advertising claims must be accurate, clear, and not misleading.

**Actionable takeaway:** Approaching label design as a compliance playbook, verifying every claim with credible data, is paramount.

## 4. FDA and FTC labeling requirements for cosmetics

Regulatory clarity is the invisible backbone of a successful cosmetics brand.

In the U.S., the FDA and FTC set the standards for what can be said and how products must be presented.

A good product must pass regulatory tests under the Food, Drug, and Cosmetic Act, with the burden of safety and accurate labeling falling on manufacturers and distributors.

Knowing the law and demonstrating compliance are essential.

There is no blanket pre-market review for cosmetics.

Continuous compliance through solid testing, robust documentation, and readiness for recall is crucial to maintain brand integrity.

Building a proactive process that monitors every new item, assesses its impact, and implements changes quickly, protects your private label and keeps it pristine.

Ensure all product ingredients are accurately listed and clearly visible on packaging, adhering to fundamental transparency principles.

Focus here on maintaining rigorous label accuracy, ensuring all claims are truthful and substantiated, and implementing proactive measures for regulatory monitoring and change control.

- Write a concise label template covering Product Identity, Net Quantity, INCI, Manufacturer/Address, and Warnings.
- Implement a simple checklist for verifying INCI listings.
- Build a voluntary fragrance/allergen disclosure plan to enhance transparency.
- Establish an annual audit cycle for label text versus formulas and claims.

**Real-world context:** brands that publish clear ingredient lists and honest disclosures tend to earn quicker trust from retailers and customers.

By embedding these practices, your private-label brand can compete confidently while staying compliant.

**Quick-start checklist:**

- Confirm that no pre-market approval is required for your product category.
- Ensure INCI listings are present and accurate.
- Verify manufacturer/distributor information is correct.
- Attach all necessary warnings.

Plan for sustainable labeling and verifiable sustainability claims.

## 5. Ingredient transparency and full ingredient declaration.

Ingredient transparency is paramount for packaging and labeling, serving as a cornerstone for building consumer trust and demonstrating ethical stewardship.

Clearly declared ingredients empower consumers to make informed choices, particularly concerning allergens, dietary restrictions, and personal values.

This not only enhances brand credibility but also mitigates potential health risks and ensures regulatory compliance.

## 6. Allowed vs restricted claims and substantiation

Product claims on packaging and labeling are critical for setting accurate consumer expectations, establishing brand credibility, and ensuring regulatory compliance.

Misleading or unsubstantiated claims can erode consumer trust, lead to legal repercussions, and damage brand reputation.

Therefore, all claims, from nutritional benefits to safety assurances, must be rigorously substantiated with scientific evidence.

## 7. Sustainability considerations and packaging costs

Packaging is more than a mere container; it is a visible commitment to a brand's values.

In a market where sustainability is the norm, packaging decisions become a strategic lever for environmental stewardship, cost control, and consumer trust.

The right choice aligns materials and processes with the brand's goals, creating a foundation for smart, dependable decisions that satisfy regulators, customers, and the bottom line.

By linking packaging to the brand's purpose, companies can build lasting value while protecting the planet.

A clear plan is essential for aligning enterprise goals with sustainable outcomes.

Companies must set objectives to cut waste, boost recyclability, and reduce environmental impact, ensuring compliance with regulations.

Transparency in these goals helps avoid greenwashing while building lasting value for all stakeholders.

Balancing the environmental benefits of sustainable packaging against potential cost implications is a key challenge.

Clear, regulatory-compliant disclosures help consumers understand trade-offs, fostering trust and avoiding greenwashing. This involves ensuring traceability and communicating facts in plain language.

Packaging optimization programs should right-size packages, use lightweight materials, and eliminate superfluous parts to reduce waste and cut costs.

By balancing environmental impact with financial goals, firms can deliver long-term savings and lasting value. Evaluating sustainability across SKUs and analyzing ROI ensures green initiatives align with budgetary constraints.

## 8. Sourcing sustainable materials and suppliers

Sustainability begins with material choice and extends through the product's entire life cycle.

To guide material selection and supplier choice, concrete objectives must align with the corporate vision, focusing on reducing environmental impact, minimizing waste, promoting recyclability, and ensuring supply chain transparency and accountability.

Clear packaging objectives lead to better supplier conversations and audit readiness. Identifying sustainable materials early is essential, along with assessing supplier credentials to ensure transparency and accountability throughout the process.

Proactive risk management safeguards sustainability goals from disruption. Core actions are:

- Identify single-source risk
- Develop offsets and contingency-sourcing strategies
- Require third-party testing and COAs
- Conduct regular supplier audits

By planning for risk, teams avoid surprises and keep steady progress toward responsible packaging.

**Actionable takeaways:**

- Define 4 clear sustainability objectives that align with your mission and regulations.
- Identify at least 3 sustainable material options early in development.
- Vet suppliers that hold recognized certifications and practice transparency.
- Design products with end-of-life considerations and ensure compliance with relevant rules.
- Build a supplier-risk plan that includes contingency options and scheduled audits.

## 9. Lifecycle messaging and recyclability commitments

Packaging is a critical communication channel for environmental commitments, particularly recyclability and disposal.

Its message must be clear, vivid, and concrete, directly addressing what happens to the product and its components at the end of its life.

Brands build confidence and credibility by speaking plainly and setting clear, measurable targets for recyclability. The message must be accurate, consistent, and easy to grasp, avoiding jargon.

Standardized symbols, codes, and transparent labeling (including a QR code) are essential tools for guiding consumers on recyclability and disposal. These provide clear, credible messages that boost consumer confidence, strengthen brand reputation, and encourage reuse and recycling.

This approach ensures brand accountability and makes the path to 100% recyclable packaging clear to shoppers.

Companies should define clear recyclability targets with timelines, use plain language, maintain consistency across all touchpoints, and publish progress regularly.

## 10. Label design best practices and readability

In a sunlit shelf, a bottle speaks before you even read the label.

The first handshake between product and shopper happens here, where clarity trumps bold graphics.

A well-designed label is more than a list of ingredients; it filters essential information quickly, reduces friction, and builds trust. This instant connection becomes the foundation of practical commitment, making the product feel familiar and reliable at a glance.

The practical takeaway is to design for comprehension before aesthetics.

A strong typographical hierarchy guides the eye across the label, effectively organizing information.

Using distinct font sizes and weights allows the product name to stand out and its claims to be immediately clear and complete.

The rule of thumb is to provide shoppers with a simple hierarchy they can quickly skim and understand.

Accessible copy goes beyond good print; it means using plain language that is easily understood by everyone, characterized by simplicity and directness.

Readable claims must be succinct, unambiguous, and speak to what truly matters.

To engage a multilingual audience and demonstrate inclusiveness, ensure each technical term is accompanied by a plain-language alternative and, where applicable, a translation. Compliance with FDA/FTC regulations for all legal requirements including labels, standards, ingredients, and warnings must be ensured.

This information should be prominently displayed and easily legible to consumers, avoiding overly small print that hinders readability.

Proactive validation of legal compliance is crucial from the earliest stages of development. Embrace sustainable and transparent packaging as a modern standard, as consumers increasingly expect and value such practices.

Clear and unambiguous presentation of information regarding recyclability and ingredient transparency is essential, without overwhelming the reader.

The goal is honest communication through simple, comprehensible typography, avoiding excessive regulatory jargon that can confuse consumers.

Effective label design prioritizes a clean set of readable pointers, including necessary regulatory details, to ensure clarity and appeal.

## 11. Summary

In today's crowded marketplace, packaging is the product's first conversation with the consumer, signaling quality, building trust, and setting expectations.

Strategic alignment of packaging and labeling from the start reduces costly errors and builds a clear pathway to scalable growth.

Prioritize design elements that immediately communicate value and trustworthiness.

Packaging and labeling are strategic disciplines that impact product integrity and consumer confidence.

By choosing durable materials and designing labels that clearly communicate safety and key information, you protect freshness and ensure consumer trust in every purchase.

This proactive approach turns packaging design into a competitive advantage, ensuring your product is trustworthy and market-ready from day one.

Focus on material choices that deliver appropriate barrier performance to maximize shelf life, considering protection against moisture, oxygen, and physical stress.

Translate these choices into robust material specifications and testing protocols.

Design labels with transparent ingredient lists, accurate nutritional information, and explicit allergen declarations to foster consumer trust and clarity.

Ensure brand-consistent typography and color on labels to reinforce key messages like freshness, safety, and quality.

Prioritize simple, readable designs with quick checks for clarity and allergen transparency.

Define shelf-stability early in product development and translate it into appropriate material choices and testing.

Choose efficient packaging that protects product integrity and always optimize typography and color for strong brand recognition and recall.

## Section 2.

### Regulatory labeling, translations and cost implications, claims substantiation

The impact of a product label reaches far beyond its surface.

It serves as a vital legal commitment between a brand and its audience, securing the truth and guarding against risk.

To fulfill this role, every claim must be clear, precise, and fully documented.

All allergen and safety disclosures must be handled with the utmost diligence, following the most universal and complete codes and standards. The requirements for each product claim are laid out in detail, and the costs of certification, cross-border compliance, and efficient operation are carefully considered.

By aligning legal, business, and operational aspects across the globe, we ensure that the label truly reflects what the product is and protects both the brand and its consumers.

## 1. Labeling compliance steps and documentation

Labels are a fundamental contract with the consumer, providing truth, clarity, and reliability in product information.

Effective labeling ensures adherence to legal prescriptions and industry standards, fostering consumer confidence and protecting brands.

To uphold these principles, a robust framework for documentation and processes is essential, ensuring integrity, reliability, and effective regulatory compliance.

This framework enables effective compliance with all relevant regulations, protecting consumers and stakeholders from deception. It includes a structured approach to documentation, covering the organization, control, and change-tracking of records, which ensures clear procedures for meeting regulatory requirements efficiently.

Furthermore, establishing a defined scope for labels and packaging, supported by a secure, versioned file system and periodic audits, is critical for traceability, accountability, and maintaining up-to-date information, thereby reinforcing integrity, transparency, and demonstrating ongoing compliance.

## 2. Translations and localization for the global market

First impressions matter, and in private-label packaging they matter more than ever.

The label is the product's opening statement to the world, so it must be legally correct, true to the brand voice, and easily understandable locally.

To reach the target market on your terms, you need a clear grasp of the regulatory landscape, whether you sell cosmetics in the United States or under the European Union's Cosmetic Regulation (EC No. 1223/2009).

By defining the scope of translation and localization early, you can ensure that your packaging is credible, compliant, and ready to succeed in any market.

Start by deciding what must be translated and what can remain unchanged.

The product name, description, and any ingredient list that is required by law should be translated first.

Label elements that are purely informational such as warnings, cautions, and claims can often stay in the original language if they are not legally required to be translated.

This early decision saves time and money by avoiding costly last-minute changes.

Regional norms also play a powerful role.

Color choices, imagery, and naming conventions vary from one market to another, sometimes more than the words themselves. For example, white may symbolize purity in the West but carry different connotations in parts of Asia.

Understanding these cultural nuances helps you design packaging that resonates locally while staying compliant.

In short, identify the mandatory translations, keep non-translatable elements consistent, and tailor visual elements to each region's norms.

This balanced approach keeps your brand credible and compliant across all markets.

Recognizing that symbols and images carry diverse meanings across markets, establishing a consistent brand identity is paramount. To achieve this, a centralized glossary is essential.

This glossary should define product names, claims, and technical terms, ensuring a unified vocabulary and protecting our brand voice consistently across all languages.

Establish a robust packaging quality-assurance system, leveraging certified translators and comprehensive Service Level Agreements (SLAs).

Conduct regular audits to ensure the correctness, consistency, and fluency of all localized content.

Develop a detailed market map and allocate budget for translation, quality assurance, and regulatory fees from the project's inception.

Implement parallel compliance checks to maintain consistent package standards.

### 3. Claims substantiation processes and evidence

In the crowded aisles of private-label cosmetics and supplements, claims like "reduces wrinkles" or "supports immune function" are common.

However, every product claim must be backed by robust, repeatable evidence and be ready for regulatory scrutiny.

This is not merely a best practice but a legal and ethical imperative, as regulatory bodies such as the FDA and FTC closely monitor product labeling and advertising to protect consumers from misleading information.

Unsubstantiated claims can lead to significant penalties, including product recalls, substantial fines, injunctions, and severe reputational damage.

A successful private-label program therefore hinges on establishing product consistency, tested efficacy, and readiness for review. This involves rigorous scientific substantiation, which often requires a combination of in vitro studies, consumer perception data, and, where applicable, clinical trials demonstrating the claimed benefits under specified conditions.

Maintaining clear, realistic, and well-documented claims is crucial for brand protection and regulatory compliance, forming an indispensable audit trail for all marketing and labeling materials.

## 4. Allergen labeling requirements

Allergen disclosure is fundamental to label design, packaging, and consumer trust.

Adhering to legal frameworks and regulations protects your brand and keeps consumers safe, requiring a detailed understanding of specific allergen classes and regional rules.

This includes understanding the practical requirements for allergen disclosure, such as market-specific labeling, formatting rules, and handling cross-contact.

Essential practices involve clear disclosure of potential allergen exposures, ongoing tracking of ingredient compositions, and accurate multilingual labeling, considering regional rules and translation requirements.

Furthermore, maintaining robust documentation, implementing strict cross-contact controls, and thorough manufacturing procedures are vital for ensuring product safety and consumer trust, encompassing comprehensive controls and required attestations.

## 5. Disclaimers and safety warnings

In health and wellness, trust is paramount, making disclaimers and warnings essential guardrails.

These statements are critical for protecting against legal risk, clearly defining product limitations, and ensuring promises remain reliable and transparent.

To achieve this, it is crucial to communicate product usage, contraindications, and potential risks with absolute clarity, preventing misunderstandings and minimizing legal exposure.

All such statements must be pure, precise, and truthful, meticulously avoiding any suggestion of cures or guarantees.

It is paramount to emphasize that general health information provided is not a substitute for professional medical advice.

Comprehensive allergen statements are also critical, and all warnings, especially regarding allergies and potential reactions, must be translated accurately by certified professionals.

Budgeting for both professional translation and thorough legal review is essential to ensure compliance and clarity.

## 6. COAs and batches, and ingredient declarations

COAs, batch numbers, and ingredient declarations form a critical system for product safety, traceability, and consumer trust throughout the supply chain. These elements go beyond regulatory requirements to provide essential records that confirm results, enable recalls, and facilitate clear communication with authorities.

COAs are indispensable for verifying product attributes like purity and potency, while batch numbers are crucial for unique identification, traceability, and rapid recall of products.

The synergistic use of COAs and batch numbers ensures thorough documentation, testing, and tracking of every product lot, creating a robust safety net for manufacturers.

Ingredient declarations provide vital transparency regarding product composition and allergen information, empowering informed consumer choices.

Balancing transparency with robust regulatory adherence is crucial for accurate product labeling and preventing misrepresentation.

Compliance with stringent labeling regulations is fundamental, benefiting manufacturers with sustained trust and market integrity, while non-compliant practices incur severe consequences.

• Regular testing and analysis of critical parameters are vital.

- Accurate record-keeping of production, testing, and analysis is essential.
- Transparency in communicating ingredients and allergen information to consumers is paramount.
- Continuous compliance with evolving laws and standards is required.

### Key Principles

Maintain a clear, integrated ledger linking COAs, batch numbers, and declarations for each product line.

Periodically review COAs, batch numbers, and declarations to ensure ongoing compliance with relevant regulations.

Ensure consistent and accurate reporting of ingredients and allergens on a regular basis.

## 7. Imports/exports labeling and regulatory alignment

A strong brand is crucial for international market effectiveness and establishing a superior global standing.

For private labels, and indeed any brand aiming for cross-border success, the key lies not merely in clever packaging, but in meticulously meeting the specific laws of each market.

Compliance with diverse and rigorous international and local regulations is imperative for successful market entry and sustained operation, transforming potential hurdles into strategic opportunities rather than obstacles.

By adopting a disciplined approach to every regulatory change, whether originating domestically or in a new country, brands can expand confidently across borders, avoiding costly adaptations or fines.

Required information includes ingredient lists, preparation instructions, freshness claims, and any warnings or advisories.

For Canadian food products, bilingual script is mandatory and must be accurately reproduced on packaging. This requires a robust translation process to maintain regulatory compliance and clear consumer understanding.

Maintaining precise records of all translations, approvals, and changes is crucial for ensuring compliance and facilitating audits.

This process is absolutely essential.

In markets where foreign-import and foreign-export work is conducted, translation, reprints, and audits are not optional; rather, they constitute the backbone of compliance. By carefully planning these activities, the risk of failure is reduced, and costs are kept under control.

A coherent cross-border branding strategy, built on a clear labeling scheme, protects against regulatory pitfalls and ensures that the most critical elements, those that regulators scrutinize most closely, are handled correctly.

The practical implication is clear: it is essential to plan for anticipated costs rather than reacting to unexpected issues.

A solid, scalable labeling program will ensure operations remain compliant and efficient.

Start with a centralized labeling playbook that maps country requirements, translations, and approvals.

Build a transparent change-control system and audit-ready documentation.

Budget for translations, reprints, and audits upfront, and reassess as markets evolve.

## 8. Sustainability labeling and eco-certifications

In a market crowded with claims, transparency is key.

Sustainability certifications go beyond a simple badge, serving as a system of trust that aligns with global regulations and provides assurance of a product's environmental and ingredient standards.

They build consumer confidence in product claims and choices.

While eco-certification involves costs, the benefits are substantial: independent verification boosts consumer trust, creates market differentiation, and aids regulatory alignment.

As products reach new regions, accurate multilingual labeling becomes essential to maintain credibility and consistency of claims and seals.

A coherent, sustained commitment to sustainability should thread through every touchpoint, from product pages to packaging copy, ensuring a unified and complete brand story.

## 9. Cost-optimizing the packaging and labeling

In the private label world, packaging is more than a shield for a product; it is a strategic lever that, if built well, shapes costs, compliance, and consumer perception.

The foundation you lay determines how lean, compliant, and credible your brand appears in the market.

This section provides a cost-conscious baseline and explains how every choice can be measured against the primary cost drivers.

The main drivers fall into three buckets: material costs (plastic, glass, paper and their finishes), machine operations (tooling, setup, cycle times), and design complexity (intricate shapes, tight tolerances).

Each decision trades off protection, sustainability, and cost, and a well-conceived, highly ornamental design can increase tooling and cycle times, so balance is essential for a lean, compliant, and credible product.

End-of-life costs, whether from recycling or disposal, add to the total cost of ownership and can influence both regulatory compliance and consumer perception. To keep decisions grounded, track these key metrics:

- **Cost per unit**: total packaging cost per item, including materials, production, and end-of-life considerations.
- **Packaging efficiency**: the ratio of packaging material to product weight, highlighting waste and maximizing opportunities for optimization.
- **Compliance rate**: the share of packaging that meets regulatory requirements, reducing rework and penalties.

Complementing these performance insights, rigorous attention to regulatory alignment for label content is essential.

Aligning label content with regulatory requirements ensures that claims and disclosures remain accurate, protects the brand's reputation, and keeps the product compliant.

Food labels must comply with FDA regulations, including nutritional labeling and allergen warnings, whenever changes occur.

By consolidating all multilingual information into a single master label, we can translate once for all markets, saving time and reducing the risk of errors during updates.

Choosing the right packaging format, whether a flexible, biodegradable option or a cost-effective design, helps balance protection, compliance, and environmental goals while meeting consumer expectations.

This approach not only cuts costs but also ensures that every claim is scientifically supported and sustainably verified.

Let the verifiable certifications—ISO 14001, FSC, and the like—serve as a foundation for your packaging strategy.

Build a modular labeling system with interchangeable components so you can keep SKUs low and reduce reprint costs.

Start by establishing a packaging baseline that covers cost per unit, efficiency, and full regulatory compliance.

Use a master multilingual label to cut translation effort and errors.

Evaluate every packaging format for total conversion cost, not just unit price, and rely on third-party credentials to substantiate sustainability claims.

This approach balances protection, compliance, and environmental goals while meeting consumer expectations and keeping costs in check.

## 10. Case study of packaging compliance

In a world where a single label can determine a product's fate, packaging is more than protection, it is a visible commitment to safety, legality, and trust.

This chapter follows a packaging-compliance initiative through a real-world lens, concentrating on a scenario that demands the strictest adherence to regulatory requirements and industry standards.

The goal is not merely to pass audits but to build a resilient system that guides every packaging decision, from material choice to final delivery.

Case Study Overview: Packaging Compliance Scenario, Scope, Objectives, and Success Metrics for the Initiative.

The scenario adopts an end-to-end view of the packaging supply chain, illustrating how each link contributes to overall compliance and confidence.

Every raw material, component, and process in the supply chain is governed by universal rules that shape our ethics, standards, and commerce.

Selecting materials that meet these laws ensures they can be recycled, are biodegradable, or safe for use.

A robust system must control every supplier input, monitor manufacturing and assembly, and enforce compliance at each step.

This holistic approach not only keeps regulations alive and active but also identifies and mitigates risks of non-compliance, protecting the company from penalties and reputational damage.

The result is a clear, end-to-end view of packaging compliance that aligns policy with practice and safeguards the entire packaging supply chain.

Achieving efficiency and cost-reduction is paramount, particularly within the context of packaging compliance, as it directly involves streamlining operations to mitigate significant expenses.

This encompasses optimizing processes, leveraging technology, and improving resource allocation – for instance, by optimizing packaging design and material selection to meet regulatory standards efficiently – to reduce costs associated with packaging non-compliance, such as fines, penalties, and legal fees. It also aims to eliminate inefficiencies like rework, wasted materials, and lost productivity.

By doing so, organizations can lower operational overhead, enhance profitability, and improve overall financial health and resilience.

*Metrics of Success* are a clear, measurable program guide to progress and decision-making, providing essential insights into compliance performance. These include:

- Compliance Rate: the percentage of packaging materials and products that meet the regulations' requirements.
- Savings in Penalties and Reheats: reduced penalties for compliance improvements.
- Time-to-Market: better time to market driven by better compliance systems.

Complementing these metrics, key operational strategies and initiatives for achieving robust compliance and efficiency are:

- Analysis of Suppliers: undertake a thorough review of your suppliers' practices to foster learning and deeper understanding.
- Qualification and Training: ensure your suppliers are adequately informed and equipped to understand and act on compliance requirements.
- Process Optimization: implement systems to streamline and improve inefficient or problematic processes.

## Label Translation and Compliance

Achieving global label compliance necessitates robust legal expertise, adherence to translation regulations, and a dedicated leadership structure for translation.

While initial investment in regulatory standards may seem substantial, it is justified by significant long-term benefits, including enhanced market confidence, expedited approvals, and tangible cost savings.

Accurate labeling is fundamental for meeting government standards, ensuring compliance, and realizing financial gains.

Expedited time-to-market, streamlining the product journey from concept to consumer.

Demonstrable business impact through quantifiable cost savings and efficiency enhancements, supported by empirical data.

Industry examples, such as Unilever and Procter & Gamble, illustrate how standardized packaging, disciplined governance, strategic supplier selection, and precise labeling establish a cohesive system.

This system safeguards consumers, builds brand trust, and provides a sustainable competitive advantage.

The synergy of key components, materials, suppliers, processes, labels, and substantiation, forms a comprehensive package.

This holistic approach upholds brand integrity, establishes a unified standard, and enhances market responsiveness.

## 11. Takeaway

On the shop-floor, a label is a promise a testament to scientific integrity and transparency for discerning customers.

Design labels that clearly disclose ingredients, enabling informed consumer choice, and plainly state net weight or quantity.

Prioritize clear warnings and cautions where necessary to build trust and ensure product understanding.

When designing labels, ensure clear ingredient disclosure.

Craft claims that accurately describe product benefits and are supported by evidence.

Anticipate that translating labels and packaging for new markets can be costly, requiring proactive budget planning.

Mitigate translation accuracy risks by implementing robust QA processes and native-language reviews to preserve meaning across languages and cultures.

Ensure all claims are supported by evidence-based statements and, where applicable, third-party testing.

Plan for third-party testing during product development, pre-launch, and for ongoing quality control, budgeting for typical timelines of 2-6 weeks and costs ranging from $500 to $5,000 or more. Proactively budget for packaging localization, reprints, and necessary label updates.

**To keep labels current, plan these allocations:**

- Packaging localization: 10-20% of total packaging costs.
- Reprints: 5-10% of total printing costs.
- Regulatory updates: 2-5% of total regulatory costs.

**Actionable takeaways:**

- Map each product's labeling path early, planning for clear disclosures and effective claim communication to build consumer trust.
- Build a QA cadence for translations and substantiation, with a documented testing plan.
- Reserve budget lines for third-party testing and ongoing regulatory updates to sustain brand credibility.

# Chapter V

## Regulatory & Legal Framework

### Section 1.

### *Overview of FDA, FTC and GMP requirements, third-party testing, compliance documentation, labeling laws, disclaimers, and international considerations*

In bringing dietary supplements and cosmetic articles to market, the creative engineer must abide by the rules of science, lest sweat turn into blood and fumes burn his hands.

He must also heed the regulations of agencies that hand over his bottles of vitamins and lotions, and the labels on his wrappers.

To navigate this complex terrain, one must learn the precise ways of working for supplements and their manufacturing requirements, which are both independent of and dependent on government inspectors and the FTC.

Only by understanding how this special system of regulation works can you chart the road you shall travel.

## 1. FDA overview of supplements and cosmetics

In a crowded market, the quiet truth is simple: every product that touches your body carries a thread of trust and safety.

The FDA is the conductor of two major product lines, dietary supplements and cosmetics, each governed by its own set of rules.

Private-label manufacturers know that compliance is more than a legal formality; it is a competitive advantage that builds consumer confidence.

Understanding the regulatory scope and key distinctions between supplements and cosmetics helps you navigate the market with clarity and confidence.

Cosmetics fall under the FDCA and are defined as products for beautification, cleansing, or altering the appearance of the body.

Knowing exactly which category your product belongs to is essential, as it determines the labeling requirements, safety testing, and inspection procedures you must follow before the product reaches consumers.

The FDA's focus is on ensuring a sound quality foundation and verifying accuracy, so that only safe, compliant batches reach the market.

Supplements demand rigorous testing for identity, purity, and potency to support ingredient claims.

While cosmetics also follow GMPs, the focus shifts to safety, cleanliness, accurate labeling, and product integrity.

Both sectors rely on third-party tests, audits, and thorough record-keeping to ensure that every batch is safe, compliant, and trustworthy for the market and the consumer.

The labels must clearly state identity, provide a complete ingredient list, and include a supplement facts table, demonstrating that everything is accurate and fair.

Beyond these foundational FDA requirements, comprehensive compliance demands attention to global standards, especially for export.

Companies must ensure a clear statement of identity and an accurate ingredient panel.

Proactive compliance also includes identifying the correct product category (supplement or cosmetic) and understanding all applicable regulations, both domestic and international, such as the European Cosmetics Regulation No. 1223/2009 for products destined for the EU. Building robust GMP-type processes for identity, purity, potency, safety, labeling, and sanitation is paramount.

Plan early for product development and claims, ensuring all assurances and substantiation are readily available.

Establish robust post-market monitoring and an efficient system for reporting any adverse events.

When exporting, adhere to the compliance standards of the destination market and consider seeking third-party testing as a signal of confidence and a commitment to safety.

## 2. FTC advertising guidelines and substantiation

Before the product hits the shelves, its true test begins long before flavor, scent, or packaging coalesce.

It is the regulatory set that protects consumers, guides brands, and shapes every claim we make.

The FDA and FTC are the two branches that act for the benefit of people, ensuring safety, efficacy, and truthful labeling.

Below is the road map of who watches what, how you demonstrate quality, and what it takes to succeed with integrity in a crowded market.

This shows the essential regulatory functions you must perform to speak authoritatively on your own terms.

The FTC oversees advertising claims, demanding substantiation and preventing misleading practices.

Just as our advertising must comply with FTC guidelines, our product labels also demand meticulous attention to detail and regulatory compliance.

Labels must be precise and compact.

Typical requirements include ingredient lists, nutrition information, allergen warnings, directions for use, and any necessary disclaimer or disclosure.

We should be diligent in verifying that each label meets FDA standards and, where applicable, the regulations of foreign markets.

Keeping a systematic audit of all ingredients and claims helps us avoid omissions and ensures compliance across all regions. This approach protects us from costly mistakes and maintains the integrity of our product information.

### Advertising Substantiation: FTC Guidelines, Truthful Claims, and Substantiation

Standards require that advertisers back every claim with competent, reliable evidence. This often necessitates robust data from independent, third-party testing.

When choosing a third-party lab for this purpose, select one with established credentials, proven experience with similar products, and transparent methodology to ensure the credibility of results.

Ensure claims are truthful, supported by the most robust data, and accompanied by clear disclosures when necessary.

A private-label brand thrives when GMP, labeling accuracy, third-party testing, and honest advertising align from day one.

The proof is in the records you keep, the tests you perform, and the clarity of every claim you publish.

**Quick takeaways:** map claims to the correct regulator (FDA vs FTC) early; build a vigorous GMP program and maintain a thorough documentation system; use independent labs for credible testing; keep labeling and disclosures consistent with safety and truth standards; and plan for international rules from the outset.

### 3. GMP and manufacturing controls

In private-label manufacture the story of a product starts long before the label is ever printed.

Good Manufacturing Practices (GMP) provide the discipline that guarantees consistency, ensuring each batch meets the same high standard.

The process begins with rigorous control of incoming materials and a formal qualification of suppliers, followed by audits and continuous monitoring to confirm that the suppliers' systems perform as promised.

By protecting consumers, preserving brand trust, and creating a stable foundation for growth, GMP keeps the product's quality uniform and its value intact in an increasingly competitive market.

Process controls ensure that production runs adhere to a strict schedule, that equipment is calibrated and recalibrated on a defined timetable, and that critical process parameters stay within the established limits.

Every batch must generate a complete batch record, tracing every action from raw material to finished product. Such a record is indispensable for root-cause analysis, confirming whether a failure was an error or a coincidence, and for maintaining consumer confidence.

Checklists document the SOPs for all essential processes, while regular calibration and maintenance of machinery keep equipment in optimal condition.

Capturing critical parameters and any deviations in each batch provides the systematic ledger needed to identify and eliminate defects before they reach downstream stages.

In-process testing involves systematic sampling and analysis at various stages of production, ensuring that quality standards are maintained from the moment raw materials are introduced.

Third-party validation, conducted by regulators or independent auditors, provides objective verification that established standards are consistently met and that products comply with all GMP requirements.

We take the matter in a controlled and orderly fashion, tracing the materials and products we handle so that we can quickly return to their source when quality exigencies arise.

A strictly controlled change-control system evaluates, approves, and implements changes, while traceability systems track materials and products as they move, enabling identification if a quality issue surfaces.

Regular audits and inspections, internal, external, and third-party, keep us alert to gaps, and the Corrective and Preventive Actions (CAPA) that run the ship make it a real-world possibility to act on any problem.

This systematic approach turns each audit and inspection into a guide, allowing us to look back, learn, and ensure that genuine issues are addressed promptly and effectively.

CAPA should become a daily habit, with clear owners, timelines, and measurable results. By anchoring private-label manufacturing in these GMP foundations, brands protect consumers, earn retailer confidence, and become long-term winners in a crowded marketplace.

### 4. COAs, batch-records, QA documentation.

In the fast-moving world of supplements and cosmetics, the true strength of a brand lies not in clever branding or packaging but in the quiet, unglamorous backbone of COAs, batch records, and QA documents.

When these elements are robust, the brand can stand its ground during inspections, weather recalls, and regulatory scrutiny, all while proving its quality.

A Certificate of Analysis (COA) is a formal record that documents a product's quality, purity, and freshness. Its creation standards and format are detailed further below.

Batch records are the complete files that document the production run for a single batch.

QA documents live within a larger quality-management system and include policies, procedures, and records that show compliance with regulatory requirements and industry standards.

For detailed insights into batch record contents, lot traceability, and QA documentation controls, please refer to the comprehensive sections that follow.

### Why COAs, batch records, and QA documents matter

1) Compliance – regulatory bodies such as the FDA and FTC require clear evidence that products meet safety and labeling rules. COAs, batch records, and QA documents provide that evidence.

2) Consistency – standardized testing, processes, and controls reduce variability, ensuring each batch performs as intended.

3) Traceability - if a problem arises, you can trace the product back to its raw materials, the factory, and the specific batch, enabling precise action and faster resolution.

**COA Creation Standards and Format:** A comprehensive COA should present the following information in a clear, concise manner:

- **Test Methods**: Detailed descriptions of the analytical techniques used.
- **Results**: Numerical data and observations.
- **Acceptance Limits**: Criteria for pass/fail decisions.

- **Lot Number**: Identification tied to the tested batch.
- **Issuing Laboratory**: The facility that performed the tests.
- **COA Validity Period**: The timeframe during which the COA remains applicable.

**Batch Records and Lot Traceability:** For complete traceability and regulatory readiness, batch records should capture the following:

- **Batch Record Contents**: What was produced, with dates and quantities.
- **Lot-to-COA Linkage**: Direct connection between the batch and its COA.
- **Complete Lot Traceability**: Ability to trace from finished product back to raw materials.
- **Change Control**: Procedures to document and approve process or record changes.
- **Audit Readiness**: Clear, organized records that withstand regulatory review.

**QA Documentation Controls and Retention:** Effective QA documentation requires adherence to the following:

- **Document Control Systems**: Centralized management of all QA documents.
- **Versioning and Approvals**: Clear history of updates and authorized sign-offs.
- **Retention Requirements**: Retention periods aligned with GMP and FDA/FTC expectations.

**Third-Party Testing Alignment and Certificates:** For many manufacturers, external laboratories play a key role. Practical steps include:

- Coordinating with qualified labs to conduct the necessary tests.
- Ensuring COAs accurately reflect test reports from those labs.
- Managing and distributing COAs in line with regulations and customer agreements.

**Actionable Takeaways:**

- Maintain a robust traceability chain from finished product to raw materials.
- Implement strict change-control procedures with documented approvals.
- Keep audit-ready records and a centralized document control system.
- Align retention schedules with regulatory requirements.
- Coordinate closely with third-party labs and ensure COAs are accurate and compliant.
- Conduct thorough COA, batch-record, and QA document checks to uncover gaps in linkage and audit readiness.
- Establish an informal change-control and version-control system for all QA documents, setting a baseline that defines standards for third-party laboratory qualification and prevents misreporting.
- By integrating every product record and procedure, you create a framework of compliance, consistency, and trust that will secure long-term partnerships with your customers.

### 5. Claims substantiation and labeling rules

Imagine launching your first private-label line of supplements and cosmetics by building on a foundation of proven evidence, clear communication, and disciplined compliance.

This section introduces the critical role of claims substantiation and labeling, which are not optional features but the core of every product you offer.

A comprehensive understanding of regulations and claims is essential: the Food and Drug Act mandates labeling for dietary supplements and cosmetics, while the FTC monitors advertising to prevent deceptive practices.

Following Good Manufacturing Practices, securing third-party testing, and fully proving quality and safety are fundamental steps.

By establishing trust, evidence, and pure, transparent communication from the outset, you create a solid base that can be expanded upon with confidence and integrity.

Beyond these national rules and fair competition standards, robust regulations ensure fair competition and prevent deceptive practices.

**Key Regulatory Bodies and Standards provide the framework:**

- FDA: Establishes labeling rules and the kind of claims that can be made, along with language that is truthful and not misleading.
- FTC: Monitors advertising to ensure it reflects product reality and does not mislead consumers.
- GMP: Provide the baseline for production quality, process controls, and traceability.
- Third-party testing: Independent verification of ingredients, potency, purity and stability supports credibility.
- Fair competition: Rules against deceptive or unfair practices help protect consumers and brands.

Detailed requirements for claims substantiation and documentation are outlined in the subsequent sections.

Claims substantiation requires maintaining comprehensive dossiers on all claims to demonstrate they are true and not misleading, backed by the amount, type, and rigor of evidence.

A practical approach is to assemble a living file that includes testing results, method descriptions, data, conclusions, date-stamped records, details on how evidence was obtained, who performed it, when, and under what conditions.

This robust dossier becomes the backbone for inspections, audits, and consumer inquiries. Furthermore, labeling content must faithfully reflect the ingredients, quantities, warnings, and uses disclosed in the claims.

Mastering the various categories of claims is essential: health claims, nutrient-content claims, and food-claims each describe how the product relates to disease risk, vitamin and mineral content, or overall nutrition.

Structure/function claims describe how a product affects the normal structure or function of the body without implying disease prevention or treatment.

Advertising and labeling must meet the same substantiation standards. Inconsistencies between what is claimed in ads and what appears on the label can lead to enforcement actions and erode consumer trust. Therefore, messaging should be harmonized across packaging, website copy, social media, and promotional materials.

Disclaimers such as "not evaluated by the FDA" and safety statements must be clear, accurate, and proportionate to the claim being made. Risk statements should communicate uncertainties without deterring informed choice.

International regulatory considerations apply to all these elements.

When exporting, account for country-specific labeling rules, import alerts, and translation needs—noncompliance can lead to seizures, fines, or reputational damage.

Plan early for multi-market labeling, cross-border claims, and local consumer expectations.

Build a claims dossier system from day one, recording evidence types, sources, and dates; establish a practical third-party testing plan and keep a record of results.

Set up labeling and advertising checklists to ensure consistency across all channels and map the international labeling requirements for your top markets to avoid costly revisions later.

## 6. Disclaimers and warnings, etc

Labels serve as both compass and contract in the private-label world, guiding consumer choices, protecting health, and shielding the brand from risk.

Adhering to specific disclaimers and warnings, such as FDA requirements for supplements, is crucial for meeting regulatory obligations and maintaining customer trust.

For comprehensive details on disclaimers and warnings, refer to the detailed guidelines on global labeling requirements.

Allergy labeling and ingredient transparency are essential for any product applied to the skin or consumed orally.

The FDA requires that every potential allergen, peanut, tree nut, milk, egg, fish, shellfish, wheat, and soy be clearly listed, and that the full ingredient list be disclosed. This transparency builds trust and protects consumers from unexpected reactions.

By providing accurate, easy-to-read information, manufacturers meet regulatory requirements while maintaining credibility with their customers.

Structure-function claims, which describe how a product supports normal body function, are permitted but must never claim to diagnose or treat disease.

Additionally, cosmetic warnings and safety precautions are essential to set clear usage expectations and prevent adverse effects.

For comprehensive details on permissible claims, cosmetic warnings, and other safety precautions, refer to the detailed guidelines on global labeling requirements.

Planning for global labeling from the outset, rather than as a supplemental add-on, is critical.

Labels must always be translated into local languages and meticulously checked against the specific requirements of each target market to preserve uniformity across brands and product lines. Consult regulators to ensure all disclaimer and warning statements are accurate and compliant.

For dietary supplements, the FDA requires a disclaimer stating the product has not been approved and that the FDA is not a medical authority, which prevents implying medical endorsement and clarifies legal boundaries.

Structure-function claims, which describe how a product supports normal body function, are permitted but must never claim to diagnose or treat disease; when uncertain, frame claims around general wellness or daily support.

Additionally, precise safety warnings and cosmetic precautions are essential, including external-use allergy risks, warnings against applying to damaged skin, and clear instructions for handling potential sensitivity or irritation.

By addressing these comprehensive requirements, you protect consumers, maintain product integrity, and effectively meet jurisdiction-specific labeling rules when expanding into global markets.

### 7. Remember those procedures and adverse event reports

Every recall is a disciplined, cross-functional process that protects people, keeps markets honest, and maintains order and safety. It begins with the discovery of a defect or contamination, the report of an adverse incident or injury, or the failure to meet regulatory requirements.

The owner of the product initiates the recall, setting the chain of events in motion. This coordinated effort, detailed in the following sections, ensures operations remain under strict control and trust is pre-served.

**Manufacturer:** The manufacturer initiates the recall, informs distributors and retailers, provides recall instructions to consumers, and maintains comprehensive tracking and documentation of the recall process.

**Distributors and retailers:** Distributors and retailers act on recall instructions, halt distribution of affected lots, and assist with consumer communications.

**FDA:** The FDA oversees the recall, ensures regulatory compliance, and offers guidance and support to the manufacturer throughout the process.

**Timelines:** Establishing clear timelines is critical for rapidly reducing risk and protecting people during a recall.

– Notify the FDA within 24 hours of discovering a potential recall.

– Initiate the recall within 48 hours of notification to the FDA.

– Complete the recall within a reasonable timeframe, usually 30-90 days, depending on the scope and severity.

**Record-keeping:** Meticulous record-keeping is essential, including maintaining batch-lists, recall logs, and tracking systems for all affected items.

Escalation thresholds and decision-making authority must be established to guide the recall process effectively.

Prompt notice and recorded action for every incident are paramount.

The recall system must clearly define decision-making authority, communication channels, and notification chains.

Maintaining thorough record control and traceability ensures all actions are documented, provides accurate information to regulatory authorities, and empowers timely, transparent decision-making compliant with established thresholds.

Post-Recall Corrective Actions (CAPA) and Adverse Event Reporting are crucial to closing the loop on every recall and fostering continuous improvement.

After a recall, it is essential to implement corrective measures based on thorough root-cause analysis. Verified actions confirm the success of these measures, ensuring the issue is resolved and preventing recurrence.

Promptly capturing adverse events is vital for informing risk assessment and regulatory reporting. This involves immediately documenting adverse events, assessing their severity, determining reportability, and submitting reports to relevant authorities like MedWatch.

Effective recalls hinge on clear triggers, shared responsibilities, and swift timelines.

Robust documentation and traceability enable quick reactions and provide confidence with regulatory certainty.

Ultimately, CAPA and MedWatch reporting serve as critical learning opportunities, strengthening future product safety and compliance.

## 8. International export/import considerations

When a private-label product crosses oceans, you are not simply moving inventory—you are stretching your brand into a new legal and cultural ecosystem.

The opportunity is real, but so is your responsibility to protect your assets, satisfy local requirements, and keep your experience consistent with your customers.

What are successful ventures doing in practice?

They blend smart IP protection, meticulous compliance, and collaborative adherence with competent partners. Register your IP in all the countries you plan to enter. Protect your ideas first. Secure your trademarks, copyrights, and patents as soon as you can. It helps curb counterfeit activity and prevents your brand from being used in unauthorized ways.

Learn the local IP laws, file early, and monitor filings in your priority markets.

Real-world consumer brands protect their marks across borders to preserve long-term value, often using the Madrid System for international trademark protection. This lets you file a single application that covers multiple countries, ensuring consistency and efficiency.

Register your marks in each target market and evaluate the Madrid System for its cost-saving benefits.

Early protection prevents costly disputes and downstream bottlenecks when you scale. Establish cross-border priorities compliance, labeling, and documentation to keep your trademark filings up to scratch and deter counterfeiters while safeguarding design rights worldwide.

Exporting private-label products requires a tight alignment between export and import rules.

**Focus on three core priorities:**

**Compliance** – understand the safety standards, consumer protections, and customs clearance requirements in each destination.

**Labeling** – match the language, format, and content to local regulations so the product is legible and compliant.

**Documentation** – keep a reliable trail of origin certificates, invoices, shipping records, compliance certificates, and testing and inspection reports. Every document must meet the destination's legal standards.

Additionally, pay close attention to taxes, duties, and HS codes, keeping margins in mind.

In every case, consult a trade expert or a customs specialist, and then work with a trusted broker to ensure accurate classification and smooth clearance.

Partner with accredited manufacturers and laboratories that meet local standards and Good Manufacturing Practices.

Real-world brands rely on vetted labs to verify product safety and performance before market entry, so take your product seriously and maintain a rigorous quality-management record for every market, ensuring all aspects meet the destination's legal standards.

## 9. Documentation and recordkeeping best practices

For regulated products, effective documentation isn't just a requirement—it's the linchpin of success.

The difference between navigating challenges and achieving your goals often lies in the files you keep.

A robust documentation system provides a practical backbone, standing up to FDA/FTC standards, GMP practice, and the scrutiny of auditors. It is not a vanity project but a working tool that clarifies decisions, protects products, and earns the trust of regulators and partners.

When done right, it records what was done, when it was done, and by whom, providing a solid foundation for compliance and continuous improvement.

A robust record-controlled system ensures all documents are reviewed, approved, and distributed in a controlled manner.

Maintain a comprehensive change history log, detailing dates, times, the individual who made the change, and a clear plan for implementing each change.

Controlled access to records is essential, with privileges granted only to an authorized class of personnel. Procedures for sharing information with internal teams and external partners must be clearly defined and secure, as a well-regulated system is paramount for security. Additionally, develop clear batch protocols outlining plans for testing, sampling, and acceptance criteria.

For labeling and packaging, verify the accuracy of the label and the integrity of the packaging before it reaches the market.

Implement standard templates and checklists, and ensure teams consistently use them to avoid errors.

An effective labeling and packaging system, with necessary precautions, enables teams to operate efficiently without compromising accuracy. It also ensures all stock is visible at a glance and that regulated brands rely on consistent, standardized forms.

Third-party testing and record-keeping—including storing Certificates of Analysis (COAs), certificates, and reports, must be handled with confidentiality and precision. Compliance schedules and approval records should be maintained rigorously, even when outsourcing testing.

In regulated zones, cross-functional teams must collaborate closely, following these standard guides to minimize confusion and protect brand integrity.

All results must be controlled and deposited as trusted parts of the record, following clear procedures that keep the contents secure and prevent outdated items from lingering.

A well-defined retention schedule ensures that records are kept only as long as they remain useful, after which they are properly disposed of.

This approach preserves the integrity of the brand and complies with law and policy, providing a simple, reliable system that is easy to follow and maintain.

## 10. IP basics and the trademark

When a brand expands to mass sales, its most precious asset is its private label—a built-for-purpose identity that customers recognize, trust, and remember.

Intellectual property (IP) is not an abstract concept here; it is the practical framework that keeps innovations orderly, protects the brand, preserves its value, and enables growth. This section provides a comprehensive overview of IP basics and trademark protection.

A solid IP strategy starts with a clear understanding of what IP covers, how it supports what you sell, and what it actually protects.

To safeguard the unique aspects of your offerings and establish credibility, you must know the types of IP available.

Trademarks protect brand identity—names, logos, and taglines—ensuring distinctiveness and consumer recognition.

Patents cover products that are novel and non-obvious, protecting unique inventions and designs.

Copyrights guard original materials, including packaging, which signal the uniqueness and identity of your product rather than generic offerings.

By aligning these IP tools with your product strategy, you preserve value, prevent confusion, and secure a foothold in the marketplace based on distinctiveness, not just price.

**Aligning IP Protection with Product Strategy**

To secure your brand and protect its value, follow these essential steps:

1. **Thoroughly search for the right trademarks:** Check all known classes and jurisdictions for infringement to ensure distinctiveness.
2. **Decide on appropriate trademark classes:** Classify products and services (e.g., for cosmetics and supplements) and cover all product lines and packaging.
3. **Create a Brand Protection Plan:** Register marks in key markets, actively monitor sales channels, and take swift action against counterfeits.
4. **Evaluate patent opportunities:** Assess the novelty and non-obviousness of unique formulations and, if applicable, consult with legal counsel to pursue patent registration.

5. **Guard copyrights:** Protect original branding materials, including logos, packaging designs, and content.
6. **Secure your domain and web presence:** Keep all domains and ensure your brand's web presence is consistent and unmistakable to avoid online confusion and cybersquatting. Map each brand to at least one effective protection tactic and build a monitoring plan to catch violations early. This comprehensive approach safeguards both the mark and the consumer, securing a competitive edge in new markets.

### Common Threats to IP

Infringement: Unauthorized use of IP can dilute a brand and damage reputation.

Counterfeiting: The production and sale of unauthorized copies erode trust and harms the brand's image.

Cybersquatting and domain-name confusion: When bad names proliferate, the meaning of a good brand is lost, leading to consumer confusion and reputational damage.

A disciplined IP framework protects growth. For example, a cosmetics line that registers a trademark for its name and distinctive trade dress on packaging reduces the risk of imitators.

A startup evaluating a novel formulation for patent can secure its unique edge and expand into new markets.

### *11. Takeaways*

### Actionable Strategic Imperatives:

- Integrate compliance as a proactive brand differentiator, not a reactive checklist, to build enduring consumer trust.

- Treat each product category (e.g., foods, drugs, cosmetics, supplements) as a distinct regulatory track, requiring specialized expertise and dedicated operational approaches.
- Future-proof your brand by designing compliance frameworks that anticipate international market entry and diverse regulatory landscapes.
- Leverage robust documentation and a "compliance library" not just for audits, but as a strategic asset to accelerate product launches and market expansion.

## Section 2.
### Third-party testing, audits, compliance roadmaps

The path from product concept to consumer trust is paved with rigorous verification and unwavering commitment to standards.

In the cosmetics and supplement industries, safeguarding quality and compliance is paramount.

First, select a reputable third-party laboratory, then interpret the Certificates of Analysis and match the results to the specifications.

Next, conduct stability testing to confirm shelf life and ensure long-term product integrity.

Finally, maintain GMP certification, perform supplier audits, and keep thorough documentation to stay audit-ready.

This systematic approach builds confidence in every product that reaches the consumer.

It also facilitates new product regulatory compliance, supports the establishment of robust protocols for adverse event reporting, and ensures thorough preparation for international shipment.

### 1. Lab testing and COA interpretation

In the world of private label, the promise travels with each bottle—safety, quality, and accountability.

The most effective way to back it is with third-party laboratory testing, not just for regulatory formality but as an investment in credibility with retailers and consumers.

By setting a high bar and making independent lab testing the baseline, you build trust and protect yourself from liabilities, giving you the bargaining power to defend your product's integrity.

This commitment to rigorous testing lays the foundation for a healthy, credible private-label business that stands out in a competitive market.

**The payoff is clear:** fewer recalls, a stronger brand reputation, and a smoother path to scale.

Start by selecting labs that meet ISO 17025 accreditation, ensuring a competent quality-management system and credible technical competence.

CGI and GLP credentials are the gold standard for disciplined, traceable, and reliable data.

For businesses selling abroad, verify that the lab can meet the specific market requirements.

Keep the list short, request method-validation documents and COAs, and use those certificates to gauge clarity and practicality.

A well-chosen COA is the proof that testing meets the specification, limits, and units you need to trust your product's integrity.

When reviewing COAs, first confirm that the results match the defined standards and the appropriate reporting units for the substance.

Verify that the limits listed are the ones you need and that the intended use is clearly reflected.

Cross-check the COA against the batch records— the lot number on the COA should match the internal lot records, and the limits should be consistent with those set for the batch.

Look for any outliers; if they appear, ensure they are explained and that the testing scope was adequate. This quick verification step prevents mislabeling and guarantees that the product's integrity is upheld.

### Have a robust COA verification procedure

Cross-reference every COA source with your own records, confirm the results against the specifications, and resolve all errors before releasing the product.

Assign a verification owner, establish a checklist, and require a second review for high-risk categories such as allergens and contaminants.

Audit readiness and data integrity are critical: keep traceable COAs, secure storage, and complete audit trails.

Ensure data integrity by controlling access, backing up documents, and maintaining up-to-date inventory records for recall readiness.

Define a clear testing frequency and sampling plan and determine how often each lot should be tested to maintain product quality and compliance.

A clear plan, built upon robust lab selection and verification processes, keeps surprise delays in check and aligns with the product's risk profile and market requirements. Implement a Protocol for Non-Conformities (PNC) to provide practical escalation paths and notification procedures, preventing a long-winded, painful "locked-out" process.

This integrated approach, which includes diligent COA verification and the use of checklists with clearly defined owners, ensures that products are released promptly and in compliance.

Ultimately, this delivers both transparency and efficiency, safeguarding data integrity while maintaining product quality and regulatory readiness.

Integrate COA management seamlessly with your product specifications and batch records, securing the rigorous test trails they must follow.

Embed your defined testing cadence and sampling plan directly into your launch calendar and establish non-conformity protocols from the outset as part of your overall quality management.

Ultimately, private-label brands that publish COA-backed claims on retail shelves leverage them as a clear seal of approval, not merely a vague promise.

This practice not only protects the brand but also drives shelf commitments as the business scales, demonstrating an unwavering commitment to safety, quality, and accountability.

## 2. Stability testing and shelf-life validation

The value of a cosmetic or supplement product lies not only in its color, fragrance, or promise, but also in its purity, strength, and performance.

A critical factor for maintaining these qualities is shelf life, the period during which the product remains stable, safe, and effective from manufacturing to consumer use.

To ensure this, rigorous testing of the material's chemical, biological, and physical qualities is essential.

By carefully studying and protecting shelf life, we guarantee that the product delivers its intended benefits throughout its entire consumer journey.

**Our goal is clear:** to confirm that a product remains stable and effective throughout its intended shelf life.

Stability testing reveals how formulations degrade, guiding optimal packaging and storage strategies, and helping manufacturers maximize performance while mitigating risk.

Its regulatory relevance is significant: agencies such as the US FDA and the European Chemicals Agency (ECHA) require stability testing to verify product safety and efficacy.

The data also underpin Good Manufacturing Practice (GMP) compliance, demonstrating a rigorous quality-control process and a commitment to consumer protection.

Establishing an effective stability-testing program requires building it on solid, practical pillars: the composition of the formulation, the packaging, the storage conditions, and, crucially, the physical, chemical, and microbiological properties of the product.

### Types of Stability Testing

To accurately assess shelf life, it's essential to determine the appropriate testing methods: real-time, accelerated, and stress testing. The timeframe for these tests is determined by the product's intended shelf life.

Acceptance criteria are established for every stability-related property, and the specific testing types and durations are chosen in accordance with regulatory requirements.

- **Real-time stability testing** evaluates the product under normal storage conditions for extended periods (typically 12 to 36 months), directly mirroring its expected shelf life.
- **Accelerated stability testing** exposes the product to elevated, stressed conditions (e.g., higher temperatures or humidity) to predict its long-term stability more quickly.
- **Stress testing** involves even more extreme conditions to force degradation and identify potential weak points in the formulation.

A comprehensive stability profile is built by applying the right mix of these tests, guided by industry standards and regulatory rules.

Understanding the differences between real-time and accelerated testing is crucial for accurate shelf-life determination.

Accelerated stability testing, while conducted over shorter periods, provides valuable predictive data on a product's potential long-term behavior.

The most robust stability programs blend both real-time and accelerated approaches.

This combination allows for the capture of degradation pathways and, where possible, demonstrates how performance under real-world conditions can be safely assured.

The goal is to translate stability data into reliable shelf-life criteria, ensuring product quality throughout its lifespan.

Developing a comprehensive stability testing schedule is paramount.

Companies can either establish internal capabilities to conduct these tests or enlist the aid of qualified third-party laboratories. The objective is to consistently verify that products meet their promised quality and performance attributes from manufacturing through distribution and consumer use.

Thorough auditing and meticulous record-keeping are indispensable for any stability testing program.

Laboratories must maintain comprehensive records of all testing protocols, raw data, results, and conclusions. Such detailed documentation is crucial for demonstrating compliance during regulatory inspections and for upholding product quality standards.

A robust plan for stability testing and ongoing quality control ensures adherence to legal requirements and builds consumer trust.

## 3. GMP certifications and supplier audits

Before the label is peeled back, the foundation is laid by the supplier's behind-the-scenes work: the checks, the records, and the tested ingredients that link raw material to finished good.

In the private-label world this is the role of GMP certifications and supplier audits, practical standards that turn quality into everyday practice and give regulators, retailers, and customers confidence in what ends up on the shelf.

These certifications act as both a shield and a compass, helping you keep risk in check and ensuring baseline compliance from start to finish.

Certification programs set a minimum bar, while supplier audits verify that the bar is met in real operations, not just in policy documents.

The result is safer products, fewer recalls, and clearer accountability across the supply network.

To build a reliable supply chain, define clear criteria for qualification and a sensible audit cadence.

Evaluate factors such as each supplier's GMP compliance history, quality-control processes, and overall risk profile.

A risk-based approach lets teams focus energy where it matters most, enabling initial qualification and then regular re-audits, often yearly or bi-annually, to ensure ongoing compliance.

**Practical check:** tailor audit frequency to risk tier, not just volume, and keep a consistent check on audit cadence to maintain a solid chain of trust.

Third-party lab testing and GMP standards form the steadying force behind product safety. Independent laboratories confirm identity, potency, purity, and safety, and their work should harmonize with GMP standards.

Choose labs accredited by recognized bodies such as ISO or the American Association of Analytical Collaboration (A2LA).

By validating ingredients and finished products in your warehouses and factories, you reinforce regulatory readiness and build consumer trust.

Prepare your compliance program with clear, actionable steps:

- Corrective action plans: state explicit obligations to correct non-compliance and assign responsible owners.
- Accountability: designate a clear owner for each item.
- Deadlines: set realistic milestones to track progress.

In a written plan, you establish a clear routine that keeps you abreast of audits, supplier changes, and regulatory updates.

The documentation becomes a transparent trail that supports audits, negotiations, and continuous improvement.

Audit your own records and certifications at every level of the company and certify third-party tests and corrective actions.

By building a solid baseline with GMP certifications, supplier audits, and third-party testing, you give your clients and regulators confidence in your processes and demonstrate that you are a leader with a clear vision.

## 4. Audit trails and QA workflows

In the private label world, the story of a product begins long before it sits on a shelf.

The quiet backbone of this journey is the audit trail and the quality assurance (QA) workflow, meticulously following every step from the first material cue to the moment a customer holds the finished item.

This comprehensive framework protects regulatory compliance, preserves data integrity, and creates a transparent record of all activities, ensuring every detail is visible and trustworthy.

Central to this system, the audit trail provides verifiable evidence of every transaction, guaranteeing transparency from material sourcing to the finished product.

This robust traceability allows you to quickly ascertain who did what, when, and why, promptly answering any doubts about a specific batch.

By establishing compliant processes that record each activity, from sourcing, production steps, and testing to packaging and distribution, private label brands create a clear product lineage.

This lineage not only meets regulatory requirements but also upholds internal company standards.

Mapping each stage to a precise record facilitates a simple lookup, revealing the full history of any unit, while clearly defined roles in QA and compliance maintain an organized and trustworthy workflow.

A clean, well-documented system is crucial for preventing gaps and delays. It ensures every QA check is performed correctly, assigned to the right person, and recorded in real-time with tamper-evident storage.

This meticulous approach guarantees that all controls, versioning, and documentation remain intact and auditable throughout the product's entire life cycle.

Effective lot tracking is another critical component. Assign a unique identifier to each lot and continuously track its journey through the entire process, keeping a living record of material movement, processing steps, test results, and final disposition.

This detailed log enables swift recalls and precise investigations whenever a quality issue arises, ensuring rapid response and containment.

Following any identified non-conformance, the Corrective and Preventive Action (CAPA) workflow is initiated. This process systematically recognizes non-conformances, identifies root causes, and drives the implementation of necessary corrective and preventive actions.

The CAPA cycle concludes with thorough verification that the measures have successfully prevented recurrence, thereby restoring confidence in the supply chain and satisfying auditors.

**Summary Takeaway:** By embedding traceable processes, clear roles, sound recordkeeping, robust lot tracking, effective CAPA flows, and proactive audit readiness, private label brands build trust with customers, regulators, and partners—setting the stage for sustainable and scalable growth.

## 5. To regulate what you say, labeling, compliance

In the world of medical technology, a great idea starts with a blueprint.

The real difference-maker is a comprehensive regulatory compliance roadmap that turns ambition into a compliance-ready, market-ready product.

By defining product scope early, you can accurately classify whether a claim falls under cosmetics, a dietary supplement, a medical device, or another category, and understand the specific tests and permissible claims each classification requires.

This upfront clarity significantly cuts risk, expedites approvals, and keeps teams focused from concept to launch.

To ensure your product meets all legal and market expectations, it's crucial to establish accurate claims and testing protocols early in the preparation and labeling process.

This includes engaging with a Third-Party Testing Plan from day one, securing an independent laboratory, and defining a robust protocol. Proactive third-party validation builds essential credibility with regulators and ensures claims are substantiated, even if the initial protocol details are still being refined.

External validation, especially by accredited laboratories, reveals true product performance and builds essential credibility with regulators.

Companies demonstrate trustworthiness by substantiating claims, whether for a cosmetics line or a medical-device maker that tests materials and sterilization processes.

This confidence is reinforced by a clear "Structured Compliance Milestones" calendar. This roadmap lays out every filing, audit, renewal, and re-certification on a definite timeline, from pre-market clearance or approval, GMP certification, and label and claims validation, through ongoing post-market monitoring.

Successfully managing these milestones ensures real-world brands avoid last-minute scrambles and can spot problems early.

By meticulously documenting each step, including pre-market clearance, GMP certification, label and claim validation, and ongoing post-market monitoring, companies demonstrate continuous adherence.

Robust record-keeping and a formal audit-and-corrective-action loop reinforce that compliance is a living process, not a one-time check.

This disciplined approach keeps regulators and partners confident that the brand is prepared, allowing the business to focus on growth rather than firefighting.

Coordinating contracts with laboratories and manufacturers is essential for a smooth roadmap. These agreements should precisely spell out scope, service levels, intellectual property (IP) protection, and confidentiality.

Clear, enforceable terms prevent disputes and safeguard product integrity and business interests.

Look to industry examples where precise Service Level Agreements (SLAs) and well-defined IP clauses thwart friction during scale-up. Furthermore, ensuring trademark, labeling, and claims alignment maintains consistency across product names, packaging, and marketing communications.

Develop comprehensive labeling and claims validation checklists to sustain FDA/FTC compliance throughout the product life cycle, minimizing mismatches between what is marketed and what the evidence supports.

A unified approach, as demonstrated by leading cosmetics and supplement brands, highlights the value of coherence across all touchpoints.

The framework for a robust compliance roadmap is completed by mapping risk assessment and contingency planning.

Identify potential disruptions, such as supply issues, regulatory changes, or recalls, and map clear escalation paths.

A robust contingency plan saves crucial reaction time and preserves customer trust when unforeseen events occur. Synchronizing compliance requirements with each phase of product development is paramount.

Every milestone reached not only enhances your product's capability but also strengthens your readiness for regulatory scrutiny, instilling greater confidence in engineers when product launches occur and endure.

What we all need is a real-world model of disciplined, practical planning on this journey.

## 6. Adverse event reporting processes

Beyond proactive planning and readiness, an equally critical component of maintaining consumer trust and regulatory adherence involves robust adverse event reporting processes.

In the world of cosmetics and supplements, safety data is not a rumor whispered in a corner but a production parameter that shapes trust, compliance, and growth.

When an adverse event (AE) occurs, a structured path is activated: entries, reviews, and actions flow from the earliest signal to the formal response.

This chapter explains how AE reporting becomes an efficient channel of protection, improvement, and accountability, defining AEs and showing how they become a matter of law, just as they are for drugs and other regulated products.

The process begins with the first signal, moves through recognition and documentation, and culminates in decisive action that safeguards consumers and upholds regulatory standards.

Clear definitions eliminate ambiguity and ensure consistent triage across teams.

Standardized data capture is crucial, covering every detail from product name and batch/lot to onset date/time, symptom description and severity, patient demographics and exposure, co-administered products or confounding factors, and reporter information and location.

A uniform record set cuts errors; speeds triage and supports credible analyses for both internal and external reporting.

This disciplined approach protects consumers, satisfies regulators, and enables decisive action when it matters most.

The clear deadlines and well-defined roles keep teams focused on investigations,

Corrective and Preventive Actions (CAPA) initiation, and regulatory submissions. By setting explicit boundaries, each member knows exactly what to do, which eliminates confusion and prevents oversights.

When a potential issue is spotted, the team immediately shifts attention to that case, ensuring that corrective actions are taken swiftly and that regulatory channels remain open and compliant.

A robust regulatory channel is essential for AE reporting.

In the United States, MedWatch handles consumer safety reporting, while CAERS manages cosmetic-related adverse events.

These channels require ample documentation and timeliness.

Downstream actions must include thoroughly probing the root cause, documenting corrective actions taken, and communicating these actions to stakeholders. A clear escalation path must be defined.

All actions, including regulatory reporting (MedWatch, CAERS, and recalls as necessary) and other downstream activities, must be meticulously logged for future reference and linked to the CAPA process for lasting improvement.

## 7. Remember now readiness and product remediation plans

In the fast-moving world of consumer goods, a recall is far more than a mere setback; it is a test of an organization's readiness to protect people, preserve trust, and respond with discipline.

This comprehensive guide outlines a practical, action-oriented approach to recall readiness and product remediation, blending risk management, regulatory awareness, and brand stewardship.

The goal is to be proactive, anticipate issues, mobilize quickly, and act decisively, so that harm is averted and confidence is maintained.

To translate theory into action and establish a repeatable framework for recall readiness, organizations must define key operational components.

This begins with establishing a dedicated, cross-functional recall team responsible for swift mobilization and effective management. The team's initial steps include thoroughly assessing all available inputs, from consumers, regulators, and business partners, to determine the validity and scope of potential recall events.

Critical to this process are clearly defined recall triggers and thresholds, which prompt immediate action. Common triggers include:

• Product defects or contamination
• Labeling errors or omissions

Failure to comply with regulatory requirements, consumer complaints, or adverse event reports trigger the need for a structured remediation approach.

Remediation playbooks standardize the initial steps to contain and address a recall, including:

- Quarantining affected products
- Fixing or reworking products
- Testing and verifying product safety and efficacy
- Verifying product integrity and authenticity

Once initial containment and verification are complete, comprehensive product remediation and repackaging protocols are implemented to restore full product integrity and safety, involving:

- Thoroughly restoring product integrity where necessary
- Validating all rework and repackaging processes
- Safely redistributing compliant products

Regulatory reporting and timelines require timely notification and documentation.

Notify agencies such as the FDA and FTC within specified deadlines and provide thorough records to support the actions taken.

Third-party testing audit readiness ensures reliability by maintaining accredited labs, accurate records, and certificates to pass audits.

Beyond immediate response, robust root-cause analysis identifies systematic failures and informs preventive controls, ensuring recurrence is prevented.

Thorough investigations uncover the true cause and enable corrective measures.

A well-structured recall readiness program balances people, processes, and information so that when a recall occurs, the response is quick, precise, and effective.

Throughout the process, customers will be informed promptly about recalled goods and any related compensation, ensuring transparency and trust.

## 8. Label claims, compliance checks, and internal reviews

Labels carry more than words; they carry trust.

In foods and dietary supplements, every claim is a contractual promise with the consumer and with regulators.

A misstep can ripple into recalls, expensive fines, and lasting damage to a brand's credibility.

The antidote is a disciplined, repeatable system that turns regulatory expectations into everyday practice.

### Establishing Essential Checks for Label Claims

A well-built checks framework begins with a standardized workflow that assigns clear ownership, defined steps, and concrete checkpoints. This makes the path from idea to label claim transparent and verifiable.

The claims verification workflow includes:

- Conducting a preliminary review of the claim to identify potential regulatory issues.
- Gathering and analyzing supporting data, including scientific studies and regulatory guidance.
- Evaluating the claim's compliance with relevant laws and regulations, such as FDA guidelines.
- Managing internal approvals and signatures, including preparing and signing reports and documentation before publication.
- Recording every approval and maintaining detailed records for future audits or investigations.
- Conducting a routine review and update of all documentation to ensure claims remain sharp and accurate.
- Maintaining a constant pulse on regulatory changes, monitoring the latest interpretations and modifications from agencies like the FDA.

Proactively address any regulatory change or new information, ensuring your claims program is prepared for Third-Party Audits and remains ahead of scrutiny from consumers, retailers, and investors.

To be thoroughly auditable, a robust claims program should function like a well-kept library: every statement must be traceable to its source, every source meticulously documented, and every file recording who accessed or modified it, and when.

This meticulous record-keeping is crucial for demonstrating compliance and building trust.

To build a strong claims system, create and maintain a centralized repository for all supporting data, scientific studies, and regulatory guidance.

Schedule routine reviews for this documentation, with triggers for updates tied to any regulatory changes.

Prepare third-party audit packets in advance, including all source data, validation records, and compliance documents.

Ultimately, treat all label claims as verifiable commitments rather than mere marketing promises, thereby establishing a solid foundation of compliance that strengthens brand value for both consumers and regulators.

## 9. Export paperwork and global regulations

From the shelf of your kitchen-cabinet to distant retail shelves, the leap into international markets hinges on more than a great product.

It relies on a disciplined plan, careful preparation, and a process that clarifies every requirement beyond the point of sale.

An export readiness assessment serves as a compass for private-label brands: it reveals regulatory gaps, confirms documentation needs, and charts optimal routes, partners, and terms for smooth cross-border movement.

Real-world examples, Kirkland Signature, Amazon Basics, Trader Joe's private-label lines, demonstrate what is possible when compliance, branding, and logistics align. Mapping regulatory scope and country-specific requirements ensures seamless entry into diverse markets.

Before exporting, you must understand which rules apply to your product in each target market.

This means labeling, packing, and safety standards differ by jurisdiction; the European Union enforces strict food-safety and labeling rules, while the United States has its own set of requirements.

Make a list of the most important items you need for your category, anticipate changes, and build in time to accommodate them.

Keep an official checklist for every country of interest to ensure compliance at every step of the export process.

Common export documents include commercial invoices, bills of lading, certificates of origin, and export licenses.

Keep them accurate and complete errors log, can trigger delays, fines, or even rejection at the port.

Start by examining your target market and distribution channels to understand buyer requirements and identify routes and ports that offer the best price and fastest delivery.

Build a checklist that covers every country of interest, and verify each document's fields, currency details, and product particulars before shipment. Doing so avoids long delays and ensures a smooth export process.

Selecting the right distributors, co-packers, and freight forwarders, along with clearly defined freight terms, is crucial for successful delivery.

Thoroughly vet potential partners by assessing their experience, reputation, and capacity.

Verify their certifications and ensure their capabilities align with your cargo and operational needs.

Document all agreements meticulously; robust communication channels between your operations and partners are vital for managing the entire supply chain.

Furthermore, ensure the accuracy of Harmonized System (HS) codes for customs duty verification, and that all HS export certificates are provably correct and well-documented.

Accurate labeling and country-specific documentation are essential to prevent hold-ups at customs.

Proper translation and meticulous attention to country-specific documentation will significantly reduce the risk of delays at ports of entry.

The international protection of intellectual property abroad is also essential; protecting trademarks in target markets (e.g., via USPTO, EU-IPO, or local authorities) and swiftly enforcing infringements will be critical for your brand's security.

To put these principles into practice, utilize this eight-point readiness checklist:

—Confirm product classification (HS code) for target markets
—Map regulatory requirements for labeling, packaging, and safety
—List required export documents and assign owners
—Identify target routes, channels, and potential partners
—Vet distributors, co-packers, and freight forwarders
—Define freight terms, payment terms, and delivery schedules
—Verify destination labeling and translation needs
—Protect IP with timely trademark registrations and monitoring.

The real-world takeaway from these insights is to be ready and use these steps to create a practical map before systems are deployed and shipments go overseas.

This proactive approach benefits retailers, private-label manufacturers, and the growing tide of American enterprise entering the global market.

10. Insurance and regulatory risk management

In the cosmetics and supplements aisle, a single product can derail a brand after launch, turning a costly misstep into a costly recall.

Behind every trusted SKU lies a disciplined, practiced approach to risk that catches issues before they become incidents, turning regulatory demands into an advantage.

**This section outlines the framework:** how risk management preserves continuity, how insurance underpins compliance, and how a living system of controls keeps your company ready for audits, lawsuits, and the inevitable surprises at every stage.

### Insurance and Regulatory Risk Management

The best way to manage risk is to treat it as a routine discipline, not a reaction to rare trouble.

A well-planned strategy covers regulatory compliance, third-party testing, and audits, acting as a shield that protects operations, cash flow, and brand reputation.

When executed properly, it turns potential disruptions into manageable events and keeps the project's momentum steady. Insurance plays a key role in this framework, providing financial security against the liabilities that arise from product development, distribution, and storage.

Product liability insurance, for example, covers losses or injuries linked to defects or contamination.

Together, disciplined risk management and robust insurance coverage ensure that a company remains ready for audits, lawsuits, and the inevitable surprises at every stage.

### The Role of Insurance in Regulatory Compliance

- **General Liability:** guards against third-party claims for bodily harm, property damage, or personal injury.

- **Recall Costs Insurance:** covers the costs of a recall, including notification, retrieval, and disposal.
- **Errors and Omissions Insurance:** shields against claims of negligence, errors, or omissions in development, labeling, or marketing.
- **Cyber Liability Insurance:** addresses data breaches and cyber incidents that threaten sensitive information.

Aligning Insurance Coverage with GMP Compliance and Labeling Claims GMP compliance costs and labeling accuracy are costly and visible risks. Insurance should reflect those realities and any enforcement penalties.

### Consider:

- GMP Compliance Costs: training, equipment, and facility upgrades necessary to meet standards.
- Labeling Error Contingencies: re-labeling, re-packaging, and notification expenses.

### Enforcement Penalties:

-Fines and penalties imposed by regulators when non-compliance occurs. A dynamic calendar keeps risk controls current and comprehensive.

### Build in:

- Policy Renewal Dates: keep these at all times.
- Audit Cycles: keep auditing in line with your schedule.
- Regulatory Changes Alerts: stay aware and adjust promptly.
- Testing the Timing: validate your controls and GMP compliance at defined intervals. Map your readiness against inspection and audit:
- Internal Controls: check and test them for effectiveness.
– Supplier Audits: ensure they are conducted on schedule.

- GMP Checks: examine every corner of the supply chain for compliance. The Incident Response and Recall Plan is a constant rhythm that keeps the organization prepared for any event.

**The key elements are:**

- Clear Roles and Responsibilities, assigning incident response and recall leadership.
- Notification Protocols: alert regulators, customers, and stakeholders in a timely manner.
- Customer Communications: transparent messages that address concerns and preserve trust.
- Financial Buffers: reserve funds to cover recall and crisis costs.

## 11. Actionable takeaways:

Start with a real-time risk map covering product development, labeling, testing, and data handling.

Align insurance policies to likely GMP costs, labeling contingencies, and penalties you might face.

Create a living calendar that refreshes annually and after every regulatory change.

By adopting these principles, cosmetics and supplement brands can shrink their liability, maintain compliance, and shield the bottom line while delivering safe, trusted products.

**Strategic Imperative:** Embed a "living compliance roadmap" that continuously verifies product claims through independent audits and rigorous third-party testing, transforming regulatory diligence into a source of undeniable brand authenticity and market leadership.

# Chapter VI

# Finding and Vetting Manufacturers

## Section 1.
## Domestic vs. overseas production, vetting partners, MOQs, contracts, IP

For any product creator, the initial strategic decision is critical.

This choice defines not only the production territory but also the entire approach to bringing a product to market. Initial cost and time-to-market are largely determined by this market entry strategy.

A secure supply chain is ensured through diligent partners and detailed logistical arrangements, accommodating diverse climatic zones and operational requirements.

### 1. Domestic vs. offshore production

In the private-label world the very first decision is not the feature set or the packaging, but where to produce the product.

Geography dictates the cost, speed, risk and the sequence of moves you must make, and that choice becomes the foundation for every subsequent decision, materials, timing, quality, price.

Domestic production is faster, more controllable and lets you test and tweak your goods on a daily basis, but it is also more expensive per unit.

By manufacturing within your own country you reduce shipping risk, enforce quality more freely and can bring a product to market in days rather than weeks.

The proximity often gives us the advantage of quicker iterations and tighter feedback from colleagues and stores, while labor costs can erode profits in regions where wages are high.

Offshore production may offer a window of opportunity for certain products, but the ramp-up can be slow starting with a single line means coordinating components over long distances.

You'll need to manage careful quality control, protect intellectual property, and keep teams well-coordinated to avoid trouble.

In short, domestic manufacturing lets you test and tweak goods daily, reduce shipping risk, enforce quality more freely, and bring a product to market in days rather than weeks, but it comes at a higher per-unit cost.

Regulations for cosmetics and supplements differ significantly by country.

For instance, U.S. FDA regulations for dietary supplements involve specific rules regarding permissible claims, ingredient lists, and labeling.

The EU has distinct requirements for cosmetics.

Ensuring compliance is essential; however, navigating the complexities of regulatory requirements, including the time and cost involved, can pose significant challenges.

Careful consideration should be given to partner selection, as Quality Control and IP Protection depend heavily on the region.

When evaluating foreign suppliers, if their local Quality Assurance (QA) system meets the desired standards, it is often satisfactory. However, offshore suppliers frequently necessitate a rigorous QA process, certification, and guaranteed IP safeguards.

It is essential to verify the quality of your partners at every stage of your project.

Keep good relations of trust and confidence so that your partner can provide constant certainty, traceability, and conformity to your requirements.

Vetting should include diligence, certifications, references, and adherence to standards.

Conduct thorough due diligence: request certifications, verify references, and confirm the partner's ability to meet regulatory and quality requirements.

Map the procedures for QA, IP protection, and compliance history to your product's environment.

Define ownership, confidentiality, QA responsibilities, pricing, change orders, and termination rights in the contract.

Engage legal counsel early to clarify these terms and avoid confusion.

Finally, consider offshore MOQs and scalability, ensuring that minimum orders fit your forecast and that the supplier can scale with your needs.

Offshore MOQs can constrain early launches, but they also give you a clear view of your supplier's capacity and help you plan for growth.

By setting realistic minimum orders that match your forecast, you keep the flexibility to scale without being locked into a single contract.

Keep communication and culture at the forefront, regular updates, shared language, and a mutual understanding of risk will keep the partnership strong.

Diversify your sources and regions to build supply-chain resilience and stay alert to changes in demand or regulatory environments.

With these practices in place, your minimum orders will stay aligned with your needs and your supplier will be ready to grow with you.

## 2. Finding manufacturing partners, directories, brokers, referrals

A founder pins a promise to a wall: quality, consistency, and speed.

He then charts a path to make that promise real, placing a trusted manufacturing partner at the helm.

This opening section offers a practical framework for selecting and vetting manufacturers, guiding you through the process until you secure a reliable partner such as the American Factory.

The result is shorter lead times, higher standards of quality, and stronger regulatory compliance—advantages that give you real power in the market.

To ensure a reliable manufacturing partner, thorough credibility and capability checks are essential. This includes conducting financial due diligence by reviewing statements and credit reports to gauge stability, and performing site visits to assess facilities, equipment, and quality control (QC) processes.

Additionally, investigate:

- **Certifications:** confirm ISO 9001, FDA compliance, or other relevant standards for your product.
- **Client references:** speak with previous customers about performance.
- **Audits:** schedule regular audits to enforce ongoing adherence.
- **Real-world note:** brands that insist on visible QC practices and third-party certifications tend to reduce post-launch surprises and preserve margins

While general vetting practices apply universally, working with overseas manufacturers introduces specific considerations.

Longer lead times and potential communication problems can arise, as can the complexity of regulatory compliance and quality control. Import duties and tariffs add another layer of cost.

In practice, many brands begin with domestic prototyping to move quickly and maintain tight control, then scale overseas once the product and demand mature.

Patience with early testing pays off when the product hits the market with a solid track record of quality.

### MOQs and Minimum Order Quantities

- MOQs shape cash flow and inventory risk; negotiating them keeps your launch on track.
- Sample runs: test capability and quality with small batches.
- Staged orders: grow quantities as you validate demand.
- Align with your launch plan: ensure MOQs fit your marketing and sales schedule.
- The contract is where protection and clarity live.

### Key provisions

- Non-disclosure agreements (NDAs) to guard ideas.
- Clear ownership of designs, specifications, and data.
- Termination clauses and dispute-resolution mechanisms.
- Intellectual property clauses should cover licensing, royalties, and post-termination use.
- IP ownership and licensing boundaries are clearly defined, ensuring that rights and obligations are unambiguous.
- Termination provisions and exit strategies are kept in place to safeguard continuity and protect both parties.

**Practical tip:** build exit steps and data-handover mechanisms early, so that in both good and bad times you can transition smoothly. Work with reliable, experienced partners who understand your industry and can help you manage costs and supply.

**Real-world illustration:** Patagonia balances supply and access with transparency, while Apple relies on tight IP protection and rigorous supplier standards to maintain scale and trust.

Decide on your domestic strategy, weighing speed, cost, and control before each move.

When executing this strategy and expanding, conduct rigorous credibility checks (including site visits and audits), start with a small sample run before staging orders to scale, lock in IP protections and termination terms in clear contracts, and build a network of credible directories, brokers, and referral partners to support your growth.

## 3. Vetting criteria and certifications (ISO, NSF, GMP)

In a world where every link in the supply chain can influence the final product, consistency is not a luxury but a guarantee.

It becomes the quiet backbone of trust, ensuring that partners across continents and time zones know they can rely on you.

This section lays out a practical framework for establishing baseline procedures and certifications that set the benchmark for quality.

By defining standards up front, you avoid missing critical parameters that could imperil performance, safety, or perception.

The result is a network that delivers with clarity, accountability, and traceable results, making you the trusted choice wherever the chain collides.

I am never satisfied with perfection at every turn, but I do value transparent, auditable consistency that can be checked every inch, every day.

ISO 9001, the cornerstone of quality management, signals to your partners that they can consistently produce goods and services that meet customer expectations and regulatory requirements.

In addition to ISO 22000 for food safety, consider real-world, take-home checks for your partners.

Third-party certifications from NSF International, which often follow NSF/ANSI standards, provide independent verification of safety, quality, and GMP practices, ensuring that your supply chain remains reliable and trustworthy.

These certificates give you an extra layer of confidence that a partner's ingredients and processes are safe and meet stringent requirements for quality and efficiency.

**Practical note:** verify not only the certificate itself but also the scope of the products it covers, the warehouses where they are produced, and the traceability of any deviations and corrective actions.

Every GMP inspection must be thorough, and a detailed, auditable trail of control results, deviations, and corrective actions can significantly reduce recall risk and make issues easier to manage.

This level of transparency is essential for reliable, trustworthy supply chains.

A quality contract establishes clear responsibilities and standards for both parties, and a regular on-site audit is the best way to verify that those standards are met.

The audit should include a thorough inspection of the supplier's processes, a review of ISO certifications and any industry-specific standards, and a detailed record of any non-conformances.

Corrective actions must be documented, traced, and followed up to ensure that deviations are resolved before they can affect the product.

Traceability—through batch records, audit trails, and corrective-action logs—provides the safety net that reduces recall risk and makes issues easier to manage.

By keeping a transparent, auditable trail of control results, deviations, and corrective actions, the supply chain remains reliable and trustworthy.

- Confirm that third-party certifications from NSF International (such as those based on NSF/ANSI standards) for the products and facilities are valid and applicable.
- Review GMP-related documentation: QC tests, batch releases, deviations, and CAPAs.
- Establish and sign a formal QA agreement, including audit dates and responsibilities.
- Ensure robust traceability: lot numbers, COAs, and retention timelines.
- Make consistent quality a measurable goal across all partners, backed by documented processes and evidence.
- Demonstrate competence and commitment through certification and active quality management.
- A proactive QA framework protects the brand, builds trust with customers and partners, and safeguards the supply chain.

### 4. MOQs, lead times, and capacity planning

The clock that swings three different tempos!

The product's launch date, the supplier's production cycle, and your cash-flow calendar, guides every decision in this book.

In the section we outline five key levers that shape both timing and money: MOQs, production runs, lead times, capacity planning, and contract terms.

Understanding how these pieces fit together is the difference between a launch that glides into the market and one that stumbles on day one.

MOQs are the minimum quantities a supplier requires in a single order, and production runs determine how many units you ship at a time.

By aligning these levers, you can turn a launch that flutters into a freefall into the ocean into a launch that rises and floats freely.

They anchor the supplier's planning, the buyer's inventory, and the economics of the first wave.

A larger MOQ can boost profit and justify the cost of storage, but it can also tie you up with excess stock.

The key is to negotiate flexibility in MOQs—buy a little larger or a little smaller—so you protect your price structure while staying responsive to demand.

By keeping MOQs as small as feasible, you avoid stranded inventory and preserve a favorable cost base, turning a launch that might falter into one that rises and floats freely.

A real-world note: start with a small pilot batch that uses reduced MOQs, then scale up quickly as demand becomes clearer.

Lead time, the interval from placing an order to its arrival, affects every stage: testing, certification, and QC windows. Because delays ripple through these stages, buffer planning is essential.

Document each supplier's MOQs and calibrate their buffers to the testing windows so that approvals don't become schedule killers. When a test or certification fails, hold the buffers so that subsequent approvals remain on track.

This approach lets you buy only what you need, avoid stranded inventory, and keep the launch responsive and cost-effective.

The best tactic is to pair buffer buffers with phased launches, freeing up the initial SKUs and the stock awaiting final sign-off, thereby reducing overall launch risk.

Capacity planning across lines and packaging means mapping the throughput of each production line and the packaging path.

It's about spotting bottlenecks, slow lines, packing stations, or labeling queues and then, with the size of capacity per line and packaging option, setting realistic MOQs to gain resilience in a crisis.

If a line cannot meet a surge, consider alternate packaging formats or parallel lines to keep the launch on track.

Contract terms and scalability shape how you grow, ensuring that every buffer and launch phase stays aligned with your production capacity and market demands.

Add IP protection to the designs, clear the order-procedure changes so you can adjust orders without chaos, and use holdbacks to verify quality and ensure punctual delivery.

A clean, well-defined change-order clause lets you make significant adjustments within a month, keeping cash flow steady and growth on track.

By keeping the process predictable and efficient, you protect your customers' confidence and give your business the chance to expand without delays or unexpected costs.

Build buffers around lead times, especially during testing and certification, and map out line capacity to mark early milestones. Use contract terms to protect the integrity of your timeline and grow smoothly. Align these elements to create predictable schedules and steady cash flow.

## 5. NDA, IP, and Trade Secrets

In the private-label world a single confidential insight can make or break momentum.

When you share product specs, formulations, supplier lists, or market plans with a manufacturing partner, you trade more than samples—you trade trust.

A well-crafted NDA establishes a solid legal foundation, protecting trade secrets, client data, and other intellectual property.

It serves as a secure, professional bond that guards your private information as it moves from concept to reality, ensuring that every sensitive detail remains confidential and that any breach is clearly addressed.

By signing an NDA, suppliers recognize the need to safeguard their innovations and agree to treat your intellectual property with the same care.

This trust is essential in the early stages of vetting, when many suppliers are evaluating capabilities side-by-side.

The NDA should clearly define what is confidential, who is bound, and the duration of protection, so that neither party feels like a spy or a potential thief.

By establishing these terms early, you protect your trade secrets, client data, and other intellectual property, ensuring that every sensitive detail remains confidential and that any breach is clearly addressed.

- **Permitted uses**: Clarify how the supplier may use the confidential information, if at all, and for which projects.
- **Breach remedies**: Specify the consequences of a breach—monetary damages, injunctive relief, or termination—and outline a clear notification and mitigation process.
- **Multi-supplier environments**: In tiered agreements, establish a robust vetting and asset-protection framework that protects each party's trade secrets while allowing collaboration across multiple suppliers.

Intellectual property (IP) protection encompasses various types:

- **Trademarks**: Safeguard brand names, logos, and slogans through registration, enforcement, and careful license control.
- **Copyrights**: Protect original works such as packaging art, copy, and instructional materials.
- **Patents**: Secure exclusive rights for novel inventions and significant process improvements, with attention to filing location and enforcement.
- **Trade Secrets**: Implement strict access controls, document controls, and formula safeguards to prevent unauthorized disclosure.

**Trade-secret strategy:** Limit access to only those who need it and use enforceable measures for emergencies.

- Keep your formulas strictly confidential in a controlled environment and require formal confidentiality agreements whenever they are shared.
- An NDA designed for private-label work serves as a guardrail for all confidential disclosures and protects the IP that can be disclosed.
- Define a clear scope, use precise terms, and apply tiered protections so you can vet suppliers without delaying progress.
- IP protection should cover trademarks, copyrights, and patents, while trade secrets are shielded through access control and disciplined information handling.
- Bring this framework into every supplier conversation to ensure your private-label program rests on solid, enforceable foundations.

## 6. Contract basics: terms and warranties

In the private-label world the first contract is not a formality but a compass.

It tells both sides why they are there, what they will build, and how they will handle the bumps along the way.

A well-crafted agreement provides a clear purpose, a finite scope, and a shared framework for decision-making.

It lays out the core foundations of the partnership from concept to shelf, keeping the manufacturer-partner on the right path toward its ultimate goal.

Purpose and scope are the building blocks that prevent misunderstandings and keep expectations aligned from the outset.

### Deliverables and milestones

To ensure efficient execution and prevent conflicts, clearly defined roles, responsibilities, timelines, and checkpoints will be established for all parties.

This includes detailing specific deliverables and their corresponding delivery schedules.

Payment terms, methods, and schedules will be explicitly outlined, alongside any penalties for late payment or non-compliance.

All changes to project scope or deliverables must be formally agreed upon and may result in adjustments to timelines and costs.

- Approval workflow and timelines – Impact on timeline and budget
- IP Ownership and License Rights – Protecting ideas and brand integrity matters.
- Ownership of designs, trademarks, and know-how – Licensing terms and fees – Usage restrictions and enforcement
- Warranty Terms – Quality assurance protects consumers and brands.
- Product guarantees and remedies for defects – Replacements process and timelines – Recalls responsibilities and procedures
- Indemnification and Liability Limits – Clear risk allocation supports calm decision making.
- How risks are shared and who bears what – Coverage limits and applicable scenarios
- Governing Law and Dispute Resolution – Practical framework for resolving disagreements – Applicable law and jurisdictions – Escalation paths and timelines
- Quality Assurance, Testing, Audits and Certifications – Standards and verification keep products trustworthy.
- Testing requirements and standards – Audit frequency and scope

Build the contract with your product specs in mind; the documents should dovetail.

- Define a simple change-order process to avoid drift.
- Establish clear IP rules up front to protect brand and know-how.

## 7. Quality agreements and QA expectations

For the purpose of product creation, the work that ultimately ships out is governed by a quality agreement that serves as the quiet backbone of the manufacturing relationship.

This formal contract codifies expectations and governance of quality across the partnership, laying out clear roles, responsibilities, and measurable standards.

By naming responsibilities explicitly, it leaves no room for ambiguity, ensuring that everyone in the partnership follows the same playbook and that the business knows exactly what must be done, by whom, and to what standard.

Furthermore, if the agreement specifies that batch capture and release testing is conducted, formulations are approved, and specific assays are provided to third parties under known rules, the importance of clear ownership and established levels of escalation for such issues is underscored.

It is essential that the product specifications, approved formulations, exact ingredients and concentrations, and process mechanics are clearly defined. Similarly, impurity limits, timelines, and testing methodologies must be clearly specified. For instance, the test methods deemed acceptable can be highly diverse.

Our development is guided by clear procedures to ensure consistency and facilitate objective judgments.

The agreement specifies comprehensive testing procedures, the frequency of data collection, and the mechanisms for regulatory and client trust in the process.

It further details variance correction, adherence to analysis intervals, the implementation of corrective and preventive actions (CAPAs), and meticulous record-keeping.

This clarity extends to our planning, production, and approval processes, ensuring all requirements are consistently met.

This structured approach enables practical demonstration and application.

Our actions are transparent, results are audited, records are meticulously maintained, and errors are addressed through formal corrective procedures.

This disciplined approach to IP laws keeps the alliance profitable and protects the product's integrity.

By safeguarding intellectual property, we ensure that innovations are the foundation of success while clearly defining ownership, confidentiality, and leakage safeguards.

A well-written quality agreement should spell out the company's rights, obligations, and the exact roles, standards, testing, and change-control procedures that will govern the partnership.

The real-world takeaways are evident in every "action-filled" checklist: roles, standards, testing, change control, and IP protection.

**Key takeaways:** a crystal-clear agreement that balances protection with performance is the bedrock of a thriving alliance.

Structured testing, change control, and CAPAs prevent drift and drive continuous improvement. IP protections make confidentiality and safe collaboration possible, keeping the value of the relationship intact.

## 8. Sample evaluation and pilot runs

Now your pilot begins, a disciplined round of sampling, sample testing, and pilot runs.

A well-structured pilot mitigates regulatory risk, establishes a clear plan, and provides a path to success.

A comprehensive sample covers all specifications, including packing requirements, weight, and performance metrics.

With objectives that are clearly defined, measurable, and achievable, effective decisions regarding implementation can be made.

Consistent communication with suppliers, including requesting necessary items and ensuring clear understanding of requirements and expectations, is crucial.

This process frequently involves the use of multiple samples.

To bring the variability and the true range of results, ask the supplier for 3—5 samples; a practical rule of thumb is 3—5, with a certain number of samples depending on the complexity of the product, the supplier's history, etc.

To detect batch-to-batch differences, to check that the products are not missing one or more ingredients, let the vendor pack them up and send them off to you, see if you can find a few problems, then take action.

Consistency across the samples is a sound predictor of long-term performance and helps in the long run to avoid surprises in mass production. ... What will your acceptance criteria be?

Before the pilot, pre-agree on your acceptance criteria with the supplier.

Define quality control metrics, tolerances, and decision triggers so everyone knows what constitutes "good enough" and what triggers a corrective action.

Keep the metrics neat and clear, avoiding a "good enough" trap that lets problems go unchecked.

Capture every Pilot Run in a Pilot Results and Vendor Scorecard, noting obstacles and mapping next steps.

Use the pilot data and vendor scorecard to judge the alliance and guide future negotiations, protecting your IP and keeping the contract intact.

Ensure the supplier can set proper parameters and respond quickly to any issues that arise during scaling.

Protect your intellectual property by embedding robust non-disclosure clauses, IP safeguards, and traceability requirements into the pilot agreement.

Keep proprietary information under strict control and ensure suppliers adhere to the same standards.

Conduct thorough stability testing during the pilot phase to confirm the product meets regulatory standards and to identify any issues early.

Use the pilot results to shape mass-production requirements, capacity, and schedules, allowing you to anticipate problems and launch the product safely and efficiently.

This systematic, evidence-based approach builds a solid foundation for successful scale-up while safeguarding your IP and maintaining contractual integrity.

**Actionable takeaways:**

- Define clear pilot objectives and success metrics up front.
- Request 3–5 representative samples to assess variability.
- Pre-agree on acceptance criteria and critical tolerances.
- Use a limited SKU set to test process capability.
- Document results with a vendor scorecard and protect IP with proper agreements.
- Include stability testing and plan scale-up from pilot learnings.

## 9. Red flags and due diligence checklist

Before initiating a private label brand, the inherent uncertainty amplifies the tension between ambition and risk, making it critical to identify early indicators of potential challenges.

Furthermore, once a prospective partner becomes deeply engaged, it can be challenging to maintain strict adherence to contractual terms or recognize persistent warning signs, which remain present despite initial enthusiasm.

Inconsistent documentation and missing licenses make us look backward.

To avoid this, keep the law at arm's length and maintain an up-to-date license, a confirmed GMP certification, and clear documentation of quality-control processes.

If an "excellent" set of papers appears and the site doesn't permit it, be patient and ask for inspection; chances are the place will soon be bursting with compliant partners.

Even if some documents are inoperable, don't lose sight of what's essential—licenses, certifications, proof of GMP compliance, and a documented quality-control system.

By doing so, you guard against the evils that may arise and ensure your firm stays ahead, not behind, in the long run.

To prove capacity, start with a thorough site visit: examine the equipment, layout, and process controls to ensure they meet your needs and specifications.

Check maintenance records, personnel qualifications, and the adequacy of each piece of machinery—no leaks, no hidden defects.

Verify that the costs, MOQs, and pricing are clear and transparent; any ambiguity should be resolved before committing.

Keep a documented quality-control system and protect intellectual property with proper safeguards.

By doing so, you guard against hidden pitfalls and keep your firm ahead, not behind, in the long run.

IP is the most sensitive asset in a private-label scheme and protecting it is essential.

Don't rely on a weak or unconditional NDA; instead, secure a robust agreement early in the talks and ensure it is followed through with concrete actions.

Build a red-flag checklist that covers documentation, facility access, pricing clarity, and IP protection.

By addressing these elements promptly, you lay a solid foundation of understanding and accountability that keeps your firm ahead, not behind, in the long run.

Remember to establish clear guardrails for your product categories and growth plan.

Create a concise checklist that includes charts, principles, and best-practice guidelines drawn from your own experience.

This structured approach will keep your firm on track and ensure accountability as you move forward.

## 10. Cost structures and payment terms

When you launch a private-label brand, you start by clarifying costs, payment terms, and the flow of money through every decision.

This practical groundwork lets you act immediately, whether your production is local or overseas.

You'll understand exactly what each cost means, how much it will cost to bring a product from the shores of your country, what you'll pay domestically, and what you'll pay abroad.

Knowing these figures helps you decide how much to produce at home and how much to import, ensuring the entire bill balances in your pocket.

Domestic production versus overseas production is a key factor in that calculation.

The cost of goods rises with higher labor and material expenses, while shipping can lower overall costs by reducing transport time and risk.

Duties and tariffs usually add a modest surcharge, but they are often comparable to other fees and can be simplified through efficient customs handling.

Other expenses, such as currency hedging, import filings, inspections, and packing are common to both domestic and overseas production.

Overseas manufacturing often offers lower unit costs and capital outlay, but it also introduces additional liabilities through foreign exchange and tariff exposure.

Balancing these factors helps determine how much to produce locally versus import, ensuring the final bill stays within budget.

When negotiating, keep the price drop in check against the risk of unsold stock and the cash needed to reach the MOQ.

Payment terms and schedules protect cash flow and reduce the danger of inventory piling up, thereby safeguarding your cash needs.

Typical structures include:

– **Deposits**: The initial payment to lock in materials and start production.

– **Milestone payments**: Linked to the completion of defined stages of production.

– **Net 30/60 terms**: Payment due within 30 or 60 days of invoice.

Practical cash-flow preservation tips:

- Negotiate favorable terms whenever possible.
- Align milestones with your production progress.
- Maintain a reserve fund for unexpected costs or delays.

Unseen costs to anticipate often arise after production begins, such as freight and shipping from the factory to the warehouse, which can consume significant cash.

Warehousing and storage are a major cost driver, and keeping inventory in a costly, perpetually expensive way can quickly erode margins.

Inspections, quality checks, and routine tests are essential, especially when new production lines are introduced.

Adjusting rates is unpredictable but having a price-adjustment clause tied to inflation helps prevent runaway costs.

Commodity spikes, tariff changes, and trade-agreement rules also bind us, so contracts for IP and confidentiality must be stringent to protect our interests.

## 11. Takeaway

It is certain that the greatest private-label ventures are those that begin with a clear set of goals, precise product requirements, and a practical view of the regulatory landscape.

Before you launch any other activity, ask yourself:

"What do I want the product to be?

What do I expect from it?"

Once you have that certainty, you can build a firm foundation.

Domestic production offers shorter lead times, easier communication, and stronger control over what is made, ensuring higher quality and faster response to market needs.

By starting with a well-defined vision and a solid domestic base, you set the stage for lasting success.

Prices may be high, but domestic production delivers faster time-to-market and clearer oversight.

By starting with a well-defined vision and a solid domestic base, you gain stronger control over what is made, ensuring higher quality and a quicker response to market needs.

Overseas manufacturing can offer initial savings, yet it brings longer lead times, language or cultural gaps, and more complex regulatory steps.

When weighing these factors, choose the path that aligns with your long-term goals: protect your IP, safeguard your formulations, and reduce the risk of having to worry about foreign financial or regulatory uncertainties.

This strategy sets the stage for lasting success.

Consider your audits as a solid vehicle for proving your competence and controls.

Make sure the process of auditing is a true phase of verification, not just a pre-requisite of performance.

Request references, samples, and tests, and gather critical evidence from past partners about how well they operate and what they would provide to a model.

If your contract can withstand this scrutiny, include strong clauses that protect your brand, formulations, and artwork. Ensure compliance with Good Manufacturing Practices, proper labeling, and packaging, and negotiate terms that shield your interests from market vagaries.

This approach will demonstrate your capability and safeguard your business.

You've built a solid foundation, free of doubt and ambiguity, and now you must choose a partner who will deliver reliable, compliant products and walk confidently alongside your company.

## Section 2.

### Negotiating, IP, and supplier relationships

The foundation of a successful private-label brand rests on the effective engagement of a competent supplier.

This section provides practical guidance for building strong manufacturing alliances, from the initial negotiations to long-term partnership.

We begin by defining precise negotiation goals, understanding the true cost of supplier input, and using market benchmarks to secure advantageous pricing, lead times, and payment terms.

The discussion also covers protecting the brand's core intellectual property formulas, trade secrets, and designs, through robust contractual clauses, non-disclosure agreements, and clear ownership stipulations at every stage, from early changes and joint invention to final production and renewal.

Next, we set forth the requirements for stringent quality assurance, including compliance standards, third-party testing, and thorough auditing.

We supplement these with systems for managing deviations and continuously monitoring supplier performance.

This prepares you for clear processes around change orders, dispute resolution, and the scope of co-created products.

All of this is summed up in the book itself, which you follow as you construct transparent, resilient alliances from the outset of due diligence through termination, renewal, and the management of supply-chain disruptions.

## 1. Supplier pricing negotiation techniques

In private labeling, the negotiation table is no mere sideshow; it is where margins are fixed, supplier partnerships are forged, and a brand's promise is delivered.

This section lays the groundwork for disciplined negotiations, strengthening both parties. Know how to set a realistic price, minimums, delivery times, and acceptable trade-offs, and plan what to do if the contract falls through.

Draft a concise one-page brief that outlines your targets, your price in the aggregate, your MOQs, and your contingency plan.

Understand the cost base of raw materials, labor, and overhead, and how the supplier's profit margin shapes the deal.

By keeping the discussion focused and actionable, you curb scope creep and increase the likelihood of a successful partnership.

Understand where costs are shifting—material price volatility, labor efficiency, and process improvements. Use real data: industry benchmarks, rival quotes, and current prices to anchor your concessions.

Focus on the base costs, margins, and fees to see exactly where value is created and where savings can be achieved.

By keeping the discussion data-driven and actionable, you curb scope creep and increase the likelihood of a successful partnership.

Quick practice: ask for a total cost sheet that separates material, packaging, freight, duties, and any surcharges. Build a total cost of ownership (TCO) perspective and calculate it across the buying price, freight, duties, rework, storage, depreciation, and after-sales costs.

This TCO view expands beyond the purchase price, revealing hidden pitfalls and giving you predictability and guarantees. Keep a list of your bargain-priced goods and track landed cost, damage costs, and the rate of return on end-of-life disposal. Take volume and commitments into account—your profits will be worth the effort.

Don't ignore these details; they keep the discussion data-driven and actionable, curb scope creep, and increase the likelihood of a successful partnership.

Take the time to negotiate payment terms, service levels, quality guarantees, and consistent lead times.

Build a clear menu of acceptable concessions so you can strike a balance—avoid locking into an exorbitant price for half the quality or a third of the reliability.

Ensure you secure full IP rights and protect all new products, specifications, and proprietary processes.

Demand strict confidentiality, non-disclosure, and the right to prototypes and specifications. Insist on concrete performance standards and quality assurances and be ready with remedies if those standards aren't met.

Make sure the agreement is routine, enforceable, and that the samples actually meet expectations.

In a structured, data-driven way, negotiation makes us stronger vendor partners and better products for the private label brand.

## 2. IP protection strategies for private-label formulas

Protection of private-label formulas is not a luxury—it is a practical necessity for any product that relies on unique ingredients and processes.

In a crowded market, the distinct formulation, the behind-the-scenes methods, and the data that underpin your brand give you a competitive edge. Safeguarding these elements ensures that your quality remains uncompromised and that competitors cannot replicate your secret advantage.

While patents can offer one layer of protection, trade secrets often provide the most reliable shield for the confidential information that truly matters to your business.

Trademarks and copyrights play a supporting role in branding and product identity, but the core of private-label protection lies in the interplay between patent rights and the safeguard of secrecy.

First, protection prevents copying or reverse-engineering, preserving your competitive edge.

Second, it provides a legal framework to address misuse or disclosure.

Third, a robust IP position can grow your business by attracting investors or buyers who value protected brands.

While patents offer one layer of protection, trade secrets often provide the most reliable shield for the confidential information that truly matters to your business. The benefits come with costs and a finite term, so a balanced IP strategy is essential.

Trade secrets offer the longest and most reliable protection for the confidential information that truly matters to your business. They are inexpensive to maintain—provided you enforce strict secrecy through NDAs for employees, contractors, and suppliers—and they can safeguard formulas that are impossible to reverse-engineer.

Unlike patents, which require costly disclosure and have a limited term, trade secrets can remain in force indefinitely as long as the information stays confidential. However, a balanced IP strategy should still consider patents for certain innovations, especially when the cost and time to patent are justified by the potential market advantage.

In short, keep your most valuable secrets under tight NDA coverage and use patents selectively to complement that protection.

Effective intellectual property (IP) protection is critical for competitive advantage. Implement robust legal frameworks, including clear IP ownership and protective clauses, to establish a strong defensive position. A comprehensive confidentiality strategy is paramount:

- Require Non-Disclosure Agreements (NDAs) from all employees, contractors, partners, and suppliers.
- Establish clear procedures for managing sensitive proprietary information, such as 'secret ingredients,' to ensure their secure handling and controlled access.
- Keep a good record of your audits and claims and pursue formulation patents early where the market allows. Vet covenant clauses against IP ownership and establish a clear set of ideas you can defend later. Include secret clauses in your contracts, as Coca-Cola's formula shows, protecting proprietary processes while maintaining profitability for new formulations. The right mix depends on your product, market, and resources, but a proactive approach

to patents, contracts, and secrecy will safeguard your competitive edge.

**Actions to take:**

Identify which components of your formula may qualify for a patent.
Draft a confidentiality policy and supplier NDAs.
Establish an auditable development record with version control.
Review all contracts for IP ownership and language improvements.

### 3. Change orders and lead time management

In the factory and the field, schedules are the quiet backbone of every product's arrival.

Small changes, sometimes barely noticeable, can creep over months, inflate costs, and push deliveries far beyond expectations.

The world of change orders and lead times forces us to see what has been done, what must be done, and which risks must be borne with the rigor they demand.

Change orders are formal documents that define and track scope, cost, and completion time, providing an audit trail that eliminates ambiguity around margins and outcomes.

When a new idea surfaces, the change-order process must be activated immediately, locking in approval, pricing, scope, and timing for every stakeholder, suppliers, manufacturers, and internal teams alike.

By defining the procedure in advance and circulating it widely, each party knows exactly what to expect and can plan their capacity accordingly.

A clear, transparent approval list and detailed pricing eliminate misunderstandings, miscommunications, and disputes, turning the process into a reliable, living framework that guides the project through mid-course modifications with confidence and rigor.

The lead times of the supply network impose constraints that can be mitigated by working closely with suppliers to understand production schedules, capacity, and true turnaround times.

When schedules align with supplier capabilities, the risk of delays and cost overruns shrinks dramatically. Inventory becomes a strategic asset: by forecasting potential delays and maintaining appropriate buffer stock, we can avoid rush-ups on change orders and keep production plans realistic and practicable.

This collaborative approach ensures that all parties remain fair to their brand and to the project as a whole, turning the process into a reliable, living framework that guides the project through mid-course modifications with confidence and rigor.

We must keep the IP, formulations, and trade secrets firmly integrated into the change process to protect our rights and ensure compliance with brand strategy and regulatory requirements.

Whenever a minor adjustment to formulas or packaging is needed, we should review and document the change, so it aligns with our brand's scheme and the regulatory regime.

A clear change-order procedure should be established up front, defining approvals, pricing, scope, and timing, and linked to capacity planning to account for real-world constraints.

By using historical data to forecast delays, we can build buffer-safety stock and keep production plans realistic and practicable.

This collaborative approach guarantees that all parties remain fair to the brand and to the project as a whole, turning the process into a reliable, living framework that guides the project through mid-course modifications with confidence and rigor.

These foundational actions, as essential first steps, ensure goals are achieved with minimal expenditure and mitigated risks.

## 4. Quality control milestones and acceptance criteria

In the world of private label brands, quality is not optional it is the promise you make to every shopper who picks up your product.

The early establishment of quality-control milestones serves as a compass, guiding performance, audits, and continual improvement.

These standards and protocols form a practical backbone, setting concrete goals that become the baseline for evaluation and the foundation for ongoing refinement.

### QC Milestones and Protocols: a practical backbone

The goal is not perfection on the first run, but a transparent, trackable process that flags gaps, accelerates correction, and drives repeatable results.

In real-world terms this means documenting what must be achieved at each stage, from development through final release so that every stakeholder knows the standard and the path to meet it.

By defining clear, measurable product-acceptance criteria texture, taste, and microbiological safety private-label food manufacturers can ensure consistency, meet regulatory demands, and guarantee quality for all.

A standardized matrix is generally employed, encompassing attributes, measurement methods, acceptance thresholds, and regulatory references.

This matrix establishes a common language for product development, production, and quality assurance.

The objective is to determine the optimal sample size and batch frequency to accurately quantify units of each type per batch and establish appropriate intervals for new batch production to facilitate feedback.

Testing protocols are typically designed and guided by considerations of variability, risk level, and the cost-benefit ratio of the trial. This approach yields timely, data-driven insights while optimizing time efficiency.

Note the following protocol for dealing with the problem:

For non-conforming products we must act swiftly: quarantine the affected batch, launch a thorough root-cause investigation, implement corrective measures, and establish preventive actions to stop recurrence.

The protocol should spell out each step in clear detail, ensuring that any deviation is reported, traced, and addressed before the next batch proceeds.

Maintaining reliable supply hinges on metric-based scorecards, regular supplier assessments, and real-time feedback on performance.

By combining prompt containment with disciplined investigation and proactive prevention, we safeguard quality and build trust with our partners.

Real-world brands usually run a quarterly scorecard with a monthly performance dashboard to keep their pulse steady, giving a precise view of risk and capability.

**Key actions include:**

-set up early QC milestones to anchor performance and audit.

-define product-specific acceptance criteria tied to regulatory standards and claimed specs.

-choose a principled sampling plan and batch frequency to balance rigor and cost.

-establish deviation handling based on clear containment, investigation, and corrective action.

-and set supplier ratings and cadence for the month, reviewing the system regularly.

### 5. Audit rights and IP clauses in contracts

When you launch a private label, you're stitching together a system that protects ideas, guards quality, and builds trust with every shopper who picks it up from the shelf.

The backbone of that system is a clear audit framework, rights, solid IP protection, and a practical plan that keeps your brand safe, compliant, and ready to scale.

Define scope, frequency, and inspection cadence: a plain audit scope covers financial statements, transactions, inventories, sales data, accounts receivable, and collections; it also includes inspections of manufacturing and warehouse facilities.

By laying out these concrete rules and protections, you create the foundation for a reliable, trustworthy private-label operation.

- Processes: review of quality control processes, supply chain management, and distribution channels. Audits should follow a cadence that fits risk and contract terms, with regular checks—whether quarterly or annually—to surface issues early and keep improvements on track.
- Data Access, Confidentiality, and Security: audits depend on access to relevant data while preserving confidentiality and security. Practical measures—such as NDAs, encryption, and secure data-handling obligations—create a trustworthy environment where necessary information can be shared safely.
- Audit Rights of GMP Compliance: Good Manufacturing Practice (GMP) compliance is essential for product quality. Focus areas include manufacturing controls, documentation, and facility inspections to ensure ongoing adherence to GMP standards.
- Quality systems: a review of the quality control processes and procedures, including manufacturing controls, documentation, and facility inspections, to ensure ongoing adherence to GMP standards.
- SOPs: inspection of SOPs and training records to confirm that staff are properly trained and procedures are followed.

- Corrective actions: a structured GMP review of corrective actions taken in response to quality problems, ensuring issues are addressed promptly and do not recur.
- Change control and product specification alignment: audit provisions that cover how changes are managed and how product specifications stay aligned with claims and regulatory requirements, including verification of compliance with regulatory requirements and review of specification changes affecting claims.
- Preserving IP ownership and license terms: specify ownership of formulas and other intellectual property related to the product formulations to protect the company's IP.
- Branding, trademarks, and trade dress, including licenses granted by third parties. Clear ownership terms prevent disputes and support smooth collaboration with contract manufacturers and distributors.
- IP infringement remedies and indemnities: audit rights should outline procedures for addressing IP infringement, specify damages for losses incurred by the IP proprietor, and set indemnification obligations in case of infringement.
- Exit strategies and IP transition: prepare for supplier exits or strategic shifts with procedures for asset transfer and plans to maintain continuity of supply and IP protection.

**Actionable teachings:** build your audit scope around records, facilities, and processes from day one.

- Establish NDAs, encryption, and strict access controls up front.
- Tie GMP checks to continuous improvement and worker training.
- Align all changes and specifications with the claims you make and the regulations you follow.
- Define IP ownership and license terms clearly to prevent future friction.

• Plan exit scenarios so that IP and supply continuity remain intact.

## 6. *The joint development agreements and co-creation*

A successful co-created product begins before the first prototype.

It starts with a clear framework that sets expectations, establishes authority, and protects the interests of all parties.

The collaboration between Nike and Apple, linking fitness data with their devices, illustrates the power of an integrated joint effort and shows how a well-balanced project can create a compelling experience.

This section lays out the practical framework that underpins the venture, keeping the team disciplined and on track.

Key elements include defining scope, governance structures, and decision rights, as well as objectives, deliverables, and timelines.

Roles and responsibilities are specified, clarifying who does what, who approves, and how everything is coordinated.

- Governance bodies: establish a steering group and an operational team, plus who chairs each body.
- Decision rights and dispute resolution: define who can decide at each stage and how conflicts are settled, avoiding standstills that stall progress.

IP Ownership and Allocation of Rights:

- Background IP retained by the original owner: recognize pre-existing patents, know-how and software brought into the collaboration.
- Foreground IP: identify what is created during the project, and determine who owns, licenses, or co-claims it.

Practical allocations: consider licensing paths, cross-licensing or joint ownership for jointly developed patents, trademarks, and copyrights.

- The IP inventory must be clearly defined: each party's pre-existing know-how and any newly created intellectual property. Ownership, access rights, and the ability to improve or commercialize both existing and new IP should be explicitly set out.
- Change control processes and milestones must be established to govern any modifications. These processes should be traceable, prevent drift, and be documented so that all parties can verify compliance.

The system of control and authority over the products must be robustly established, securely maintained, and diligently protected against any unauthorized access, manipulation, or information leakage.

- All limitations on revenue, expense, and supply, as well as any predefined commitments, should be pre-defined and enforceable.
- The agreement should include mechanisms for recovering delays, releasing derived efficiencies, and managing the impact of product dilatation, ensuring that the product's performance and the parties' interests remain balanced.

GMP, labeling, and claims: assign responsibility for the product's quality, safety, and regulatory compliance with clear accountability.

- INTELLECTUAL PROPERTY LICENSING – define license scope, royalties, territory, and duration explicitly to prevent future disputes and ensure commercial clarity.

**Actionable takeaways:**

- Draft a one-page scope and decision-rights matrix for your JDA.

- Create an IP map: catalog background IP, identify foreground IP, and clarify ownership.
- Build a milestone schedule with gated approvals and a change-control log.
- Establish data protection rules and a concise confidentiality framework.
- Outline roles in quality, regulatory, and licensing activities.

In practice, this framework becomes the backbone of every co-created product, guiding teams from concept to market and beyond.

### 7. Escalation paths and dispute resolution

In the world of physical products, a single dispute can ripple from raw materials to finished goods, from the first contact to the final settlement.

The remedy is not merely speed or persistence, but a deliberate escalation framework that guides each party through clear, structured steps.

A well-designed escalation tier system keeps operations moving, restores confidence, and protects the brand when tensions arise.

Define the tiers in your terms and conditions, outlining the actions each side will take—from informal resolution to formal escalation—to resolve the dispute decisively and keep the business running smoothly.

- Involvement of senior management or executive-level personnel
- Engagement of external mediators or arbitrators
- Legal action, if necessary

Document all stages related to the subject matter to ensure a clear understanding of subsequent actions.

Document in writing every component of the clause addressing intellectual property disputes, including terms for resolution, returns, and payments.

Clearly outline the procedural steps to be followed in the event of a dispute to prevent confusion and facilitate an orderly resolution process.

Subsequently, establish a 'Response Framework' that explicitly details these steps and serves as the definitive reference point for all dispute resolution procedures.

*Clear channels of communication for reporting disputes—defined in advance roles and responsibilities for employees and managers.*

The scheduled times for responding to disputes should be tied to performance deficits such as missed deliveries, payment delays, or poor quality.

When a breach occurs, the escalation triggers raise the issue to a higher level of attention.

Early legal counsel and clear contractual obligations help keep disputes fair and protect your rights, ensuring that supplier relationships remain healthy and productive.

We provide a comprehensive escalation framework, well-communicated to all, that offers a practical, repeatable method for resolving disputes.

## 8. Building long-term partnerships with manufacturers

The ultimate edge in the private-label world is the partnership that lies behind the product.

It is not just the shelf it sits on, but the team that drives it from concept to consumer.

A clear, well-defined CDMO (Contract Development and Manufacturing Organization) is the key to a smooth start, and it builds the trust that sustains long-term collaboration.

When both partners see each other as equals in growth, not merely as suppliers, the alliance becomes durable.

Discipline, clarity, shared success, and a deliberate, repeatable approach guide the entire journey from idea to launch into a new era of confidence and pride.

The elements below create a predictable, productive environment in which private-label brands can thrive.

Thorough diligence and supply-risk assessment should begin well before committing to a large transaction.

Examine the CDMO's business and controls, focusing on these key areas:

- **Financial stability**: a sound financial base supports long-term collaboration and the capital needed for growth.
- **Capacity**: proven ability to meet current demands and scale for future needs.
- **Quality systems**: robust quality management, GMP compliance, and a strong code of ethics that earn consumer trust.
- **Regulatory compliance**: strict adherence to applicable laws, including FDA, FTC, and ISO standards.

Ensure the CDMO's framework meets or exceeds industry expectations, providing a solid foundation for sustained success.

- GMP alignment: the quality system must demonstrate uncompromising rigor in manufacturing and testing, clearly reflecting the regulatory expectations of FDA and FTC.
- Supplier audits: regular, documented, independent audits to confirm compliance and drive continuous improvement.

- Clear contract terms and IP protections: define the scope of the agreement, ownership of products and processes, and explicit licenses granted to the CDMO, with provisions for breach and change control.
- Open communication and mutual problem-solving: a transparent partnership built on honesty, shared goals, and a collaborative approach to resolving issues.
- Transparent dialogue: regular touches keep both sides in line and informed.
- The issue-resolving cooperative spirit will keep us all well balanced in a governance system.
- Structured governance with regular meetings: a cadence for performance review, risk assessment, and goal setting.
- Issue escalation: clear paths for raising concerns and prompt resolution, with defined response times for decision-making and action.
- Performance-management and continuous improvement: outcomes are tracked and refined through ongoing initiatives.

Take care with your due diligence in finance, capacity, quality, and compliance.

Keep your GMP, FDA/FTC standards on the line and conduct regular audits to confirm what you are doing right.

Lock in clear contracts with IP protections and adhere to firm rules of the road.

Build open channels of dialogue and a governance structure that can grow rapidly with issues.

Tie performance to concrete measures and commit to continuous improvement. Your leader must think this way and act as a strategic partner, guiding the product road from concept to market.

The CDMO will be a valuable partner, anchoring your private-label brand on a solid foundation of consistent growth and a robust business.

## 9. *Contract termination and renewal strategies*

Establishing a private-label line requires a robust contract.

This agreement must clearly define the scope, streams, triggers, and timelines, specifying all covered SKUs, commodities, services, and add-ons.

Crucially, it must also detail the precise terms for termination triggers and the start of termination, allowing the business to manage changes effectively.

- Set timelines for notice and execution, including cure periods where appropriate (e.g., 30 days for a breach, 60 days for a market-condition shift) and a termination effective date that allows for an orderly transition.
- Anticipate real-world scenarios to reduce disputes and keep operations stable.
- Specify notice periods aligned to each termination reason (30 days for non-payment, 60 days for market-condition shifts).
- Require that termination reasons be documented and objective, ensuring fairness and predictability for both parties.
- Include process steps for the wind-down to minimize disruption to ongoing production and sales.
- Mandate written notices for any termination or renewal, with clear acceptance criteria.

When considering contract termination and renewal, critical aspects include defining clear notice periods for either party to initiate these processes.

The agreement should specify conditions under which termination can occur, such as material breach, mutual consent, or termination for convenience, alongside any associated penalties or remedies.

For renewals, it's essential to detail whether renewal is automatic or requires explicit consent, and the terms that apply to a renewed period.

Furthermore, the contract must address post-termination obligations, including the secure return or destruction of confidential data, ongoing confidentiality requirements, and any transitional support.

Standardized notice templates are crucial to prevent ambiguity and miscommunication during these sensitive phases.

Finally, the agreement should outline any costs associated with early termination or renewal, and clearly delineate the responsibilities of all parties, including data retention policies and the obligations of a supplier and its successors.

- Define the transition to alternative suppliers or back to the original owner with milestones and precise success criteria.
- The use of substitute terms or alternative arrangements is common.
- Assume responsibility for remaining issues before re-engaging with the buyer or the factory.
- Fallback options include, but are not limited to, "in-house production, substitute suppliers, partial back-runs," or other alternatives.
- Establish a framework of equitable and practical agreements, intended solely for renegotiation rather than facilitating hasty compromises.

Actionable recommendation: align the scope, triggers, and underlying reasons as closely as possible with product planning.

- Ensure proper written notice procedures and objective termination reasons are established.
- Protect confidential data through an NDA and a transparent inventory wind-down plan.
- Define IP rights and establish a clear transition roadmap with milestones and data-transfer steps.

• Create a renewal framework with explicit fallback paths to keep the brand moving forward.

## 10. Case study: supplier success stories

Real-life case studies illustrate the decisions, missteps, and turning points that shape successful brand-supplier partnerships.

They reveal how time, quality, and compliance can collide, the obstacles that arise, and the moves that remove them, providing a clear framework for ongoing success.

Every case tells a story, and that story is the key to turning a crisis into an opportunity.

By framing the supplier's challenge—whether a tight turnaround or a strict compliance launch—as a narrative with a clear purpose, we can align goals and keep everyone rowing in the same direction.

The actionable lessons that emerge from this storytelling approach are the ones that truly drive improvement, grounding abstract ideas in concrete, repeatable actions that can be applied across future projects.

Flexibility and adaptability are the core ingredients that turn a supplier relationship into a concrete, repeatable practice.

When a partnership embraces clear communication, shared goals, and an open channel for decision-making, it can respond swiftly to unexpected changes and seize new opportunities.

The real-world success of private-label alliances—such as Costco's Kirkland Signature and Amazon's Basics—demonstrates how a formal decision log, a regular cadence of meetings, and a joint risk register become the practical tools that keep the partnership on track.

These elements together create a culture of responsiveness and alignment that scales with the business, ensuring that every stakeholder moves in the same direction toward a common vision.

To drive private-label success, we invest in the latest processes and technologies that sharpen forecasting, quality control, and supplier onboarding.

We build new relationships across the supply chain to broaden capacity and create a resilient network.

Within teams, we cultivate the skills needed to design, test, and iterate quickly turning a pilot into sustained growth.

For each partnership, we document a concise one-page narrative that captures the decision, the outcome, and the next steps.

Regular quarterly reviews keep everyone aligned, while a shared risk register and a clear action plan ensure that every milestone is met and every challenge is addressed before it becomes a bottleneck.

This disciplined, collaborative approach turns a promising pilot into a scalable, high-performance private-label program.

Track the scale of supplier turnout, defect rate, lead-time variance, and regulatory milestones.

By anchoring your approach in these indicators, you prepare for stronger collaborations, quicker learning, and more tangible progress.

## 11. Takeaway

The first conversation you have with a supplier is the moment the idea turns into a tangible product, and it sets the rhythm for everything that follows.

From the outset, you must articulate a clear vision of success—specific objectives, milestones, and non-negotiables that become the north star for every encounter.

By doing so, you keep the negotiation focused on what truly matters, preventing money and time from pushing the process off course.

When both parties agree on the same goal, the discussion can proceed smoothly, free from personal tactics or distractions, and you can move forward with confidence that the outcome will match the vision you set together.

Your clear business objectives are more than a checklist; they serve as a bridge between strategy and day-to-day decision-making. Tie them to your company's goals, define the project scope, and map the milestones.

With a shared objective, every trade-off becomes a coherent path forward. Keep your KPIs SMART—specific, measurable, achievable, relevant, and time-bound—and ensure everyone has concrete examples, from quality metrics to cost of ownership.

When you protect and share your formulas, trademarks, and data responsibly, the whole story becomes transparent, and everyone knows their role.

This focused approach keeps the negotiation on track, prevents distractions, and lets you move forward with confidence that the outcome will match the vision you set together.

Protecting your intellectual property and sensitive information is crucial, especially in international business.

Utilize Non-Disclosure Agreements (NDAs) and carefully control disclosures when sharing confidential information. Always use secure channels, with strong passwords and encryption for all correspondence, to prevent unauthorized access.

When engaging with suppliers, ensure robust agreements are in place to safeguard your confidential records and establish clear responsibilities for data security. Any leaks or breaches should result in accountability for the responsible party.

Maintain meticulous batch records, Certificates of Analysis (COAs), and documentation of arrangements with reputable labs. These records are essential for demonstrating compliance, facilitating necessary approvals, and preparing for audits, ultimately supporting your business's growth and operational freedom.

Build in price tiers, lead-time buffers, minimums, and clear change-control processes so the arrangement remains cost-effective as volumes rise.

Include contract clauses for termination and transitional support, and establish exit strategies, IP transfer terms, and transitional help to minimize disruption.

Maintain supplier relationships through regular scorecards, quarterly audits, and issue-resolution protocols, keeping operations transparent and actionable.

Plan for continual governance and performance reviews, schedule occasional KPI reviews, track problem resolution, and drive continuous improvement to reduce risk and raise capability over time.

A practical takeaway: give each supplier a one-page objective sheet covering scope, milestones, and three to five SMART KPIs.

By integrating these actionable takeaways, we can ensure a prompt and efficient initiation.

# Chapter VII

## Operations, Fulfillment, & Inventory

### *Section 1.*
### *3PL, Inventory, Cash Flow, Storage, Effect,*
### *Batch-Management*

Bringing a private-label product to market is more than just an idea; it requires a flawless, end-to-end supply chain that upholds brand standards at every turn.

From the careful selection of third-party logistics partners to the meticulous management of raw-material suppliers, every step must be executed with operational efficiency.

This includes precise inventory control, rigorous quality assurance, and effective returns handling each element contributing to a resilient, scalable system that delivers on brand promises and drives profit.

### *1. Choose 3PL partners, service models, fullfilment centers*

In the private-label world your brand lives in the gaps between product and promise – the box, the shelf presence, the customer's unboxing moment.

The right partner is the engine that makes every order feel effortless, sweeping away snags with practical rules of cost, speed, scale and regulatory fit.

Your core aim is to use these four pillars in every possible way to find the right partner for that moment.

Cost is not just the sticker price; it includes all fees, errors, corrections and compliance expenses that shape the customer experience.

Speed is not just the rapidity of picking and packing; it is the quality of the cadence of status updates, the reliability of delivery, and the ability to scale without becoming a burden.

A good 3PL must handle your volume as you grow, provide regulatory fit, and maintain consistent, dependable service across food, cosmetics, pharma, or any other sector.

The measure of a 3PL's worth lies in its speed, reliability, and the way it supports your business's expansion without compromising quality or compliance.

Co-managed logistics lets you keep control of the core parts of your business while experts handle the heavy lifting.

By partnering with a 3PL that follows GMP, HACCP, ISO and other certified standards, you gain a clear audit trail, up-to-date documentation, and a proven record of compliance.

This safeguards you against recalls, fines and reputational damage.

Additionally, look for robust IT integration and data-sharing capabilities so you can monitor performance and maintain regulatory readiness in real time.

Ensure that your 3PL can integrate seamlessly with your ERP and WMS, and that it can exchange inventory, order, and shipping data through a robust API.

A healthy integration will reduce misbills, stockouts, and late orders, keeping operations running smoothly.

Pay close attention to the 3PL's geographic coverage and capacity limits so they match your territory and volume needs.

You will build a checklist of goals, certifications, integration capabilities, geographic reach, reference sources, and SLA metrics, before you enter negotiations.

## 2. Inventory planning fundamentals

Beyond securing the right 3PL partner, the enduring success of private label brands critically depends on astute inventory planning.

Private label brands appear on the shelf, but their success begins long before a product reaches the cart.

The foundation of inventory planning lies in forecasting demand, understanding the product's life cycle, and managing the costs of holding and storing inventory. When done well, this turns demand into reliable supply, keeps operations cost-efficient, and satisfies customers. Poor planning, on the other hand, leads to stock-outs, excesses, and frustrated shoppers.

The art and science of inventory planning for private label products is therefore essential to ensure that demand is met without waste or loss.

Begin by analyzing historical sales data, identifying market trends, and accounting for seasonal fluctuations to project future demand.

The objective is to ensure the availability of the correct products, in optimal quantities, at the appropriate times, thereby mitigating the risks of stockouts and excess inventory.

Defining Service Level Targets by Category: Service level targets specify the desired percentage or frequency with which demand should be met without delay.

For private labels, the prescribed classification significantly impacts costs and customer demand.

Maintaining excessively low stock levels, potentially influenced by pricing strategies that do not adequately cover inventory costs, can result in stock-outs.

Should market volatility lead to surplus inventory, proactive inventory management and reduction strategies become essential.

They should reflect lead times, demand variability, and service targets while considering carrying costs, storage, handling, and maintenance.

Set appropriate limits to ensure agility without locking capital in excess inventory.

Batch tracking ties inventory to a specific batch or lot, and expiration control regulates items with limited shelf life.

This is essential for private-label products such as food, cosmetics, and other perishable or time-sensitive items.

Proper batch and date controls reduce waste and support reliable stock planning. The lot-level traceability system should allow you to pinpoint where and how items are stored and moved, ensuring accurate and efficient inventory management.

By tracking every batch, you can verify freshness, execute recalls, and meet regulatory requirements with speed and accuracy.

This protects consumers from the adverse effects of out-of-time production and poor warehouse management, boosting brand integrity and consumer trust.

For private-label programs, choose products that integrate seamlessly with 3PLs and suppliers.

A single, harmonized view of inventory across e-commerce, retail, and wholesale whether in SAP or spreadsheets aligns production and logistics, cuts stockouts, and keeps cash flow steady throughout the day.

To optimize cash flow, establish clear reorder points that serve as critical financial triggers, not just inventory signals.

These reorder points should be integrated with your pricing strategy and ordering frequency to manage holding costs effectively and ensure timely cash conversion.

Analyze the balance between Capital Expenditure (Capex) and Operating Expenditure (Opex) in relation to these reorder points and lead times.

This analysis will reveal how swiftly cash moves through your operations and where capital is being utilized.

Proactive monitoring of these interconnected elements is essential for forecasting cash requirements, optimizing resource allocation, and maintaining financial agility across all business functions.

Use forecasting tools that link with 3PLs and suppliers.

**Practical next steps:**

–Create a simple demand profile for your top 20% of SKUs, noting life cycle stage, seasonality, and upcoming launches.

– Define your service-level targets for fast movers vs. slow items.

– Map your minimum stock levels and expiration risks, then tighten thresholds where needed.

– Pick a forecasting tool that can share data with your 3PL and key suppliers.

– Establish a one-page inventory dashboard that harmonizes data across channels and highlights cash flow impact.

## 3. Cash-flow management for bootstrapped start-ups

This section of the practical plan begins with the rhythm of cash in and out.

For a private-label brand, the first 90 days set the tone for what we can and cannot do.

By mapping that rhythm and all the timelines of every item that could last, I see what we have and what we lack, gaining a clear sense of the risks and opportunities.

Knowing the flow lets me identify the drain and the advantage, and I can seize every opportunity that the cash pool presents.

Outflows cover all the expenses you can think of—advertising, suppliers' fees, freight, and the costs of production and packaging.

Start by recording the following:

- **Cash inflows:** expected revenue from each product line, any batch-based pre-sales, and the timing of the receivables.
- **Cash outflows:** production and packaging charges, marketing tests, fees, and vendor payments with their terms.

Construct a 90-day snapshot and update it weekly.

For a kitchen gadget line with 30-day supplier terms, list every purchase and sale by month, tagging each item with its term and due date.

Check the schedule daily and weekly and adjust if orders or terms change.

## CAPTURING EXPIRATION TIMELINES

To effectively manage inventory, it is crucial to know the expiration dates of products and their expected shelf life.

Businesses must maintain comprehensive records in their ledger, detailing stock levels, quantity dates, renewal points, shelf-life dates, and lot dates, as expired or obsolete inventory depreciates value and depletes capital.

A well-maintained expiration log should encompass all this information, offering the significant advantage of preventing costly errors and mitigating risks. It is imperative to record the expiration and billing dates of all products.

Furthermore, implement a system of timely reminders to prevent overbooking space, overcommitting capital, and engaging with inexperienced or unreliable manufacturers.

Align production schedules with forecasted demand to minimize waste.

## CREATING A CASH FLOW FORECAST

A forecast projects cash inflows and outflows for the next 90 days, highlighting gaps before they bite.

Use a simple spreadsheet or accounting tool to map:

- Monthly inflows by product and channel.
- Monthly outflows by cost center (production, marketing, admin, logistics).
- Net cash position, plus a running reserve target.

A straightforward forecast lets you spot shortfalls early and test how changes in pricing, terms, or promotions will shift the bottom line.

**Actionable takeaways:**

- Build a 90-day forecast with explicit assumptions (sales growth, term changes, seasonality).
- Include a cash reserve equal to 2-4 weeks of operating costs.
- Review and adjust weekly as orders and terms evolve.

## BEST PRACTICES FOR MANAGING CASH FLOW AND EXPIRATION RISKS

- Regularly review and update your forecast to keep it relevant and fresh.
- Maintain a cash reserve equal to 2–4 weeks of operating costs to cover surprises.
- Avoid over-negotiating supplier terms; keep an eye on expiration dates and readjust production accordingly.

- Use just-in-time (JIT) stock holding when feasible to reduce tied-up capital and minimize waste.
- Keep your minimum reserve target in mind during the monthly forecast review.
- Adjust collection rates, renegotiate terms, and readjust production as needed to stay out of a jam.
- Scenario planning: best case, sales and cash flow rise together; worst case, lower sales and cash-in-hand; most likely case, slower sales but cash-in-hand.
- Be practical and proactive; keep your response playbooks ready for all scenarios.

The discipline helps you react rather than panic.

**Actionable takeaways:**

- Outline concrete actions for best, worst, and most likely cases.
- Rehearse trigger points that prompt a predefined response.
- Use scenario outcomes to refine forecasts and inventory plans.

By building a clear, disciplined view of cash flow and expiration risks over the next 90 days, you lay the groundwork for a private label brand that moves with confidence and clarity through the coming quarter.

### 4. Warehouse operations and batch tracking

The warehouse is not a mere stock room; it is the engine that guarantees reliable quality, timely dispatch, and compliant operation.

When goods arrive, they are inspected with a clarity that affirms their standards, and when they leave, the brand can trust that they are not only correct but also on schedule.

A disciplined warehouse keeps its inventory, records its movements, and tracks each batch, ensuring that every item reaches its destination exactly as needed.

This disciplined approach frees the brand to focus on growth, reduces risk, and becomes the backbone of a successful product line.

The linkage to regulatory compliance keeps your brand visible to the public, gives you real-time insight into what's in stock, where it is, and how it moves through the supply chain.

By establishing robust batch numbers and traceability, you can link ingredients, production dates, and storage locations into a single, unique batch ID—such as P-XYZ-20250420-003.

Every unit in the warehouse references this ID, allowing instant identification during audits, recalls, or regulatory checks.

This system not only simplifies recalls and expiry-date management but also provides a clear, auditable trail from factory to store, freeing the brand to focus on growth while reducing risk.

Keeping accurate batch records is of the highest value to the chain of traceability, assuring uniform quality and making it easy to reconstruct the history of any item.

By following FIFO and expiration controls, you always use the oldest stock first, keeping shelf-life and return policies in check.

The system also supports quarantine and recall procedures, ensuring that spoiled or unsafe goods are never sold again.

This clear, auditable trail from factory to store frees the brand to focus on growth while reducing risk.

By effectively isolating and quarantining compromised stock (using methods such as barcoding, scanning, and warehouse management systems), a rapid and organized resolution is achieved, preventing further inventory contamination.

This approach, combined with optimized manual handling and packaging, enables quick and complete packing, centralizes inventory, and creates an auditable trail for compliance.

Our system excels at maintaining accurate and efficiently moving stock, with regular Inventory Audits and Cycle Counts consistently identifying and correcting discrepancies.

Routine checks help keep stockouts, overstocks, and shrinkage under control, but they are only part of the solution.

To make inventory management truly effective, I develop a simple ID schema and ensure every item is recorded with it—no matter where it comes in or what it is.

I then apply FIFO logic to the best locations or dates, using clear expiration or obsolescence indicators.

A dedicated quarantine area and a fast-track recall system, along with a standard communication template, keep potential problems isolated and quickly addressed.

Investing in barcoding, a user-friendly scanning system, and a free or integrated WMS gives the visibility needed for accurate, auditable inventory.

This approach keeps our growing cosmetics or food brand clean and compliant season after season, while regular audits and cycle counts correct any discrepancies that arise.

The most successful teams' pair practical, easy-to-use systems with disciplined routines, ensuring accuracy without hindering growth.

Strong batch tracking, disciplined stock rotation, clear quarantine and recall procedures, barcode-enabled movement, and regular audits form a cohesive framework.

Together, they enable precise control, regulatory compliance, and reliable delivery to customers.

## 5. Expiration dating and rotation strategies

In a busy product world, the clock is a silent, relentless competitor. Its ticking is not just a number but a signal of quality, responsibility and cost.

This section lays down a practical principle for expiration dating and rotation that lets your inventory stay fresh without burning away, keeps your people safe, and keeps the business on a firm line.

By adopting First-Expire-First-Out (FEFO) across finished goods and ingredients, you can dispose of items efficiently, avoid recalls, and satisfy regulators.

The clock may be silent, but its message is loud: act now on the item with the shortest remaining shelf life.

When you treat aging data as a priority rather than an afterthought, you turn it into a powerful driver for inventory efficiency.

By focusing on the earliest expiration dates and moving those items first, you reduce waste and keep the shelf stocked with fresh goods.

Brands that excel in this area—whether in consumer products, perishables, or even livestock—view expiration dates as a living metric, not a static figure.

They maintain a clear record of when items are sold or bought, ensuring that the most obsolete or spoiled goods are handled first.

This disciplined approach not only satisfies regulators but also protects the brand's reputation and keeps the supply chain running smoothly.

Identify items approaching expiry and label them clearly in the warehouse.

By tracking every product's date and combining this data with FEFO (first-expired, first-out) and age information, you can ensure that the most obsolete or spoiled goods are handled first.

This disciplined approach not only satisfies regulators but also protects the brand's reputation and keeps the supply chain running smoothly.

Working closely with third-party logistics partners helps maintain the order and efficiency required for effective warehousing practices.

Regular audits and transparent data exchange with third-party logistics partners are essential for maintaining product freshness and regulatory compliance.

Major retailers rely on real-time visibility of inventory and expiration dates, so an inventory management system that tracks dates and sends automated alerts is critical.

Train staff to respond promptly to these alerts, disposing of products before risk escalates, and keep recall readiness at the highest level.

Prioritizing items with the shortest remaining shelf life through FEFO principles and rigorous traceability is essential to protect the brand, satisfy regulators, and ensure a smooth supply chain.

## 6. From one batch and lot to the next

On the shelves of modern commerce every product carries a story where it came from, how it was transported, who handled it along the way, and what it is made of.

In an era of tighter recalls, stricter regulations, and growing consumer demand for transparency, two disciplines stand out as the essential framework for tracing, valuing, and optimizing inventory: serialization and SKU management.

Serialization assigns each batch a distinct identifier, enabling precise tracking through production, distribution, and delivery, while SKU management provides the structure for cataloguing and controlling stock.

Together they form a practical system that supports compliance, improves visibility, and enhances overall supply-chain efficiency.

SKU-management locks each variant into a unique code, keeping stock levels, performance, and assortment tightly on track so that any issue can be dealt with quickly and safely.

By assigning a non-reusable serialization identifier to every batch, you ensure that each lot can be traced all the way through production, distribution, and into the market.

This clarity of cause and effect frees you from the inevitable recall of a bad batch and makes it easier to prove every step of a product's life.

Linking SKUs to product metadata completes the system, providing a practical framework that supports compliance, improves visibility, and enhances overall supply-chain efficiency.

Tying SKUs to rich product metadata, specifications, variants, and packaging details, makes it easy to answer questions instantly, align inventory with market signals, and keep accurate records of sales, procurement, and customer service.

By establishing clear naming conventions prefixes for category, suffixes for packaging, and a numeric sequence for variants you create a scalable system that counts stock, replenishes it, and reports accurately across the supply chain.

When every SKU is bound in this way, batch-level traceability becomes the norm, enabling recalls and QA procedures to be handled with speed and precision.

This practical framework supports compliance, improves visibility, and enhances overall supply-chain efficiency.

When a problem arises, the affected batch can be isolated, reducing the risk of loss and financial drain.

By fusing serialization with ERP and WMS, the flow from stock to the next batch, to new shipments, and to demand becomes orderly and efficient. This integration keeps inventory fresh, limits unnecessary purchases, and delivers a product the market can trust.

Every recall, audit, and regulatory requirement is secured in the system, enabling swift action when needed.

The result is a more stable supply chain, greater confidence in production cycles, and clearer compliance for both present and future operations.

Set a unique, non-reusable ID for every batch, link the SKUs to the product metadata, and standardize naming.

Integrate serialization with ERP and WMS to automate stock updates, proactively manage expiration dates, and keep all documentation current.

This ensures recalls and regulatory checks are handled swiftly, keeping the supply chain stable and the company's reputation intact.

## 7. Returns handling and reverse logistics

Returns are not the end of a sale; they are a gateway to better products, stronger systems, and lasting brand trust.

How you handle them is a fine line that can shape margins and set the bar for customer satisfaction.

When returns are poorly managed, they drain resources and damage reputation.

The goal is a practical, repeatable process that protects your value while keeping customers confident in your brand.

Returns handling and reverse logistics cover the entire path from product return and exchange to restocking, disposal, and compliance with labeling and claims.

The core activities are:
– Receiving and processing returned products
– Inspecting and determining their condition
– Providing refunds, exchanges, or store credits
– Restocking and replenishing inventory
– Disposing of damaged or expired items.

A clear, regulation-aligned return policy is essential. It should specify eligibility, timeframes, restocking fees, required documentation, and ways to minimize disputes.

Communicate this policy through your website, packaging, and customer service so customers know what to expect before they buy.

Key components of a practical return policy include:

– Eligibility criteria for returns and exchanges (what qualifies and what doesn't)
– Timeframes for returns and exchanges (e.g., 30 days from delivery)
– Restocking fees or penalties
– Required documentation (order numbers, receipts, photos of defects)
– Methods for returning products (in-store, mail, carrier pickup)
– Procedures for handling damaged or defective items

Real-world note: brands like Zappos have built trust with straightforward returns, while Patagonia's approach emphasizes clarity around repairs and responsible disposition.

- Your policy should be concrete and customer-friendly without inviting abuse.
- Restocking, disposition, and inventory reconciliation
- Quarantining returned products to prevent inventory commingling
- Inspecting for damage or defects
- Repackaging for resale when possible
- Updating inventory records to reflect changes
- Reconciling discrepancies between records and physical stock
- This discipline prevents phantom stock, reduces lost sales, and supports accurate forecasting.
- Handling expired or damaged products

## 8. Quality control at fulfillment

A good product may shine in one moment yet slip when the steps that move it from warehouse to customer falter.

To prevent this and ensure brand integrity and customer satisfaction, it is crucial to codify procedures, define clear handoffs, and implement proper checks and balances throughout warehouse operations.

By establishing a robust matrix of operation with clear standards for consistent execution across picking, packing, labeling, and recalls, and ensuring alignment with quality standards and effective change control, we create a firm, reliable core that protects brand integrity, ensures smooth, accountable shipments, and keeps the buyer happy all the time.

Practical considerations include pairing quick in-line checks with periodic deeper audits and ensuring that frontline officers of each unit have the right to flag issues without fear of repercussions.

Traceability and end-to-end tracking are not luxuries; they are risk-management tools.

Barcoding across products and shipments gives immediate tracking and recall, allowing the item to be traced back to its origins and speeding corrective action.

The records kept at all levels of the supply chain ensure you see the problem at the source as soon as the culprit leaves.

For verification of product consistency, tie third-party QA certificates to lots so that retail and government auditors can confirm consistency for you.

Linking certificates to specific product lots ensures compliance with approved standards, satisfying regulators and buyers by bridging factory quality assurance with retail expectations.

The system facilitates proactive inventory management, allowing checks before expiration to prevent the sale of unsellable stock and protect brand reputation.

Rigorous adherence is essential; the system provides expiration alerts, triggers corrective actions, processes refunds, and implements preventative measures to avoid recurrence.

This comprehensive approach supports effective trials and policy alignment.

Regular trial shipments verify fulfillment accuracy ahead of the major campaigns, confirming your operations can scale.

Return and refund policies that apply to us must match inspection results to our results, so we must have our expectations match what is being done, and with these things in mind, we can always be assured that we are doing our duty by the quality of the checks and the good of our customers.

## 9. Forecasting and demand planning methods

While trial shipments and policy alignment ensure operational integrity, truly mastering the complexities of the consumer goods market requires robust forecasting.

The world of consumer goods is more chaotic than we realize, and a good forecast is the difference between a smooth operation and a costly mismatch.

Brands like Coca-Cola, Dell, and Procter & Gamble juggle the demands of retail stores, distributors, call centers, and everything in between, timing everything with remarkable precision.

A short-term forecast guides weekly replenishment, giving the business confidence to respond swiftly to a rapidly changing climate.

By extending the forecast horizon and integrating more channels, companies can increase revenue and avoid the pain of stockouts or excess inventory.

In short, a well-crafted forecast is the sweet nectar that keeps supply chains humming and profits growing.

**Quantitative methods form the spine of the forecast.**

Grounded in historical data and seasonality, they rely on time-series analysis, regression and related techniques to extrapolate past patterns into future needs.

The math is precise, but it rests on clean data, clear definitions and transparent assumptions about how the market tends to behave.

Yet numbers alone do not tell the full story.

By supplementing quantitative work with qualitative inputs—customer feedback, market research, sales-force insight and dialogue with dealers—we achieve a more complete vision of likely demand and potential disruption.

This honest synthesis of hard data and human insight keeps supply chains humming and profits growing.

By openly discussing lead times, capacity limits, and batch sizes, the company reduces stockouts and unnecessary buffers.

We maintain a shared cadence, calendar, and regular data exchanges, and conduct frequent reviews.

This keeps the supply chain flowing smoothly, allows quick response when pressure builds, and prevents the line from becoming too slack.

The goal of the stock-take is to be prepared and resilient, so that when demand shifts we can act swiftly, close leaks, and keep goods moving efficiently.

The key is to blend a balanced mix of service and cost, supported by a robust forecasting engine. Start by establishing a multi-horizon cadence and solid data governance. Combine quantitative forecasts with qualitative market signals and align with manufacturers on lead-time and their own schedules.

Build scenarios and safety stock for each expiration date, so the system runs more coherently and harmoniously, turning principles into tangible results.

## 10. Scalability considerations for growing brands

With a robust forecasting engine in place to balance service and cost, the next critical step for a growing brand is to establish a scalable fulfillment architecture.

Your first ink on a product page marks the beginning of a journey.

Growth comes fast, and expectations rise just as quickly, so a robust fulfillment architecture is essential to keep promises to customers.

Design a scalable system that can handle increasing volume, maintain service levels, and adapt to changing market conditions.

Start with a clear vision of future capacity, analyze past sales data, market trends, and the promotional calendar, and use those insights to forecast inventory needs.

This approach will keep your brand strong, and your operations aligned with demand as you expand.

By understanding seasonal fluctuations and promotional spikes, brands can align inventory with customer demand, avoiding overstocking or shortages.

Practical steps include forecasting product lifecycles, identifying peak periods, and building a buffer for critical items.

The goal is a balanced baseline plus a contingency for unexpected surges.

A modern, modular tech stack underpins this strategy, offering real-time visibility into inventory levels, order status, and shipping updates, with clear dashboards and scalable, integrated solutions.

I have a well-chosen stack, not only because it supports the current load, but also for its survival as processes mature and new channels emerge.

It is this that makes it so essential to find partners that can be scalebound, with a commitment to such a solution, as well as to partners who can cover the various problems in the market–and who also bring flexibility, reliability, and a common vision of what it is to do the customer a favor, even as the conditions of market turbulence change.

Build your own system of relationships that will promote proactive communication, transparent problem-solving, and rapid adaptation to the changing demands of the seasonal stage.

Key considerations:

- Visibility: Does the setup provide real-time insight into inventory, orders, and shipments?
- Flexibility: Can the system absorb more and adapt to changing conditions?
- Partnerships: Are scale-mindful 3PLs and stakeholders in place with clear SLAs and measurable KPIs?
- Capacity planning: Have long-term needs been defined, with plans for seasonal fluctuations and promotional spikes?

By aligning these elements, a private-label brand can manage soaring volume without sacrificing service levels, freeing leadership to focus on growth and customer satisfaction.

Take-aways:

- Build a capacity model that covers baseline demand plus a buffer for spikes.
- Choose a tech stack that is modular, integrated, and transparent.
- Establish scalable partnerships with clear SLAs and measurable KPIs.
- Regularly review flexibility, visibility, partnerships, and capacity plans to stay ahead of demand.

## 11. Takeaway

When a box arrives at your door it becomes a brand moment in real time.

Fulfillment is more than just moving products from shelf to doorstep; it is the promise that your business keeps to its customers.

A 3PL partner can be an excellent extension of your team, handling warehousing, transportation, and freight forwarding so you can focus on building trust and scaling your operations.

The moment the package arrives is a tangible reminder that the journey from production to delivery has been completed successfully, and it reinforces the integrity of the brand you are building.

The right partner must meet GMP standards, provide traceable batch control, and scale with your growth, ensuring that storage, handling, and shipping remain clean, safe, and reliable.

Key considerations for 3PL selection include:

- GMP compliance: verify that the provider consistently prioritizes product quality and safety.
- Batch control: choose a partner that records inventory by batch to preserve integrity and traceability.
- Scalability: ensure the partner can absorb peak demand without service disruption.

Effective cash-flow forecasting and inventory management are also critical; they determine how quickly you can turn inventory and allocate capital, keeping your margins healthy.

- Anticipate Capital Needs: Identify gaps to secure funding or adjust stock levels.
- Ensure Profitability: Prevent overstocking or stockouts that erode margins. Regular projections of demand, safety stock, and lead times are essential to avoid cash crunches.
- Demand Forecasting: Predict demand accurately to align replenishment with reality.
- Safety Stock Management: Keep buffer levels that absorb variability without tying up cash.
- Lead Time Optimization: Shorten delays to reduce holding costs and improve product availability.
- Inventory Tracking and Management: Maintain rigorous batch and expiration tracking to support traceability and compliance.

- Batch Tracking and Expiration Tracking: Monitor movements and dates to preserve product integrity.
- FEFO and End-to-End Traceability: Prioritize earliest-expiring stock and enable recalls with minimal disruption.
- Storage Optimization and Inventory Organization

Simplify every aspect of your store and economize space by adopting standard SKUs or lots where appropriate.

Organize stock by lot, by allocated space, and by expiration date to reduce spoilage and obsolescence.

The clear SOPs and KPI monitors give the store holder a transparent view of performance and lay a solid foundation for future success.

## Section 2

### Scaling ops sustainably; storage; cross-docking; vendor management

Receiving products promptly in your shop-bay is crucial for profitability and long-term customer trust.

Mastering the flow of goods allows you to understand demand, optimize stock levels, and ensure smooth operations.

By building an inventory system that accurately forecasts market fluctuations, you can establish an interconnected and intelligently managed supply chain.

This approach ensures products are in the right place, maintains healthy shipping and cash flow, and makes the business both profitable and reliable for customers. Implementing such a system requires following proven principles of successful business management.

### 1. Inventory growth strategies and replenishment cycles

Before your product reaches the shelf, a quiet system quietly evaluates whether it will meet the customer's needs.

In fast-moving markets, the gap between success and a missed forecast can be costly.

The book opens with a practical framework for growing inventory intelligently—so you can expand profitably without over-spending or hoarding excess stock.

By linking demand signals, supplier capacity, and storage constraints, you keep the system up to date and ready for the customer's pulse, ensuring you never miss a sale or waste resources.

To build a scalable growth strategy, accurate forecasting of demand and seasonality is essential.

Analyze historical data, promotions, product life-cycle, and seasonal patterns.

By knowing these factors, you can anticipate fluctuations and adjust inventory accordingly raising stock ahead of peak promotions or trimming it during slow periods.

Employ advanced analytics and machine-learning models to sharpen the precision of demand estimates and inform inventory decisions.

The goal is to predict when demand will rise or fall and respond with appropriate replenishment timing.

Establish safety stock and reorder points that reflect these insights, ensuring you never over-stock or miss a sale while keeping inventory fresh and balanced.

Building on strategies for safety stock and efficient replenishment, effectively managing total inventory across diverse operational points presents a distinct challenge.

As a strategic solution, implementing cross-docking allows for centralized control of all incoming inventory from its point of entry, streamlining distribution and coordinating dealer activities effectively.

This integrated approach reduces lead times, increases inventory turnover, and optimizes supply chain responsiveness to meet strategic objectives.

Maintaining direct control over these processes ensures operational alignment across all stakeholders.

Once a day, keep the same rhythm show how inventory turnover, lead time, and fill rate are not just numbers but the result of a linked framework: demand, supplier capacity, and storage constraints.

Forecast with data, seasonality, promotions, and lifecycle factors all year round, and demonstrate mastery of safety stock and reorder points.

Cross-docking is a useful tool, but the key is to maintain a supplier community by tracking KPIs and keeping everyone on the same page.

This approach cuts lead times, lifts turnover, and pushes supply to the edge of the curve, keeping everything within our control and ensuring a smooth, data-driven operation.

## 2. Cross-docking and fulfillment optimization

On a bustling dock, a single decision can set the course for a day of supply-chain efficiency.

Cross-docking turns that insight into practice goods arrive inbound and are immediately transferred to outbound shipment, eliminating long-term storage.

The result is rapid fulfillment, lower handling costs, and sharper delivery times.

This opening chapter lays the foundation for a cross-docking operation that meets real-world needs.

Choosing the right facility is key: a dedicated cross-dock site, designed solely for this purpose, offers firm, cost-effective control and the flexibility to adapt to changing demands.

The decision is to choose a mix of product mix, volumes, and geography that keeps capacity in step with sales plans.

For brands like Amazon and Walmart, dedicated centers deliver consistent, speedy flows with less waste and higher efficiency.

For smaller firms or broader product families, a central hub is often the best starting point.

By matching vendor slots to forecast demand, shipments can be booked to align with production or outbound windows, reducing congestion and overstocks.

The clarity of the signals from delivery teams allows adjustments when forecasts change, ensuring the operation remains responsive and cost-effective.

The efficient docking of goods is greatly improved by a system that reduces time at the station, allowing transport partners and suppliers to pick up items early and load them onto trailers promptly.

This keeps stock clean and prevents overstocking or spoilage.

By integrating WMS and ERP for real-time inventory visibility, the warehouse can stay responsive, maintain a steady cost structure, and avoid the pitfalls of excess inventory or long waiting times.

Organizations typically leverage a warehouse management system (WMS) and an enterprise resource planning (ERP) system as foundational components of their operational infrastructure.

These integrated systems are crucial for ensuring accurate and timely planning and execution in inventory and logistics management.

The effective implementation of WMS and ERP solutions is a well-established practice across diverse industries, demonstrated by successful applications in large-scale retail networks.

Optimizing the utilization of these systems is fundamental for enhancing operational efficiency and supporting strategic business objectives.

- Choose your optimal cross-docking strategy, whether devoted or centralized, and implement a forecast-driven inbound schedule that precisely aligns supplier timing with your cross-docking windows.
- Establish fixed-dock windows to maximize throughput and minimize storage time.

• Invest in real-time visibility and WMS/ERP integration to streamline cross-docking operations, formalize vendor management with robust SLAs and audit procedures, and maintain fulfillment efficiency with appropriate contingency stock.

## 3. Vendor managed inventory and consignment basics

Vendor-Managed Inventory (VMI) reframes how a growing physical-products business treats its stock, treating inventory as a shared resource between supplier and buyer.

By placing the supplier in direct control of inventory management, VMI pilots stock levels to meet demand, cutting stockouts and smoothing flow.

The result is a tighter link between what customers want and what sits in the dark corners of the warehouse.

The core idea of VMI is to win by turning partners into true collaborators, not just contractors.

This means choosing reliable vendor partners who have a solid track record with firms of your size and are eager to work openly.

Establish data-sharing protocols early whether through secure portals, APIs, or regular reports so vendors can see real-time stock positions and act decisively. Set clear SLAs, access to supply signals, and audit rights to align inventory with demand, reduce carrying costs, and keep the supply chain in harmony.

Define KPIs such as fill rates, lead times, and inventory turnover, and set clear expectations for performance reviews.

Give the vendor visibility into demand signals sales data and forecasts so inventory decisions align with actual market direction.

Negotiate audit rights to verify adherence to SLAs, identify improvement opportunities, and protect both parties.

Clarify pricing for inventory holding and service charges and address potential supply disruptions that could impact terms.

This framework ensures VMI performance is monitored, risks are managed, and both sides benefit from a transparent, data-driven partnership.

Build a risk-based framework that starts with routine KPI monitoring open or close stock, fill rate, days of inventory, shrink, and supplier performance.

Discipline keeps the partnership focused on value and prevents drift.

Real-world touchpoints, such as Procter & Gamble and Dell, illustrate how these brands have turned supply chains into engines of reliability rather than bottlenecks.

Take action immediately to map your goals, align partners with the right mix of quality, discipline, and cooperative spirit, and move toward a full contract that covers ownership, duties, returns, fees, and all other essential terms.

This approach ensures VMI performance is monitored, risks are managed, and both sides benefit from a transparent, data-driven partnership.

- Establish a simple, ongoing KPI review cadence and a risk register.
- Define target fill rate, lead time window and inventory-turn benchmark
- Decide data-sharing format and frequency (real-time vs. near real-time).
- Draft a concise SLA with measurable KPIs and review dates.
- Outline ownership, risk and returns in the VMI contract.
- Set up a KPI dashboard and a quarterly risk review process.

### 4. KPIs for warehouse and logistics performance

In the bustling warehouse, numbers grow faster than the space can hold.

When a business shifts from artisanal picking to large-scale fulfillment, the change isn't just about larger stock or faster forklifts it's a disciplined system of measurements that shows what works and what needs tweaking.

Core warehouse KPIs become the backbone of this system, guiding decisions that compound over time into greater efficiency, accuracy, and cost discipline.

The first step is to establish baseline metrics: track accuracy, speed, and cost from day one.

Inventory accuracy and cycle-counting frequency are critical regular cycle counts keep stock right and prevent items from slipping out of sight.

Track accuracy, speed, and cost from day one. Keep inventory accurate and perform cycle counts regularly this keeps stock right and prevents items from slipping out of sight.

Make batch-level correctness certain so products are stored in the correct quantities, reducing picking and packing errors.

Label any wrong items immediately to discover root causes before they reach customers. Measure and monitor these metrics to see how the cost of holding stock affects revenue and to identify ways to improve efficiency and effectiveness.

By staying on top of accuracy, speed, and cost, you create a clear path to better inventory management and higher customer satisfaction.

On-time delivery rate to customers shows fulfillment speed against promises, a direct signal of customer satisfaction; storage utilization and space efficiency keep a warehouse from becoming a storage maze; occupied versus available cubic footage reveals how well space is used and where to reconfigure.

Cross-dock throughput and handling time measure the speed of transfers between inbound and outbound flows, exposing opportunities to streamline logistics and transportation.

Vendor performance and return logistics complete the ecosystem; vendor performance and missed deliveries score suppliers on reliability and lead times, helping solve supply gaps before they disrupt service.

Return logistics efficiency and reverse flow track how smoothly returns through the system, reducing waste and reclaiming value.

**Actionable takeaway:**

Build a cockpit of KPIs as you begin.

Define baselines, assign owners, and set a cadence of review.

Create simple dashboards that highlight gaps in accuracy, speed, and cost, and use them to drive continuous improvement.

Focus on a core set of KPIs around inventory accuracy, batch correctness, and labeling.

Track efficiency indicators such as shipping variance, dock-to-stock time, and carrying costs.

Include performance metrics for on-time delivery, space utilization, and cross-dock throughput.

Evaluate vendor reliability and reverse logistics to close the loop on the supply chain.

## 5. Cost control and optimization in fulfillment

Efficient fulfillment is crucial for timely and cost-effective online purchases.

When it arrives intact and within budget, the business grows; when it falters, the cost curve rises and wasted space becomes a problem.

This is why we must build a cost-efficient supply chain that is an integrated architecture, not a collection of isolated tactics.

Think of it as a real-time system of interlocking building blocks that supports the entire operation, from warehouse to customer.

By focusing on this foundational architecture, you can keep the supply chain resilient, efficient, and ready for any challenge.

You no longer need perfect inventory levels to avoid overstock and shrinkage—real-time visibility does the heavy lifting.

Leading companies run their ERP and WMS in tandem, pulling data from every department into a single, integrated view.

This eliminates delays, and alerts tied to inventory, shipments, and other key metrics keep issues simmering before they spiral.

By deploying this system, manufacturers trim storage costs, shorten cycle times, and cut waste, allowing leaders to act before problems become serious.

The result is a resilient, efficient supply chain that's ready for any challenge.

When thresholds are reached too late or discrepancies arise, managers can act swiftly to prevent costly mistakes.

Low-stock alerts trigger immediate action, while variance alerts prompt quick adjustments in picking or receiving.

By standardizing sizes and materials using common pallets, packing, storage, and service capacities handling becomes faster, and landed costs drop.

Lean packaging strategies that minimize waste not only keep the supply chain cleaner and safer but also reduce space, freight, and fuel expenses, ensuring that products arrive protected and costs stay low.

By simplifying components and adopting smarter shapes, waste is reduced, returns are streamlined, and carbon impact is lowered.

A thoughtfully designed layout that incorporates cross-docking and batch-picking cuts walking distances, speeds up put-away and picking and frees up warehouse space.

Cross-docking moves items directly from receiving to shipping, eliminating the need for intermediate storage and accelerating throughput.

Batch picking consolidates orders into a single cycle, allowing pickers to work more efficiently and boosting overall productivity.

Together, these strategies keep the supply chain cleaner, safer, and more cost-effective while ensuring products arrive protected and on time.

Contracts, KPIs and quarterly reviews are the tools that keep a vendor accountable and competitive.

By integrating these metrics into a modern WMS, you gain real-time visibility into stock, shipments and discrepancies, and you can act on the data before problems arise.

Use the system to trigger alerts for out-of-stock items, wrong sizes or packing errors, and to streamline the pick-and-pack process.

This approach replaces the old paper-and-pencil methods with a lean, data-driven workflow that improves service levels, reduces costs and ultimately boosts the bottom line.

- Optimize Automated Storage and Retrieval System (AS/RS) density and accuracy to enhance efficiency and reduce operational costs.
- Implement a vendor management playbook with clear contracts, KPIs, and quarterly reviews to control costs and ensure optimal service levels.

## 6. Technology enablers: WMS, ERP, and analytics

Behind every private-label product lies a system that must grow on its own terms growing when demand swells, when shelves fill, and when performance gaps become opportunities.

The system, carefully programmed and tightly linked to every element of the package, becomes the nerve-center of the operation.

Think of it as the daily engine that manages inventory, stock replenishment, picking, packing, receiving, and more.

Technology is crucial for organizing and automating warehouse operations, including the handling of stocks, replenishments, and e-commerce fulfilment.

When the operation is built on this foundation, good performance is not a fluke; it is the result of a well-structured, technology-driven system that scales with demand and keeps every routine running smoothly.

The data-driven KPIs illuminate how to grow with confidence.

By tracking throughput, service levels, and ROI, a private label brand will know where bottlenecks are, where improvements can be made, and who will be willing to do what.

However, comprehensive tracking of every transaction necessitates substantial resources for data analysis and strategic financial management to truly inform scaling decisions.

**Cross-docking to Rapid Replenishment**

Define KPIs that tie throughput, service levels, and ROI to your growth plans.

- Look at cross-docking as a means of rapid replenishment, with real-time visibility.

- Set vendor SLAs and dashboard monitors to run regularly.

- Start with simple automation but expand as the operation grows.

- Pay attention to the little things that matter most.

## 7. Managing risk in supply chain operations

Even with advanced technology and automation driving efficiency and growth, the inherent complexities of supply chains mean that managing risk remains paramount.

In the world of physical products, a single snag can ripple through the entire chain, affecting brands and customers alike.

How a company prepares for, detects, and responds to risk determines whether a promise to customers becomes a costly delay or a lasting trust.

This section lays the foundations for risk management in supply chains: proactive controls over every link, supplier, warehousing, logistics combined with constant observation, assessment, and adherence to the rules of the game.

When firms build systems that anticipate disruption, they protect customers, preserve competitive advantage, and keep the supply chain running smoothly.

A robust, systematic approach blends visibility, disciplined processes, and practical measures from contractual agreements with suppliers to the day-to-day routines of distribution and transit planning.

Risks associated with each supplier are rated by danger profile and criticality, allowing the team to prioritize where to focus resources and who should lead the effort.

By continuously tracking inputs, monitoring progress, and scoring hazards on a daily and monthly basis, companies maintain a clear view of risk and can respond swiftly before problems become costly delays.

This disciplined, data-driven framework is the foundation of effective third-party risk management.

Regular supplier audits, paired with focused corrective-action plans, bring deficiencies to light and allow prompt fixes.

By scoring risk and concentrating on high-risk vendors, companies can detect gaps early and address them before they grow into costly problems.

Dual sourcing adds a layer of redundancy that protects against supply disruptions, ensuring that quality, reliability, and lead times remain stable.

This disciplined, data-driven approach keeps risk under control and lets firms respond swiftly before issues become costly delays.

Dual sourcing not only keeps the production line moving but also injects fresh competition into the supply base, driving continuous improvement in quality and service.

By maintaining multiple suppliers, firms can rely on cross-docking and buffer-stock strategies to reduce handling and transit times while cushioning against delays.

A well-documented contingency plan complete with compliance checks and clear playbooks ensures that, when an emergency strikes, the response is swift, coordinated, and cost-effective.

This disciplined, data-driven approach keeps risk under control and protects quality, reliability, and lead times from disruption.

All regulatory controls demand auditable records and accessible documentation that align with FDA/FTC and GMP standards.

Establish provenance trails, version control, and traceability so that inspectors can verify compliance with confidence.

Strong documentation builds trust, smooths inspections, and mitigates penalties for non-compliance.

Build a unified risk framework that spans suppliers, storage, and transport categorize and monitor by risk and criticality and focus on mitigation.

Use audits and corrective actions to keep third parties aligned, score performance with KPIs and early-warning signals, and create redundancy (dual sourcing) and buffers to absorb shocks.

Prepare incident plays and robust documentation to shorten response times and assure compliance when a crisis strikes.

### 8. Build vs buy; insourcing vs outsourcing fulfillment.

When you dream of launching your own label, the vision is only half the story.

The other half unfolds in the warehouse, in the box, and the moment the customer opens the package.

Your fulfillment decisions shape the operational rhythm, your satisfaction, and ultimately the bottom line long before the product hits the market.

Choosing whether to deliver the product the first time or to build it in-house is a matter of control, cost, and confidence.

This practical framework lets you judge whether buying or building in-house best fits your vision and tastes, ensuring that the fulfillment process supports the brand you want to create.

In-house fulfillment provides enhanced protection, end-to-end visibility of inventory and shipping, and flexibility for customization, leading to greater control over product flow.

While in-house operations require direct investment and management, outsourcing can transfer these operational burdens to a partner.

Effective management is crucial for optimizing fulfillment operations.

Key benefits often include enhanced control, robust quality assurance, improved package protection against breakage, end-to-end process visibility, and the flexibility to create specialized packaging.

However, these operations can be capital-intensive, involve significant fixed costs, and present ongoing operational complexities.

When considering outsourcing, selecting a partner with substantial capacity and resources is essential.

- Costs: Compare labor, equipment, warehouse space, shipping, and overhead for insourcing against service fees, technology, and savings from volume for outsourcing.
- Risk tolerance: How comfortable are you with handling sensitive customer data, inventory containment, and shipping accuracy?

**Vendor Selection and Governance**

If outsourcing, set clear guardrails:

• Service Level Agreements (SLAs) outlining shipping times, inventory accuracy, and customer service standards.
  • Compliance with data protection and product safety regulations.
  • Audit rights to verify performance and controls.

Data security measures to protect customer information.

Real-world context and practical steps: brands that excel in fulfillment often start with this framework, then test and iterate.

**Actionable points:**
–Set yourself up for maximum speed to market:
-Map your strengths to fulfillment choices and forecast the impact in shipping to market.
  –Build a cost model that captures all direct and indirect expenses, including your direct costs, for both paths.
  –Establish governance criteria early if you go to outsource, including data security and audit rights.

### 9. Contingency planning and disaster recovery

While carefully optimizing fulfillment choices and establishing governance for insourcing or outsourcing are crucial for efficiency, it's equally vital to prepare for the inevitable.

When disruptions strike, the way we respond in the world of physical products is as much a product of our actions as the products themselves.

We must not wait for the inevitable shock; instead, we should test and refine our defenses before it hits. Start with a thorough risk assessment and business-impact analysis to identify what can go wrong and what it will cost to do it right.

Then, evaluate whether the danger lies within our control or requires mitigation.

By preserving margins, honoring commitments, and protecting the brand promise, we build a practical contingency framework that keeps us ready for any disruption.

This material provides a common understanding of when to act and how to scale the response as conditions change, outlining the specific actions required for effective crisis management.

It is a veritable goldmine of takeaways to remember for the next time our lives are thrown upside down and we must act now.

- List the top 10 risks by likelihood and impact.
- Define them as "hot" and "cold," set trigger points, and always have a fallback in case of interruption.
- Diversify stock away from a single source yet keep a buffer ready—you can never be too generous with your inventory.
- Map the critical paths so you know what to do in the latter case and how much the cost of action will be borne by the enterprise.
- Choose a "pack" to store excesses from a single supplier in case a crisis arises.

By preserving margins, honoring commitments, and protecting the brand promise, we build a practical contingency framework that keeps us ready for any disruption.

- Every critical SKU must be mapped to two viable backups, with contact and lead-time data.
- Keep minimum safety-stock levels low while tying them to performance and maximum lead-time and use a flexible stocking system so you can swap quantities quickly.
- Shortened cycle times and resilience in transit follow naturally from this approach.
- Find at least two cross-dock opportunities in your facilities and keep the channel open for rapid movement.

- Have a pre-set recall order ready for customers; pre-registered re-call steps, notices, and customer-facing messaging make a differ-ence.
- Maintain visibility across stores and be ready to change direction so you never miss a fresh recall step.

Predefine recall steps, regulatory notices, and the customer-facing messages you'd use if you were responsible for recalls.

Create a set of highly convenient response channels, including emer-gency recall templates and incident-specific reporting for a disaster zone.

Establish a clear workflow with incident categories, escalation tiers, and a single point of contact for response and reporting.

Define insurance tiers, outline gaps, and quantify the financial risk to ensure you have the contingency needed to cover the most ruinous losses.

Set funding and authorization levels for crisis use, then conduct reg-ular testing, drills, and supply-chain exercises to keep the framework val-idated and the team prepared.

After each drill, review the results and update your plans accord-ingly.

This disciplined approach ensures you remain ready for the most dis-ruptive events and can respond with confidence.

### 10. Considerations for global logistics

Beyond preparing for disruption, successful global operations also demand a highly efficient and resilient logistics framework.

In a world of shared markets and rapid fulfillment, the first act of a private-label brand is to devise a logistics framework that moves goods efficiently, in a steady and measurable way, while holding itself account-able to sustainability.

A well-delineated global plan does more than set up networks; it maps the territories, identifies central distribution hubs, and aligns warehousing needs with green partners.

The International Network becomes the map of the region, guiding the choice of transport modes rail, sea, or air to minimize environmental impact and cost.

By doing so, the brand not only meets logistical demands but also builds trust and compliance with responsible practices.

Eco-friendly packaging: design for minimal waste with biodegradable materials that protect goods while enabling efficient shipping.

Use European regulations, emissions targets, and compliance deadlines as guideposts to shape decisions.

Place strategic warehouses to cut transportation distances and reduce the overall carbon footprint.

Assess regional storage needs and lead times, forecasting demand shifts and seasonal variations.

Standardize documentation and customs compliance by creating consistent HS codes, invoices, Certificates of Origin, and labeling guidelines.

- GMP compliance: verify that all products meet Good Manufacturing Practice standards and labeling requirements.
- Choose scalable fulfillment partners with global capability to support operations across multiple continents.
- Capacity: ensure the partner can handle demand fluctuations without sacrificing service.
- Lead times: confirm that the partner can meet scheduled delivery windows consistently.
- Quality: rely on a partner with a proven track record of reliability and accuracy.
- Regulatory compliance: align the supply chain with regional rules and customs procedures, using cross-docking to streamline flows and reduce costs.

By building a thoughtfully defined international network, standardized documentation, regional-focused planning, and scalable partners, companies can create a resilient logistics backbone that supports private-label growth and sustainable warehousing.

This robust operational spine supports sustained growth, ensures the consistent fulfillment of customer promises, and provides the essential foundation for all future strategic initiatives.

## 11. Takeaway

Scale is a disciplined craft; as a private-label brand grows it becomes a strategic field where capacity, cost, and service levels must be balanced across storage, fulfillment, and vendor systems.

It is an effort to design operations that are efficient now and ready for tomorrow's demand, not just faster today.

By focusing on storage efficiency and cross-docking, we cut waste, reduce handling and storage costs, and improve the customer experience.

Concrete steps include:

- Implement a cross-docking strategy to reduce handling and storage costs.
- Design the warehouse layout to minimize distance, using vertical space to enlarge capacity.
- Build a strong foundation of efficient storage and cross-docking that will support future growth.
- Invest in a warehouse management system (WMS) to efficiently manage and track your inventory, optimize inbound flow, facilitate cross-docking to reduce storage time, and accelerate replenishment for faster fulfillment, thereby avoiding the need to expand your physical footprint.

- Utilize the WMS to gain comprehensive visibility into all available SKUs during inbound and outbound processes, enabling optimal selection and management across your entire distribution area.
- Select a WMS with visibility across your entire territory and a disciplined onboarding process.
- Ensure the onboarding process is free of surprises and performance deficiencies.

Successful consumer brands formalize expectations with co-packers and contract manufacturers, tying quality to incentives and delivery to penalties.

Data-driven inventory planning bridges demand and supply: forecast demand, set min/max levels, and automate reorder triggers to cut stockouts and overstock.

Integrate with your ERP/WMS for accurate, real-time visibility so every stakeholder stays aligned.

Transparent and compliant operations build trust—align with FDA, FTC, GMPs, and third-party testing, and maintain traceability and documentation from raw materials to finished goods.

This disciplined, visibility-centric approach keeps onboarding free of surprises and performance deficiencies.

Make good use of third-party testing; keep everything well-documented, maintain traceability from raw materials to finished goods, and build a corrective reaction for every issue that arises.

By documenting all corrections, you create a reliable base for growth and prevent repeated failures.

This disciplined, visibility-centric approach keeps onboarding free of surprises and performance deficiencies, while aligning with FDA, FTC, GMPs, and third-party testing standards.

# Chapter VIII

## Sales Channels & E-Commerce

### Section 1.

*Platforms overview: Shopify, Amazon, WooCommerce, High-level, building a converting site, listing optimization, pricing psychology.*

The choice of e-commerce platform is the very thing that defines your business.

It determines how customers will interact with your products, how efficiently you will run operations, and how profitably you will grow. In this book we survey the unique strengths of the major platforms Shopify, Amazon, WooCommerce, and High-level providing practical insight into which mix of products will thrive on each.

Beyond platform selection, we cover strategies for optimizing listings, ethical pricing psychology, and strict channel regulation.

We also dive into user-centered design, search-engine optimization, and continuous A/B testing to boost conversions and build a trusted, competitive home base in the marketplace.

## 1. Overview of major platforms

The platform you choose becomes the backbone of your private-label business.

It shapes margins, speeds you to market, and determines how customers find and trust your products.

The four major options—Shopify, Amazon, WooCommerce, and GoHighLevel—each bring distinct advantages that fit different strategies and product categories.

Shopify offers full ownership of storefront design, a rich ecosystem of themes and apps, and complete control over the checkout flow.

Amazon delivers unmatched convenience, a powerful built-in user interface, robust SEO, and a vast customer base.

WooCommerce gives you the flexibility of a self-hosted solution with extensive customization options, while GoHighLevel provides an all-in-one marketing and automation platform that can streamline operations.

By examining each platform's strengths and aligning them with your goals and constraints, you can build a solid foundation that supports growth, protects margins, and builds lasting customer trust.

Amazon's advantages are clear: a massive reach, built-in trust, and instant access to a huge customer base.

Trusted fulfillment options simplify operations and improve delivery reliability, making it easier to launch a new brand quickly and establish credibility.

The platform is fairly cost-effective and flexible, allowing you to customize the store for every customer need.

For marketers, Amazon offers a funnel-driven approach that ties CRM data to commerce activity, giving you full control over the customer touchpoints while keeping operations streamlined.

When evaluating platforms, consider three core dimensions:

- **Margins** – assess transaction fees, hosting costs, and other expenses that affect profitability.
- **Regulatory considerations** – ensure compliance with relevant regulations and industry standards for your product category.
- **Launch velocity** – measure how quickly you can set up, test, and scale a store on each platform.

Pricing psychology also varies by platform.

Amazon's pricing algorithm factors competitor pricing, customer demand, and sales history, influencing how often and aggressively prices move.

This insight helps you set signals, discount norms, and perceived value that resonate with your audience.

Shopify and WooCommerce give you greater agility in pricing, letting you experiment with points, bundles, and promotions more freely than ever.

By testing these options, you learn which prices are too low for customers and which are too high for your margins.

Use the Platform Selection Framework margins, regulatory considerations, and launch velocity to shape your choice and protect profitability.

Plan your pricing with the platform in mind so you can maintain margins while meeting demand, ensuring your strategy stays both profitable and resilient.

## 2. Shopify, as a base for D2C brands

I begin my opening address with a simple, practical schema for converting the store space that lies in your control into something more enduring and profitable.

At the heart of this scheme is Shopify, the platform that gives your enterprise its strength. It is a central hub for managing your store, its catalog, inventory, and orders, all in a single, centrally-operated dashboard where errors can be checked and productivity boosted.

When the data is in balance, the brand can focus squarely on what matters most to its customers: the products and the bottom line.

By owning its catalog, prices, and inventory from one point, the D2C brand reduces errors, saves time, and enhances productivity.

This is the essence of Centralized Store Management.

This unified control room keeps the brand's supply chain in perfect alignment across all channels, ensuring rapid replenishment, accurate promotions, and consistent messaging.

Brands like Brooklinen and Gymshark demonstrate how a well-planned system keeps inventory and pricing right where the customer expects them, so the brand can promise and deliver reliability no matter where the customer goes.

The core data fields products, variants, pricing, inventory remain under the brand's ownership, allowing it to maintain control and continuously improve the customer experience.

A robust set of templates makes all the difference for visual consistency.

As a store grows, maintaining a consistent look across months becomes increasingly challenging, especially for the customer's perception.

Leverage your existing color tokens and layout rules to ensure your templates are solid.

Once you decide which pages to keep, test any new page against the rest of the store to gauge consistency.

Consider regulatory-conscious product pages as a foundational element of your *Product Pages*.

Regulatory clarity matters as much as product quality, so your pages should use language that clearly states what is legal.

Consistency and branding remain essential, and a firm style will help you launch new collections more easily while keeping your store compliant and recognizable.

Shopify enables brands to build product pages that emphasize accuracy and transparency, thereby minimizing non-compliance risks and boosting customer confidence.

A clear, compliant copy complete with a concise disclosure block on each page ensures every claim is backed by a standard of truth.

Pair that with a streamlined, scalable app ecosystem that synchronizes goods, orders, and inventory into a single source of truth.

This foundation grows with your business without fracturing data.

Keep the pages simple, maintain consistent language, and let the apps do the heavy lifting so you can launch new collections quickly while staying compliant and recognizable.

In practical terms, before committing to an app, assess its data compatibility, launch timeline, and long-term maintenance costs.

Pricing psychology plays a crucial role: how your present prices anchor customer perception and can drive higher average order values without eroding margins.

A well-structured bundle, coupled with a limited-time offer, allows you to test its impact on AOV while keeping costs in check.

Furthermore, simple security indicators and straightforward return policies boost conversion and confidence.

Practically, map the checkout process, remove unnecessary fields, display clear policy links, and highlight supported payment methods.

Utilize Shopify's analytics to monitor funnels, run experiments, and refine your approach over time.

Brands that test hypotheses, regarding offers, layouts, and messaging drive iterative improvements that compound over time.

Set a quarterly experiment plan with pre-determined success metrics and a rapid review cadence.

In sum, Shopify equips D2C brands with a practical stack: a centralized storefront, scalable apps, and data-informed insights.

Through such a design system of regulatory-conscious pages and thoughtful pricing and checkout strategies, brands can build a resilient, growth-oriented operation that never fails to gratify.

**Key Takeaways:** include developing a single source of data, standardizing your visual materials, adhering to regulations, choosing scalable tools, and consistently experimenting and measuring results.

### 3. Marketplace dynamics: Amazon, Walmart, TikTok and others

Markets never sleep.

In online commerce a private-label brand survives by reading the signals that prices send, where buyers flock, and how competitors react.

Those forces, market dynamics, shape the channel mix you choose across marketplaces and direct-to-consumer (DTC) options.

The plan is to adapt the channel to all place shoppers expect, to charge for visibility and fulfillment, and to respond to the ever-shifting flow of money.

Amazon, for example, applies a referral fee plus a fulfillment fee on a per-transaction basis, while Walmart uses flat per-transaction charges, making it harder to get into the buyer's eye.

Understanding these fee structures and how listing placement works is essential to turning market signals into profitable action.

Listing placement is crucial because it directly influences visibility and conversion. Amazon relies on a sophisticated search algorithm and its massive scale, but the sheer volume and fierce competition can make it difficult for sellers to stand out.

Walmart, on the other hand, rewards free shipping and speedy handling, and its broad, loyal customer base offers a steadier stream of traffic.

Understanding how each platform's fee structure and placement mechanics work is essential for turning market signals into profitable action.

Move your high-demand items quickly to Amazon FBA and then to Walmart, leveraging each platform's strengths.

Use Amazon's reach to attract budget-conscious shoppers, while Walmart's free shipping and fast handling keep customers coming back.

Keep your product listings sharp titles, bullets, images, and packaging must meet each site's standards.

By aligning your SKUs and marketing across both channels, you'll turn market signals into profitable action and maintain a steady stream of traffic.

Building on our understanding of marketplace dynamics, we now delve into specific strategic advice for this channel, particularly regarding SKU listing and platform suitability.

Significant attention is required for SKU listing and maintenance.

This channel is considerably more affluent than others, characterized by an increase in wealthy buyers and a decrease in budget-conscious consumers.

Following a comprehensive study, strategic focus should pivot to Amazon, given its suitability for specific product types and cost-effectiveness.

Strong channel foundations and effective advertising are paramount for achieving market gains.

Profitability planning is the cornerstone of any successful channel strategy: forecast margins across each channel and adjust pricing and marketing budgets accordingly.

Next, focus on list optimization and compliance, test titles, bullets, and images rigorously, and ensure every listing meets regulatory requirements.

Build credibility by securing third-party verification of your claims and protecting your intellectual property, safeguard trademarks and listings from imitators and thieves.

Finally, design a pricing and cost model that covers all fees and expenses before scaling, so you can lock in profitable margins and maintain compliance across the marketplace.

## *4. WooCommerce and custom site strategies*

In the private-label world, the storefront is more than a catalog—it is the first conversation with a customer.

The choices you make in structure, navigation, and presentation set expectations, guide choices, and reduce doubt at the moment of truth.

This section outlines a practical blueprint for a WooCommerce store designed to lift conversions, curb drop-off, and support the brand across products and packaging.

A clear, intuitive structure gives customers what they want without friction, organize products into logical categories and subcategories that reflect how shoppers think about them.

Implement a capable search tool with filters and sorting options so shoppers can quickly refine results and find exactly what they need.

Product pages must provide clear, concise information, including high-quality images, detailed descriptions, and customer reviews to build confidence and encourage conversion.

Ensure all product details are accurate and compelling.

Employ up-to-date, high-resolution visuals, including images and videos, to enhance presentation.

When offering product bundles or sales, ensure all components are clearly presented and their value proposition is evident to the customer.

Additionally, streamline the checkout process by minimizing the number of steps and required fields.

We will add to your store to keep a smooth, compliant storefront.

Look to plugin systems, APIs, and data workflows that connect labeling, testing, and CRM so you can track customer interaction and tailor follow-ups and offers.

Use plugins to enhance information and visuals, reduce ambiguity, and elevate engagement.

Be sure to have a standard checkout for both you and your guests with visible costs, making the process easy and trustworthy.

Build bundles and promotions that boost value without cluttering the page.

Plan integrations that tie your WooCommerce data to GoHighLevel while complying with all privacy regulations.

## 5. GoHighLevel and funnel-driven sites

Imagine an engine of your own, a single, disciplined platform that unites CRM, landing pages, and automation.

GoHighLevel's Funnel Builder lets you craft each landing page, capture leads, and automate follow-ups without any coding.

It gives you a single hub to manage all customer interactions, standardize marketing work, and keep every touchpoint on point. Your teams stay organized, boost efficiency, and improve the customer experience.

### Funnel Architecture: Mapping the Customer Path

GoHighLevel's approach follows a five-stage model that starts at awareness and guides prospects through the entire journey:

- Awareness: Attract potential customers and let them know what to expect.
- Discovery: Educate prospects about the product or service.
- Qualification: Test with quizzes or interactive tools to uncover interests, preferences, and pain points.
- Purchase: Facilitate a smooth checkout process.
- Post-Purchase: Request reviews, encourage repeat purchases, and solicit referrals.

### Lead Capture and Qualification with Quizzes

Quizzes qualify prospects before product recommendations.

Using GoHighLevel's quiz feature, you collect insights that enable marketing teams to customize campaigns and improve product recommendations, an approach used by Dollar Shave Club and Glossier.

### Compliance-Friendly Copy and Disclosures

Transparency, clearly listing ingredients and sources and regulatory disclosures help avoid misrepresentation.

Clear warnings and disclaimers protect customers and brands, especially for health-related products.

### Data Privacy and Opt-in Compliance

Implement secure and transparent opt-in processes for all communications, meticulously recording every interaction and ensuring consent is clearly obtained and respected.

Store this data in full compliance with industry standards, especially for direct-to-consumer brands.

Centralize the system to map the five-stage customer journey, automating messaging to deliver value at every touchpoint.

This strategic approach enables the creation of relevant upsells and post-purchase sequences that encourage reviews and repeat purchases, ensuring the overall customer experience remains clear, compliant, and genuinely focused on their needs.

## 6. Pricing psychology and price positioning

The price of a product is not merely a number it is a dialogue that shapes how people perceive value.

In cosmetics and supplements, this conversation often determines what we call the "price itself."

A smart approach starts by understanding how perception is formed and then translating that insight into a practical pricing framework.

Anchoring, or setting a reference price, is essential: for example, listing a regular price of $50 while offering a discount of $30 can create the impression of a great deal and encourage purchase.

The higher anchor creates a perception of value, guiding the eye toward the lower price.

Credible references such as competitors' benchmarks signal quality and fairness.

A supplement brand might claim its formula is comparable to a luxury product yet far less expensive, while a skincare line that promises to reduce fine lines and wrinkles can justify a higher price by delivering tangible benefits.

When the advantages of a product are clear and credible, customers are more willing to pay for the perceived value it offers.

To effectively communicate product value, highlight quality signals, effective concentrations, clinically plausible claims, and authentic user testimonials.

Establish a clear product hierarchy with distinct divisions to prevent dilution of individual offerings.

Pricing tiers, such as $20, $50, or $100 monthly for a skincare line, must provide evident and sustainable value to customers to ensure market acceptance and prevent dissatisfaction.

Regarding ethical messaging and compliance, uphold truthfulness in all communications and strictly adhere to legal regulations.

Maintain complete transparency regarding compensation structures and discounts and ensure all product claims are accurate and non-deceptive.

Avoid tactics that trick customers into thinking they're getting a better deal.

Keep your promises of fairness and truth, and use bundles, time-bound offers, and genuine urgency only when they add real value.

Test price points with controlled experiments A/B tests that track demand response and revenue impact to find the optimal balance between savings and profitability.

Always comply with platform rules, pricing parity, and minimum advertised price (MAP) regulations, and communicate clear, specific savings in every promotion.

This approach protects both your brand integrity and your bottom line.

It is advantageous to establish a system where an individual's conduct directly influences their reputation, thereby enabling a reliable assessment of their capacity to meet obligations.

Such a system ensures that actions have quantifiable consequences, facilitating mechanisms for restitution, reciprocity, or other forms of accountability, particularly in contexts where reputation determines the feasibility of agreements.

## 7. Product listing techniques

The shelves are not just about products; they are the maps that guide buyers to your listings. In a marketplace where shoppers rush through crowded aisles, the right keywords become the compass that leads your target audience to you.

Keyword research is the bedrock of a successful strategy, an art and science that uncovers the terms your customers actually search for and turns those terms into visibility, trust, and profitable sales.

By mastering platform-specific keyword research, you can craft listings that not only attract clicks but also resonate with the people who matter most to your business.

Your focus on long-tail terms is more critical than ever.

By homing in on precise phrases with lower competition, you can boost conversion and drive profitable sales.

In the TikTok and Amazon marketplace, the right long-tail keywords whether in the title, bullet points, or backend search terms help your listing appear where buyers are actually searching.

Once you've identified a target term, place it where it matters most: the title is the most powerful spot, followed by bullet points and backend keywords.

Remember, there is no one-size-fits-all approach; each placement should reinforce the intent of the search phrase and resonate with the people who matter most to your business.

Lead with the primary keyword so it jumps out immediately and tells shoppers what the product is.

- Bullets: spell out the benefits, evidence points, and compliance cues. Clear, benefit-driven bullets help shoppers grasp value quickly.
- Backend Terms: add relevant keywords to your backend fields to boost discoverability without cluttering the visible copy.

### Tools and Strategies for Keyword Research

A practical toolkit helps you uncover opportunities and monitor performance:

- Amazon Keyword Research Tool: discover relevant keywords and phrases specifically for Amazon product listings.
- Google Keyword Planner: find terms and phrases that support search campaigns and organic product discovery.
- SEMrush: gain competitive insights, keyword ideas, and performance benchmarks across multiple competitors.

### Measuring Success and Iterating

What matters most in reality: search visibility, click-through rates, conversion rates, and sales.

Use these signals to recalibrate your keyword mix, refine placements, and test new ones.

A disciplined feedback loop keeps your listings in order and competitive.

Long-tail terms are powerful for precise intent and higher conversion, but over-saturation can lead to penalties.

Keep keyword density natural and avoid stuffing.

Content should be descriptive, informative, engaging for shoppers, and compliant with platform policies.

**Actionable takeaway**: map your primary keywords to titles, top pages, and supporting fields, then test them in your top listings.

Study your metrics, visibility, conversions, sales regularly and adjust them quarterly.

By taking a disciplined, platform-mindful approach, you'll create a clearer, firmer path toward better compliance and steadier growth across your product catalog. Keep learning from the data and use those insights to build your own ladder of success.

## 8. To design a website that converts and user experience

What turns a browser into a buyer isn't luck, but a deliberate design that places the real person at the center of every click.

In a crowded marketplace, speed, clarity and trust are the foundations that make a store feel intuitive, engaging and friction-free.

By putting the customer's needs, constraints and decision points first, you create a user-centered experience that turns casual visits into confident purchases.

A well-crafted product page guides the purchaser through the buying process with clear, concise information, high-quality images, and authentic customer reviews that build credibility.

To maximize conversions, coordinate the page with trust signals security badges, transparent policies, and easy-to-find return information while delivering an immediate call to action.

Make it effortless for shoppers to take the next step and showcase a compelling value proposition that is visible at the top of the fold, so every visit feels intuitive, engaging, and friction-free.

By articulating your unique selling proposition clearly, you differentiate your brand from competitors and give customers a concrete reason to choose your product.

Keep the copy short, focused, and grounded in real-world outcomes so the message anchors quickly.

Fast load times and a mobile-first design are essential, slow pages trigger high bounce rates and squander opportunities to showcase a responsive, touch-enabled experience. Optimize each page for speed, use structured data and relevant keywords, and ensure the experience feels seamless across devices.

This clarity and performance together create a friction-free, engaging visit that turns curiosity into conversion.

Keep the checkout simple and human-centered: limit the number of inputs, use clear pricing psychology, and highlight scarcity or bundling only when it truly adds value.

Present product information, imagery, and metadata in a clean, ready-to-display format so new visitors instantly feel trusted.

Make the checkout fast, mobile-friendly, and secure, so the final moment feels natural and credible.

A crisp USP and a smooth, fast flow will keep users moving toward purchase without feeling rushed or overwhelmed.

To suit each company's own tastes and needs, the checkout must follow the proven patterns of leaders like Apple, Amazon, Patagonia, Shopify, and WooCommerce.

Apple's product pages show how clarity and beauty create trust.

Patagonia's pledges are crystal-clear on screen.

Amazon and Shopify merchants demonstrate that a fast, mobile-friendly flow drives conversions.

By adopting these best practices, measuring results, and iterating through real-world experiments, you can craft a checkout that feels natural, credible, and ethically priced for every customer.

## 9. SEO, discovery, and traffic growth

When your private label brand launches, the first sign of lasting growth is not a flashy launch but a steady flow of people who find you when they type in.

In today's market, Search Engine Optimization (SEO) is the traffic backbone for multi-channel growth, guiding discovery and conversion across your owned properties and the open-marketplace systems you operate.

This section gives you a blueprint for building a repeatable SEO strategy that scales with the brand, so growth feels less like a sprint and more like a sustainable program.

Keyword Research: The Heart of SEO

Develop high-quality content that answers questions, solves problems, and supports purchase decisions.

- Establish a clear hierarchy: page titles, descriptions, meta tags, and internal links.
- Build a coherent page structure that reflects intent and value, using evergreen content as the core hub.
- Infuse user delight with useful guides, comparisons, and aids that enrich product pages.
- Cross-link deeply between related content, categories, and page blocks so search engines can see relevance.

- Keep the focus on platform-specific SEO playbooks, Shopify, WooCommerce, etc. to fine-tune optimization for each channel.

By following this strategy, you'll make your pages more indexable, attract more interest, and climb higher in search results.

- Amazon and TikTok: Align listings with relevant keywords, high-quality imagery, and compelling copy to match Amazon's search mechanics.
- WooCommerce: Pair WordPress SEO plugins with thoughtful categories and blog content to boost discoverability.
- GoHighLevel: Use its SEO tools to optimize websites and funnels, focusing on keyword research and on-page optimization.

**Quick takeaway:** keep a platform-specific checklist on hand and review performance monthly.

Creating helpful content that answers buyer questions, addresses pain points, and demonstrates value will improve rankings and attract more qualified visitors who convert at higher rates.

The real-world examples of brand-building that all of these companies put into place are a model of content ecology that answered real-world questions, supported the product decisions of every shopper, and connected the product to their purchases, driving a growth across channels.

**Key insights:**

- Start with purposeful keyword research tied to buyer intent.
- Structure their pages with descriptive titles, natural keywords, and compelling bullets.
- Build a content hierarchy and link strategy that supports discovery and conversion.
- Use platform-specific optimization to Shopify, Amazon, TikTok, WooCommerce, and GoHighLevel.

Create helpful content that serves the buyer and reinforces the product value.

## 10. Running A/B tests and optimizing conversion rate experiments

Imagine a storefront that learns from every visitor.

In the e-commerce world, A/B testing is not a one-off experiment but a continuous feedback loop.

Giants like Booking.com are famous for testing everything at scale, shaping everything from copy to layout.

The same approach works just as well for a Shopify shop, an Amazon listing, TikTok listing, or a company's own website.

The core idea is simple: state clear hypotheses, run controlled variations, let the data speak, and then make sensible changes. A/B Testing: A Continuous Feedback Loop for E-commerce Optimization, a daily habit that turns data into decisions.

Each test should answer a question you can act on, and every channel will benefit from the lessons it offers.

Treat A/B testing as a loop rather than a one-off, and you create a process that steadily improves the customer experience while keeping the bottom line healthy.

Start with the elements that most influence purchase decisions:

- **Hero Value Proposition** – the clear message that shows why your product matters.
- **Headlines** – punchy, concise titles that describe the offer.
- **CTAs (Call-to-Action)** – buttons or links that move the customer to the next step.
- **Trust Badges** – signals that build credibility.

- **Pricing Displays** – how prices, discounts, taxes and shipping are presented.

By testing these key components in a hypothesis-driven way, you let the data speak and make sensible changes that drive real impact.

Write each test around a clear hypothesis and measurable success criteria:

1. **Formulate a Hypothesis** – e.g., "If we emphasize fast delivery in the hero, conversion will rise by X%."
2. **Set Success Criteria** – a statistical lift of at least Y% with a 95% confidence level.
3. **Design the Test** – vary only one element at a time to isolate its effect, ensure a clean split of traffic, and keep the flow simple.
4. **Analyze Results** – compare variations, interpret the lift in the context of traffic and seasonality.

You will then learn how to write a hypothesis that fits your next test and design it accordingly.

Ensuring statistical significance and reliability comes from solid math and adequate time.

To estimate the required volume, calculate the sample size needed to detect a meaningful difference.

Monitor the experiment's duration by running tests long enough to gather representative data from each segment. When analyzing results, apply appropriate statistical methods to confirm significance and guard against false positives.

Finally, consolidate insights from Shopify, Amazon, and your own site, and use them to optimize the customer experience—making the flow smoother, more authentic, and secure.

## 11. Takeaway

Few brands have managed a private-label strategy that truly resonates with shoppers.

The way a product is presented, its imagery, description, and overall presentation, shapes customers' perceptions, speeds up their buying decisions, and determines how easily they can find and purchase the item.

To achieve the right balance of control and reach, we must tailor our approach to each channel's strengths, whether that's Shopify, TikTok, Amazon, WooCommerce, or GoHighLevel, or a combination of these channels.

By aligning the product's features and pricing with the unique dynamics of each platform, we can build trust quickly, streamline the decision-making process, and drive sales efficiently.

When selling a high-end product, a Shopify or WooCommerce storefront offers a polished, controlled user experience that showcases every detail of the item. You control the data and you have the buyer's information.

This rich product page, smooth navigation, and clear pricing quickly build trust, allowing you to tailor the presentation and maintain a cohesive, craft-first identity.

On the other hand, Amazon provides the unparalleled scale and visibility to turn a premium commodity into a widely recognized brand, often with competitive pricing advantages.

By combining the meticulous design of a dedicated storefront with Amazon's broad reach, you can engage consumers at every touchpoint, social media, automated follow-ups, and targeted messaging, while nurturing relationships that lead to repeat sales.

This balanced approach lets you keep the luxury of a curated shopping journey and tightly controlled user experience without sacrificing the broad exposure that only a marketplace like Amazon can provide. Except, you do not know who the buyers are, and you can't build a buyer's list. The buyer's information is owned by Amazon.

It's crucial, however, that all products meet regulatory requirements, avoiding unverified claims that could jeopardize credibility.

- WooCommerce: flexibility and customization, a natural fit for complex product offerings and unique features that add allure.
- GoHighLevel: automation and lead capture, ideal for marketing-heavy funnels and sales acceleration.

A high-converting website starts with a clear value proposition, trust signals, speed, and mobile readiness. Build listings with concise, keyword-rich titles, sharp bullet points, and compelling images. Real-world brands show that a strong homepage, fast load times, and well-structured product pages translate into higher conversions.

**Actionable Takeaways:**

- Match product traits to the platform that best supports them, rather than forcing a single channel.
- Define audience channels early and tailor messages to each cohort.
- Prioritize regulatory compliance in every claim and listing.

The platform facilitates rapid page loading and offers a mobile-optimized user experience.

Focus on leveraging the platform's strengths in content presentation and delivery, strategically positioning each element.

This optimizes user engagement and conversion by ensuring clear, impactful communication.

## Section 2.
### Wholesale vs D2C; channel strategy; B2B; B2C

When a private-label product moves from concept to reality, the most fundamental question is how it will reach its customers.

Choosing the right sales channels is not just a logistical step; it is a strategic declaration that shapes a brand's identity, profitability, and growth potential.

The decision between a Direct-to-Consumer (D2C) model and traditional wholesale distribution determines how you control your brand's message, protect healthy margins, and accelerate market reach.

We shall cover the principal features of a firm's channel-based pricing framework:

To *secure your brand's integrity* through effective policies like Minimum Advertised Price (MAP). Your *company's good name* through effective policies like a minimum advertise price (MAP), your firm's *brand protection* against counterfeiters in everything across every platform on which it stands, in operations, in fulfillment and international expansion.

By seeing these areas, all brands can make wise judgments, build united operations, and keep what they do right, and by this, can do so consistently.

## 1. D2C vs wholesale channel models

When a private-label brand is just getting off the ground, the first decision you face is where to sell.

The choice between Direct-to-Consumer (D2C) and wholesale is the core strategic fork that will shape your margins, speed to market, and brand control.

D2C puts the product directly in the hands of customers, giving you full pricing power, immediate feedback, and a tighter pulse on market demand.

Wholesale, on the other hand, offers broader reach and faster volume, but at the cost of lower margins and less direct customer insight.

Ultimately, the path you choose will dictate how quickly you grow, how much profit you keep, and how closely you can steer your brand's future.

You can get as many messages out as possible, tinker with packaging and post-purchase experience, and keep the lights on with a clear sense of your brand story.

You can tailor messages to suit you, experiment with packaging, and shape your post-purchase experience with your own peculiar gusto.

In most cases, the retail and distributor are bypassed, for they are the only two places you can make your product truly yours, putting you ahead of the market and once more at the doorstep of your shoppers.

The trade-off is a tighter margin and less direct customer insight, but you gain control, higher margins, and speed to market.

D2C lets you set the price, edge margins higher, and own the customer, while wholesale offers broader reach and faster volume at the cost of lower margins and less direct customer insight.

Ultimately, the path you choose will dictate how quickly you grow, how much profit you keep, and how closely you can steer your brand's future.

You control the narrative, gathering actionable data that informs product iterations and personalized marketing, creating a loop that accelerates learning and repeat purchases. Wholesale is the fastest way to reach a large audience without building a nationwide store network, cutting the burden of direct-channel operations.

However, it brings margin pressure and contract terms that can't be ignored.

A common risk when mixing channels is conflict: price hierarchies can clash, damaging brand perception.

To mitigate this, establish efficient price-integrity measures such as a Minimum Advertised Price (MAP) policy and set distributor guardrails to keep the bargains in line.

This balance lets you steer your brand's future while still enjoying the broader reach and volume that wholesale offers.

Keep a vigilant eye on how discounting, promotions, and assortments play out across channels, and let the buying decisions guide where you position your brand based on your goals, resources, and target audience.

**Control:**

If shaping the brand's narrative and owning customer data are priorities, a direct-to-consumer (D2C) approach is most favorable.

Margins are higher with direct channels, giving you room to reinvest in growth. Speed to market is also a key advantage wholesale can deliver quick reach into established dealers and retailers, while a hybrid strategy lets you combine the strengths of both worlds.

Brands such as Glossier, Allbirds, and Warby Parker show how a blended approach keeps the brand at the center while simultaneously accessing data and distribution channels.

By establishing guardrails, MAP policies, contract terms, and product eligibility rules, companies can prevent channel conflict and maintain control over their margins.

The result is a practical, action-oriented framework that moves beyond initial instincts into intentional, data-driven decisions, enabling rapid breadth of reach without sacrificing profitability.

## 2. Pricing and discounting by channel

In a world where product-touching storefronts, online marketplaces, and enterprise partners coexist under a single channel umbrella, the price-book becomes your canvas—yet the numbers themselves are not the sole focus.

A channel-based pricing framework is essential to keep prices in proportion, protect margins, and preserve the customer image across all sales avenues.

Each channel brings its own costs, customer profiles, competitive dynamics, and strategic nuances, so a tailored plan for B2B, B2C, and the broader markets is required.

The key to effective price-making lies in understanding and segmenting every channel by its distinctive qualities from retail techniques to procurement cycles and then crafting a "four-way" pricing strategy that delivers profitability while keeping the brand relevant in every space.

**Pricing objectives:** Set these goals for every channel in, e.g., growth in revenues, marketplace presence or brand visibility.

**Pricing strategies:** Mix tactics to the realities of your channel, asking your willingness to pay, and your competitors.

**Pricing governance:** Guarantee your consistency, to be consistent, and to enforce rules in practice which operate both in conformity with the reality of your market and in the spirit of consistency to which they point.

Your MAP, MAP Price Parity, and Channel Governance to prevent price-driven conflicts, build a firm "framework" around the three ingredients.

- MAP policies: Clearly state the price floor in your advertising so that all channels honor it.
- Price parity: Keep prices level across channels to protect brand value and prevent erosion.
- Channel governance: Define roles, responsibilities, and expectations for each partner to maintain a cohesive pricing system.

Tiered Wholesale Pricing for Private Label Retailers

- Volume-based tiers: Offer discounts that increase with volume while rewarding long-term commitments or contract-based purchases.

- Margin protection: Set prices that preserve margins even at lower volumes, ensuring profitability.
- D2C price optimization: Test and refine direct-to-consumer pricing more extensively than a single model allows, using bundles and subscriptions to add value.

**Profitability tactics:** use price anchoring, value-based pricing, and dynamic pricing where appropriate, complemented by seasonal discounts and promotional cadences.

Plan cross-channel promotions with care, aligning messaging and timing across all channels through a clear promotional calendar.

Calibrate discount depth to drive sales without eroding value and schedule launch timing to maximize impact while minimizing overlap.

Build a channel segmentation that sets explicit pricing objectives for each space, and establish MAP, price parity and governance to reduce conflict and preserve brand integrity.

Use tiered wholesale and D2C structures to protect margins while growing share, creating a practical, scalable pricing framework that supports growth, discipline and brand strength across channels.

### 3. Brand protection on the marketplace and counterfeit risk

Protecting your brand in the marketplace is not a luxury, it is the foundation of trust, revenue, and long-term growth.

In a crowded arena where counterfeiters can appear in an instant, the impact is felt within minutes.

The solution is to build a rigorous system of Authorized Seller Networks that gives legitimate partners real permission to sell, eliminates their fears, and ensures that counterfeit substitutes cannot compete.

By enforcing strict standards of fairness and guarding every channel, you create a wall of authenticity that protects both your brand and your supply chain.

To deter counterfeits, implement serialization and QR codes so that every product carries a unique mark of authenticity.

By registering each item at every point of sale, consumers can verify its legitimacy at any transaction, turning the purchase into a trusted experience.

Educate buyers and monitor listings: explain the system, show how to spot genuine items, and guide them on what to do if something seems off.

Keep the records up-to-date and maintain a clear, transparent traceability chain that makes it hard for counterfeiters to slip through.

This approach not only protects the brand but also builds consumer confidence in every product you offer.

In practice, a disciplined rhythm of checks, small but steady, keeps the rattle down as the market grows.

Leverage marketplace protections and proactive IP enforcement, using Brand Registry tools and seller programs to shut down counterfeiters and protect your brand.

A well-orchestrated mix of safeguards, platform protections, decisive action, and legal response, keeps your brand viable and your revenue secure.

Build an authorized-seller framework with relentless vetting and a rigorous quality-control system.

Seal your supply chain with serialization, unique codes, and tamper-evident packaging to authenticate authenticity and track every step of the retail chain.

## 4. Amazon Brand Registry basics

In this crowded marketplace a tiny but ambitious brand jostles for space among the crowd.

A new product line may be excellent, yet if counterfeit copies creep in or appear in unrelated listings, the line between trust and doubt narrows.

That's where the Amazon Brand Registry comes in.

It isn't a magic wand, but it protects your intellectual property and helps shape a better customer experience on Amazon.

Amazon Brand Registry provides brands with critical tools to manage their presence and protect their intellectual property.

Key benefits include enhanced counterfeit prevention, improved search visibility and product discoverability, access to advanced advertising and content features, and greater control over listings and the customer experience.

These features collectively strengthen brand credibility and recognition.

You can enroll a brand by registering it as a fully registered trademark or by filing an application that demonstrates formal ownership before you are allowed to enter the market.

1) Set up a Brand Registry account on the appropriate Amazon page and provide basic details of the brand.

2) Submit proofs of trademark status, whether registered or in-application, along with any other required documentation.

To complete enrollment, prepare the following:

- Brand name: the official brand designation.
- Logo: a high-quality image of the brand.
- UPCs: Universal Product Codes for each product in the collection.
- Proof of use: documentation showing active use of the mark.

The registry's main advantage is tighter control over listings, preventing hijacking and keeping your brand's message and reputation intact.

By restricting unauthorized changes, you protect the accuracy of product detail pages and the integrity of images.

Access to expanded product descriptions, richer images, and Sponsored Brands banner ads in search results further boosts visibility and drives sales.

Compliance and ongoing monitoring of policy are essential, keep your registrations current to avoid lapses and maintain the benefits the registry provides.

- Confirm your trademark status (registered or in-application) and gather proof.
- Assemble your assets: brand name, logo, UPCs, and proof of use.
- Set up your Brand Registry account and begin the enrollment process.
- Plan for enhanced content and Sponsored Brand campaigns to boost discovery and build trust.
- Review registrations and policy every six months to maintain compliance and keep the benefits of the registry.

### 5. Wholesale terms, distributor agreements

When you're dreaming of a private label that bears your name on store shelves, the first real decision is how to build a wholesale enterprise.

A well-formed distributor relationship is a sure bet for rapid growth; if it's weak or ill-defined, the firm will simply drift and fray.

This section lays the foundation: set clear expectations, establish baseline duties, and recognize that channel partners are the most important strategic asset.

A solid, mutually agreed contract is not just a formality, it's the framework that defines who, when, and how you'll move products, ensuring momentum and preventing friction.

The principal object is to move what is in bulk through the system which makes people happy.

With that in place, what remains is to concentrate all your forces on making quality and innovative products.

You can be a business whose basis is more solid and sound and where at last can the distributor take the orders, accounts, post-sale services to the retailers.

Don't forget to outline delivery schedules, preferred carriers, and who bears freight responsibilities at each stage.

Clarify lead-times, packing requirements, and handling for damaged goods.

This baseline will guide actions and transactions, making communication clearer and more efficient.

It builds a shared understanding of expectations from the selling side, so everyone stays on the same page and works toward mutual goals.

Good to know that setting these details early keeps the brand in the best condition and keeps partners aligned throughout all phases.

When a brand successfully establishes a presence within a specific market, such as through prominent retail placement, it can cultivate strong distributor relationships and provide incentives like co-branded promotional materials.

Similarly, securing a regional foothold via local distributors offers significant advantages in market entry and operational stability.

Nevertheless, the demarcation of distribution territories and retail channels necessitates careful strategic planning to navigate expansion and optimize resource allocation.

Ultimately, a precisely defined distribution agreement is essential for maximizing efficiency and achieving commercial objectives.

## 6. Channel conflict avoidance and alignment

Imagine stepping into a store where the same product appears at three different prices, each with a distinct service offer.

The effect is immediate: trust eroding, margins tightening, and the customer experience faltering.

Yet the book turns to the fundamentals of channel management, showing how the various channels, working together, maintain coherence, set margins for all but the outliers, and present the true brand to their ideal stakeholders.

The key to unraveling each channel's errors lies in a disciplined, unshakable framework that lays out clear goals for wholesale, direct-to-consumer, and B2B engagement across every mile and breadth of the network.

Each channel has its own strengths and weaknesses, and each contributes to the bottom line in a distinct way.

The goal is a unified vision where every channel supports the others rather than competes.

Begin by outlining the role of each channel and the customer value it delivers, then translate those roles into clear, measurable objectives for growth, profitability, and service levels.

A disciplined MAP policy can be established on the basis of business needs, setting a floor that protects margins, prevents price erosion, and maintains brand consistency.

When customers see consistent pricing and quality across all touchpoints, the brand stays strong, and the margins grow.

A disciplined MAP policy is built on clear guidelines, defined consequences for non-compliance, and transparent monitoring.

These elements create trust, protect margins, and reinforce a premium brand position.

By limiting distribution to a select group of high-performing partners, you ensure consistent messaging and presentation.

Tiered pricing rewards channel performance and market contribution, while regular reviews and governance keep the partnership on track.

This approach strengthens brand control in key markets, drives mutual confidence, and sustains healthy margins across all touchpoints.

This sharing of data gives visibility into sell-through, inventory levels and the marketing impacts, enabling timely, data-driven decisions and continuous improvement.

The practical powers of governance cover all decisions, from the decision to give some money to a seller to the decision to give a producer some free stuff to spend.

Government of incentives and rebates is a way of doing the same thing.

Incentives can be tied to sales quotas or to marketing milestones (e.g., the seller's own mileage), to which they must *sell*, in such a way that the incentives promote the brand's goals and make their store value endure.

**Make actionable take-aways clear**: ask for the terms clear enough that wholesalers *might* not forget them.

1. Give quarterly reviews to the partner. ...
2. Set up incentive structures to match firm activities with brand growth.

## 7. Direct-to-consumer customer experience and service standards

If you open a package and read the label, every detail, from the ingredients to the return policy, can either cement trust or raise doubts.

The foundation of loyalty is built on clear, accurate, and honest communication.

Transparent advertising gives customers a realistic idea of what they're getting, while precise descriptions, high-quality images, and factual reviews reinforce that trust.

In a direct-to-consumer world, the quality of the customer experience is the bedrock on which future loyalty grows, keeping buyers coming back and reducing returns.

To make that experience truly seamless, provide complete details of what's been sourced, manufactured, and shipped on every page.

Don't just ask customers for information, give them effortless ways to do business with you.

Smooth, error-free cross-platform processing on all devices and touchpoints turns discovery into a painless checkout, making the brand feel personal and trustworthy.

The result is a brand that customers are eager to share and return to again and again.

Behaviour-based messaging, tailored offers, and relevant content make the shopping experience memorable.

This includes product recommendations, special offers, and content that aligns with individual interests across email, social channels, and site content.

**Real-world note:** keep suggestions helpful yet respectful of privacy, and adjust frequency so messages stay precise and useful.

Responsive customer service is a decisive trust builder; customers expect quick answers and effective resolution when they need them.

Proactive follow-ups after a problem can turn a setback into a loyalty amplifier.

Equip your teams with clear escalation paths and service levels to respond rapidly and maintain a clear return and refund policy.

## 8. Fulfillment options by channel

A brand's path to its customers is defined by the channels it chooses, every mile, every rhythm, every cost, and the way product finally lands in a consumer's hands.

Think of each channel as a chess piece: it has its own size, angles, and opportunities.

When you get it right, the operation becomes a competitive advantage rather than a hidden cost.

B2B wholesale fulfillment, moving large quantities of goods from business to business, differs from bulk-packaging, palletized, and scheduled deliveries in both volume and the way it is managed.

By aligning the right channel with the right strategy, a brand can achieve efficient, fast, and cost-effective fulfillment that supports its overall growth.

Many firms turn to third-party logistics providers (3PLs) to manage the complexity of B2B fulfillment.

A good 3PL can handle scale, timing, invoicing accuracy, and compliance, keeping operations predictable even for large or recurring orders.

They offer bulk packaging, palletization, scheduled delivery, and precise billing systems, while also providing fast, reliable shipping and easy return and exchange processes.

Depending on a brand's size and capabilities, it can choose to run D2C in-house or contract with a 3PL, ensuring efficient, cost-effective fulfillment that supports growth.

Effective multi-channel fulfillment necessitates quality packaging that aligns with the brand's image, especially when e-commerce platforms are integrated.

A streamlined customer experience should offer effortless order tracking, clear status updates, and simplified transaction processes.

This approach reduces customer friction and eliminates unnecessary administrative steps.

A powerful multi-channel system keeps stockouts and overstock at bay, ensuring that products are always available when and where they're needed.

By synchronizing replenishment across B2B, D2C, and marketplace channels with channel-specific packing and labeling rules, you can avoid the hassle of last-minute reorders.

Pack your packaging to exact specifications, protect the product on the way, and keep it where demand dictates.

This approach not only preserves inventory but also strengthens the brand's presence wherever customers go, giving you a reliable, efficient supply chain that serves every channel with the same level of care and precision.

## 9. The global e-commerce considerations and tax compliance

When a maker ships a lamp from Lisbon to a customer in Singapore, the product arrives before the box is opened.

The chance for real business is there, a worldwide audience waiting in droves.

Yet the rules, the costs, and the difficulties in measuring the goods create friction.

Each country treats the item differently, imposing duties and taxes that can make a seller hesitant to market it.

The opening of this global trade map lays out the common pain points and the decisions that set the momentum for expanding the physical product brand.

This is why you must sell cross-border in a way that positions your products and highlights their unique value.

The goal is to drive cross-border interest and foster profit growth while minimizing risks and avoiding unexpected complications.

Navigating regulatory and product restrictions requires you to thoroughly research your target markets to understand local regulations and potential challenges; and adapt your offerings to each market.

Crucially, managing VAT/GST and other tax considerations is paramount.

Taxable duties and prices vary widely across jurisdictions, significantly impacting overall pricing, billing, invoicing, and the application of various tax rates and thresholds.

For instance, EU VAT regulations differ by country and product category, with rates and thresholds set locally.

Understanding tax nexus, which defines a business's obligation to collect tax in a particular jurisdiction (often based on specific activity or sales thresholds), is crucial.

This also necessitates clarity on the allocation of tax liabilities and the associated costs of compliance in diverse markets.

Moreover, currency exchange rates significantly impact profit margins.

Local price, gives local perception, and processing fees can erode profitability,

Practical measures include hedging a little in your exposure, and reviewing fees, etc., etc. Shipping Duties, etc., and import duties and classifications (HS codes), determine the taxes at the border.

Coding and understanding the import rules create time and money for delivery and total landed cost.

Understand and manage VAT and GST thresholds and filing cadence.

Decide channel tax ownership early in the process. Build your pricing plan to accurately account for foreign exchange (FX) and cross-border fees.

## 10. Channel-specific marketing playbooks

A launch of a private-label line is more than a splash; it is a map that shows how you will win in every channel.

When strategy meets day-to-day action, momentum builds and stays rooted in what already works.

The result is a playbook that guides wholesale, direct-to-consumer, and marketplace efforts alike.

### Wholesale Playbook: Partnership Criteria and Terms

- Identify retailers whose values and audience match your brand and weave them into your story.
- Negotiate margins that are fair and profitable for both sides, setting a safe but firm floor for future growth.
- Let the playbook translate high-level goals into concrete, actionable steps for your team, ensuring every channel plays to its strengths.
- MOQs: Define minimum order quantities to balance production efficiency with market reach.
- Ensure compliance: Verify that retailers follow your branding guidelines and meet regulatory requirements.
- D2C/B2C Playbook: Owned Storefronts, Funnels, and CAC
- Owned storefronts: Build a smooth, engaging shopping experience on your own site.
- Funnels: Design and refine conversion paths to reduce drop-off and lift average order value.
- CAC: Craft strategies to bring in new customers through social channels, email marketing, and paid media.
- Own data: Collect and use customer data to guide creative, messaging, and product decisions.
- Optimize funnels: Continuously test variations to improve conversions and satisfaction.
- Email and retention: Grow an email list and implement retention tactics to encourage repeat purchases.

Marketplace Channel Playbooks and Channel Policies

- Listing optimization: Design clear, compelling listings that enhance visibility and drive sales.
- Compliance with platform rules: Ensure your listings and marketing practices align with each platform's policies.
- Content strategy per channel: Tailor assets for retailers and direct consumers, speaking to each audience's needs and motivations.
- Messaging guardrails by channel: Establish clear boundaries for tone, claims, and branding across every channel.
- Regulatory claims and branding: Keep all content accurate and compliant while reflecting your brand identity.

Together, this practical framework provides the means to grow a private-label brand across multiple channels, supported by a sales playbook that contains the knowledge, skills, and actions required for success.

## 11. Takeaway

In a crowded marketplace, a product's fate is decided by the channels through which it travels, whether through wholesale partners, direct-to-consumer storefronts, or business-to-business collaborations.

The brands that thrive are those that pursue a unified aim: delivering value to customers while preserving control over experience, data, and margin.

By aligning every channel to this purpose, a brand can win more customers without losing its core identity.

For example, in supplements and cosmetics, regulation, speed, and trust are the key conditions that must be met to succeed.

D2C gives you the power to control the brand experience, lift margins, and harvest rich first-party data that informs product and marketing decisions.

The strongest brands don't rely on a single path; they mix and match channels as a habit, balancing profit with control.

The goal is to keep the profit at home without sacrificing the brand experience, ensuring every channel contributes to a cohesive, high-margin strategy.

Higher margins can be realized through direct channels that optimize fulfillment, returns, and customer support.

This strategy necessitates accurate forecasting and an understanding of market *velocity* to inform decision-making.

A comprehensive approach, encompassing product offerings, customer education, and service delivery across all touchpoints, is critical for market success.

Implementing a truly coherent strategy, even with complex operational requirements, is fundamental for long-term viability.

This success is underpinned by operational excellence and a robust operating system designed for *scale*.

Consequently, it is imperative to *build for redundancy* within all critical systems.

### Actionable takeaways:

- A three-part channel framework—wholesale, D2C, and B2B—for each channel.
- Compliance and risk control early in the process (documenting, labeling, safety testing).
- A test-and-scale approach: pilot in select areas, then expand where margins, velocity, and brand growth align.
- An operating system: use checklists, partner SLAs, and performance data to steady growth.

We'll create playbooks, contracts, and performance reviews that bring you that channel-retaining, scalable procedure, ensuring you're ready when the channel goes too far or goes astray.

This comprehensive support ensures channels are effectively established, achieve sustained success, and maintain ongoing momentum.

So, when brands unite their paths, and mix them by way of some judicious mixing, they'll make something durable out of the matter.

Bulls, Nike, and Glossier, in particular, exemplify a blended approach.

While a blend of scale with direct relationship is crucial for optimal results, achieving this intricate combination requires nuanced execution.

# Chapter IX

## Marketing and Launch Strategy

### *Section 1.*

### *Pre-launch buzz, influencers, UGC, affiliates, educational content*

When the product arrives on the scene, its first impulse is to make the first stirrings of interest.

This is the prelude to the excitement of discovery, to the earnest, genuine trust that you build, and to a firm but steady presence.

I must tell you how to lay out your aims, to lay out your targets, and how to make the attractive early outreach work with you, with the creative and the producer, and with the reader and the medium.

I am not speaking here of one specific aim, but of all the aims that might come into being.

### *1. Pre-launch strategy and list-building campaigns*

Before a product reaches the customers, you set a precision compass that marks the start of the pre-launch phase.

In this stage, momentum builds, credibility is earned, and the signals that guide every move are established.

You lay out clear goals, chart the channels, and turn interest into traction, creating the first positive signs of success.

A sensible plan pairs definite targets with actual intervals, so every action has measurable worth.

This approach defines your ideal customer profile (ICP) and aligns the realistic forecast with the numerical targets, ensuring that each activity has a clear, valuable outcome.

Clearly defining the Ideal Customer Profile (ICP) is a foundational step, specifying demographics (e.g., age 25-45) and psychographics (e.g., commitment to sustainable living and wellness).

Subsequently, select pre-launch channels that directly engage this ICP and align with the product's nature.

Effective channels may include targeted email lists, specific social media platforms, and active community groups where the target audience congregates.

Prioritize the quality of reach and engagement over sheer quantity, aiming to cultivate genuine interest and resonance with the product's value proposition.

Build a long, bright, high-value waitlist from day one.

Offer early access, samples, or exclusive content in exchange for an email address or phone number.

Make the page clear and enticing, state the value you're delivering, keep the layout polished yet simple, and use crisp formats like briefs, checklists, or short videos.

Keep the copy engaging but not heavy, readable, vivid, and easy to digest.

Keep the content fresh and the page updated, so every visitor feels the excitement of what's coming next.

A sense of exclusivity or urgency to act now, publish educational content that builds authority and anticipation.

- Blog posts that illuminate problem-solving.
- Social content that demonstrates practical use.
- Email newsletters with actionable insights.
- Videos or webinars that showcase the product in context.

Ensure a well-written pre-launch contract, clear expectations, and a complete list of claims and disclosures.

Verify that all pre-launch statements comply with FDA and FTC guidelines and that partner vetting is thorough and honest.

Avoid all false advertising, clearly disclose sponsored content and affiliate relationships, and provide a detailed list of claims and disclosures.

Make sure your KPI targets and timeline charts are measurable and well-structured and map out the channels with a clean signup path that lets the data speak for itself.

Verify that all pre-launch statements comply with FDA and FTC guidelines, and that partner vetting is thorough and honest.

This will turn any thirst for information into genuine interest and set a solid foundation for a successful launch.

A compliant, clear narrative protects your trust and long-term growth.

## 2. Criteria for selecting influencer and creator partners

When a founder launches a private-label line, the success hinges on the people who represent it.

You don't need every creator, but the right ones, those whose values, audience, and craft align with your brand, will add credibility, reach, and measurable impact.

In this section we lay out a practical framework for selecting those influencers.

Start by setting clear, specific, and measurable goals.

Define what success looks like for your launch, determine your budget, and ensure each potential partner fits your target audience.

These criteria: Goals, Budget, and Audience Fit, will guide every outreach decision and keep your strategy focused and effective.

Your budget is paramount.

It covers your costs and defines the scope of your niche appeal and market relevance.

Yet, the real question is whether you truly understand who you are and who you want to serve.

Who is your target customer?

What kind of content and community do you aim to create?

Authenticity and reach will only materialize if you answer these questions.

Be inventive in your content and bold enough to match your vision with the right talent.

Remember, reach alone should not be the sole criterion, your audience fit and the value you deliver are what will ultimately define success.

All right, let's start with a Big Data-driven ranking of engagement that measures authenticity, signals, and the demographic makeup of the audience.

A clean beauty brand can thrive by partnering with micro-creators, tiny or large, who are loyal within their own communities, rather than chasing the highest follower count alone.

You must wake them up at the right time, keep their messages under control, and preserve the power of the brand's voice across channels.

Brand safety and conflict-risk vetting are essential; they prevent the brand from taking a misstep that could damage its reputation.

By tracking the quality of engagement and the tribe that carries the brand's message, you can ensure that every communication works in harmony with your vision and delivers real value to the right audience.

Putting It into Practice:

Define clear goals, budget, and target audience before outreach.

Build a shortlist of creators who demonstrate authentic engagement within your niche and score them on authenticity and audience fit.

Use a data-driven approach to select a three-to-five shortlist of ideal influencers that mirror your core customer.

Conduct a thorough safety and conflict check on past content and brand associations to avoid any lingering risks.

Approve partnerships with a transparent brief and measurable success metrics, ensuring every collaboration aligns with your vision and delivers real value to the right audience.

Real-world anchors like the bold, niche-focused lines in health and lifestyle show that careful fit, cautious vetting, and clear success metrics lead to genuine collaborations that resonate with audiences and deliver real results.

By setting a solid stage for each partnership, you ensure every collaboration aligns with your vision, brings measurable value, and positions your product for proper consideration and lasting impact.

## 3. UGC campaigns and guidelines

The biggest advantage of user-generated content is the power it gives consumers to speak out, speak in, and speak for themselves.

Authentic voices arise when customers are invited to create their own narrative and share it freely, turning a campaign from a simple exercise into a product shaped by real people.

By breaking the cobwebs that slow branded messages, you allow the consumer's voice to multiply, enriching the experience and rewarding both the brand and its audience.

In material goods, UGC can showcase real-world usefulness, reveal practical advantages, and spark authentic conversations that go beyond the surface.

The key benefits are wider reach, stronger social proof, and deeper buyer bonds.

Authentic demonstrations often convert as well—or better—than polished, brand-created content.

Make sure your product stories highlight genuine value, and clearly spell out ownership, rights, and duration so that everyone knows who owns what and for how long.

**Channel scope:** name the places your brand may repurpose content.

**Compliance anchor:** set permissions to cover all intended usages and markets.

**Establish a Content Approval Process:** an effective review flow keeps the brand voice consistent and the quality high.

Set clear timelines, application criteria, and decision-making points; the rules of conduct must specify what is authorized for accuracy, safety, and alignment with your claims.

**Review timelines:** establish turnaround windows to avoid bottlenecks.

**Quality benchmarks:** define clarity, safety, and factual-accuracy standards.

**Brand voice:** set tone, imagery, and messaging to reflect the brand.

FTC endorsement disclosure in UGC postings that reveal any material connection with a brand must comply with FTC guidelines.

Maintaining clear, straightforward, and consistent disclosure practices is crucial.

This commitment to transparency and trust establishes our brand, ensuring it is consistently clear and direct across all advertising channels, fostering trust and alignment.

Key guidelines for UGC campaigns include:

- **Brand Design:** Ensure all content is clearly branded and consistent with our established visual and textual guidelines.
- **Participant and Data Guidelines:** Clearly define eligibility criteria for participants and establish precise protocols for content tagging and data access.
- **Transparency:** Communicate clearly to all participants what information is required and what key details they need to consider.

Moderation and Safe, Compliant Content Moderation protects accuracy, safety, and regulatory compliance.

Establish clear content guidelines, define the categories of material, and specify what is disqualifying.

Use moderation rails that set a standard do/don't rule for submissions, and screen for false claims and misrepresentations.

Apply consistent standards to every entry.

A robust measurement and optimization plan tracks KPIs such as submission volume, engagement rate, and sentiment, and monitors participation rates, content quality, and contribution to brand goals. Iterate by tweaking prompts, timelines, and eligibility to improve performance.

### 4. Affiliate program design and management

The trust is the currency of affiliate marketing.

When a consumer encounters a recommendation, he wants to know who benefits and how he can make the most of it.

The rules that govern this space are not a burden but a framework that protects him and encourages long-term progress.

In the United States the Federal Trade Commission (FTC) plays a central role, emphasizing honest, conspicuous, and easy-to-see disclosures that help the reader understand the terms of the bargain clearly and openly.

Individuals or entities receiving any form of compensation, including remuneration, commissions, or free products, must clearly and conspicuously disclose these financial relationships to their audience.

This transparency is crucial to prevent deception and maintain consumer trust, aligning with ethical standards and regulatory requirements.

Compliance with disclosure guidelines, such as those mandated by the Federal Trade Commission (FTC) for affiliate marketing and endorsements, is essential.

Such disclosures must be made prominently and clearly in all relevant communications, ensuring that the audience can easily identify any potential biases or vested interests. Implementing consistent and straightforward disclosure practices is fundamental for establishing and preserving professional credibility.

When you cite performance, durability, or any other claim that influences decision-making, you must have the data to back it up and label it clearly.

Best practices for compliance call for a proactive approach: keep your records accurate, disclose links openly, and update policies and procedures regularly.

By doing so, you ensure that every action you take is as reliable as your words, giving everyone the best chance to find the truth.

This consistency builds trust and keeps you from being a fool.

**Actionable Takeaways:**
A practical blueprint for FTC-ready disclosures
Turning policy into daily practice
Technology as a catalyst for trustworthy promotion

## 5. Content-calendar and edutainment approach

When a product sits on a shelf, it can become a teaching moment.

We start with a clear map of tone, structure, and learning value so that every element is purposeful and engaging.

By treating the item itself as the lesson, we guide each detail—its form, function, and impact—toward a practical, enjoyable experience.

This framework turns ordinary objects into edutainment that captures curiosity, keeps learners coming back, and delivers real value.

**Tone:** Let the brand personality shine through in a way that feels credible and approachable. Think of brands that blend practical know-how with authentic storytelling—conversations that feel human, not canned.

**Structure:** Build a predictable yet flexible format. Tutorials, myths, and demos are the most effective templates because they deliver clear steps, debunk misconceptions, and showcase real-world results in a digestible sequence.

**Learning Value:** Every piece should offer actionable insights, tips, or information your audience can apply. The strongest edutainment leaves the viewer with a usable takeaway, not just a warm feeling.

**Outlining Goals, Formats, and Cadence for Learning:** Clarify what success looks like—boosting brand awareness, driving traffic, or generating leads—so every asset is purpose-built.

**Formats:** Pick the formats that resonate with your audience—tutorials that teach practical skills, myths that correct misconceptions, demos that showcase a product in action, and occasional live streams for real-time interaction.

**Cadence:** Establish a steady publishing rhythm that matches your audience's preferences, weekly, biweekly, or monthly, so expectations are crystal clear and consistency is maintained.

**Scheduling Content Pillars Across Channels:** Identify the central themes you want to emphasize and build a coherent brand story across all channels. Map those pillars to the right platforms—social posts, blogs, email newsletters, and video channels—so the right format reaches the right audience at the right time.

**Tutorials:** step-by-step guides, or "guidebooks", to teach a skill or yield a practical insight.

**Mythology:** Common misconceptions about your product or category.

**Demos:** Probing real-world experiments, making them relevant and marketable.

**Product Demonstrations/Use Cases:** Illustrating how an audience interacts with and perceives a product.

**Product Milestones:** Tying content publication dates to feature launches or releases to reinforce relevancy.

**Seasonal and Launch Windows:** Aligning content to seasonal trends and key markets.

**Influencer Brief Templates:** Standardized templates for providing instructions to influencers.

**Content Guidelines:** Establishing rules for disclosure, branding, and messaging.

**Disclosure Standards:** Ensuring compliance with labeling and transparency requirements.

- Set concrete goals, choose formats that fit your audience, and fix a cadence that builds trust.
- Create pillars and channel mappings to ensure consistency and cohesiveness.
- Build a calendar that ties content to milestones and seasonal opportunities.
- Use influencer briefs with explicit guidelines and transparent disclosures.

Applied example: a private-label brand can pair tutorials with demos about product assembly, debunk myths on common misuse, and schedule weekly short demos on social, plus a monthly in-depth live Q&A to reinforce trust and drive engagement.

## 6. Educational content, blogs, podcasts, reels

In a saturated market flooded with choices, a private-label brand can rise by speaking directly to the questions others shy away from answering.

The promise is clear: what's inside, why it matters, and who stands behind it.

Education begins with practical, sensible knowledge about your products and the wider category.

This means clarifying your claims, labeling ingredients plainly, and making every statement transparent and compliant with the rules.

Present the facts so clearly that consumers understand not only what the product does but why it works for them.

By showing the scientific basis and real benefits, you dispel misconceptions and build trust.

Collaborate with honest, trusted voices—experts and customers alike—to reinforce your credibility.

This comprehensive approach, blending transparency and integrity, signals competence, reduces guesswork, and establishes you as a credible and reliable source in a crowded marketplace.

In regulatory climates such as this, the content must always match the reality of the rules and speak truthfully in the real world.

**THIRD-PARTY VALIDATION AND CITATIONS**: publish customer testimonials, reviews and ratings, and back assertions with credible sources.

When you cite research or independent testing, you provide a defensible evidence base to assured readers.

Use a variety of formats, text, audio, video, to extend reach and keep content fresh.

Maintain a content calendar and deliver timely education to keep audiences engaged.

Track engagement, website traffic, social interactions, and conversions to gauge effectiveness.

Use the data to refine messaging, channels, and formats so your educational content becomes a reliable fixture in the spotlight.

**Practical takeaways:**

-create a quarterly content plan that charts topics for mutual attention and sharing.

-build an advisory panel of trusted voices for collaboration.

-record and publish at least three testimonials each quarter; and maintain a lightweight content-reuse system that lets long-form pieces transition into short formats.

By laying the groundwork for your private-label brand, you can establish a credible, value-driven presence that guides audiences from curiosity to informed preference without sounding pompous.

## 7. Manuel Suarez-inspired edutainment… (education via entertainment)

At the heart of the edutainment-driven Pre-Launch plan is a lesson that turns curiosity into trust.

It is carried aloft by stories that enlighten and amuse, and by a blueprint that blends content and entertainment at its best.

The private-label brand becomes more than a product; it is a way of saying, "I want you to go and buy this," to someone who is just getting started.

By telling the story with clear, science-backed, transparent processes, you build credibility and make your message resonate.

Structured edutainment—practical philosophy, GMP-aligned principles, and engaging narratives—creates confidence and keeps the audience eager to take the next step.

The key element is the creation of tiered content paths that move a viewer from beginner to expert.

These ladders weave through formats such as blog posts, videos, social media series, and webinars, allowing the audience to progress at their own pace.

For a beauty brand, this might mean launching a skincare routine series that starts with fundamentals and gradually introduces more complex steps, keeping the learner engaged and confident.

Regulatory-safe messaging frameworks ensure that every piece of content clearly states what can and cannot be said about the product, maintaining transparency and compliance throughout the journey.

Rather than solely relying on content that *appears* scientific, prioritize leveraging direct engagement with your customers.

This direct interaction offers valuable opportunities to gather insights, build trust, and tailor your content to their specific needs, ensuring it resonates authentically.

The most effective collaborations and content strategies are those that align closely with customer requirements.

Always ensure that information shared is accurate and presented transparently to foster credibility and trust.

Strategic 'Influencer-Edutainment' collaborations can further enhance reach and deliver educational content in an engaging and impactful manner.

Partner with aligned influencers and empower them with precise, compliant briefs.

- Leverage UGC as social proof, repurposing it into enduring funnels.

- Align affiliate rewards with education and entertainment outcomes.

**Action checklist:**

- Draft a 3-tier content ladder (beginner, intermediate, advanced) for one product line.
- Create a regulatory-safe messaging framework document.
- Identify 3–5 potential influencers and define brief templates.
- Plan a UGC challenge and a method to showcase submissions.

Design a 3-step affiliate incentive structure tied to content quality and engagement.

## 8. Email and SMS funnel design basics

In crowded markets, permission-based channels are the quiet engines that drive durable sales.

A well-constructed email and SMS funnel does more than push messages; it attracts the right audience, builds trust, and drives conversions with integrity.

In this section I lay out a practical blueprint for compliant funnels, focused on clear consent, straightforward opt-in mechanisms, privacy protections, and robust data handling.

Gather explicit permission before sending messages, keep records that show consent was given, and use simple opt-in methods that make opting out easy.

Protect subscriber data by informing them of its use before it is collected and by safeguarding it against misuse.

These guidelines ensure your funnel is effective, compliant, and built on a foundation of trust.

- Robust data handling: implement strong security, capped data retention, and clear access controls for teams.
- Lead magnet strategy: define a lead magnet that aligns with your brand and audience, offering genuine value that solves a real need.

- Relevance: ensure the lead magnet reflects your brand and targets the right market.
- Value: provide something of real worth that addresses the audience's problem and delivers tangible benefits.
- Specificity: Clearly state what your lead magnet offers and the problems it solves.

A well-designed welcome series is essential for any email funnel, it sets expectations, introduces your brand values, and establishes you as an authority.

Keep the content engaging and informative; it's the key to building trust.

Make sure the series is concise, clear, and delivers tangible value to your subscribers, so they feel welcomed and confident in what's to come.

Educational content wins, even when it's not perfect.

**Relevance** – Make sure every piece speaks directly to your audience's needs.

**Value** – Deliver insights and practical tips that truly matter.

**Consistency** – Keep the same high standard in every touchpoint; trust is built on reliability.

By segmenting your list whether by behavior, preferences, or interests you can personalize offers that resonate, saving subscribers from feeling overwhelmed or ignored.

With these ingredients in place, brands can build compliant email and SMS funnels that attract the right audience, nurture trust, and drive conversions.

The following steps will now be the bare bones of your plan:
- Map consent steps for your channels and keep a clear audit trail.
- Define your lead magnet and design the opt-in flow around it.

- Outline a 3– to 4-email welcome sequence that balances brand intro with practical value.

- Create an educational content calendar that delivers practical tips and case studies.

- Set up segmentation rules and run tests to fine-tune relevance and personalization.

Ultimately, compliance is founded on clear, documented consent and transparent data practices, and a strong lead magnet effectively filters to attract genuinely interested prospects.

Effective educational content, delivered through precise segmentation, fosters engagement and conversion without overt pressure.

### 9. Social media funnel architecture and sequencing

On the scroll-packed feed, a brand doesn't merely appear, but guides, instructs, and earns your trust.

To do this well, a practical framework is essential: a social-media funnel that moves a viewer from noticing your brand to becoming a loyal advocate.

The goal is a seamless flow, taking a viewer from awareness, through consideration and decision, to conversion.

This stage-by-stage blueprint ensures each touch-point delivers content and offers that meet the viewer's needs and questions, creating a natural, intuitive progression.

By treating every stage as part of a single, coherent journey, messaging remains consistent, value clear, and friction low, turning a casual observer into a loyal advocate with purposeful and heartfelt interactions.

By understanding how people progress, you can shape the message and the timing so that each touch-point builds credibility and momentum.

Content, Offers, and Compliance form a tight triangle: at every stage ensure your content is factual, compliant with regulatory requirements, and truly informative, not misleading.

Offers should remain relevant and compelling without exaggeration, and every claim must be backed by evidence.

The emphasis is on transparency, show how your product helps, back claims with proof, and tailor offers to the stage and the audience's needs.

This careful coordination reduces risk, reinforces trust, and guides potential customers forward.

The top-of-funnel moment is where you attract attention with value-led education, turning casual observers into loyal advocates with a purposeful, heartfelt journey.

Use your educational content to reveal useful insights, answer questions, and offer practical guidance.

Start with a blog-style post, then move to short, engaging videos and punchy social updates that keep readers hooked.

Plan a cohesive cadence across channels: let Instagram tell the visual story, TikTok deliver quick, entertaining clips, YouTube Shorts provide bite-sized lessons, and email retargeting nurture and convert interested prospects.

This coordinated flow turns casual observers into loyal advocates, reinforcing trust and guiding potential customers forward.

The goal is to create a seamless customer experience where every channel reinforces the same core messages and smoothly guides prospects from one touchpoint to the next.

Key social-media funnel channels:

**Instagram** – ideal for visually showcasing products and services.
**TikTok** – effective for engaging, short-form videos.
**YouTube Shorts** – useful for bite-sized, informative content.
**Email retargeting** – nurtures lead and encourages conversion.

Map the four funnel stages: awareness, consideration, decision, conversion and plan content and offers for each.

Ensure every piece of content is factually accurate and complies with FTC guidelines.

Design a cross-channel cadence that delivers a single, guiding experience, turning casual observers into loyal advocates and driving them forward through the funnel.

Within the marketing funnel, a structured progression can be designed to guide customers from initial brand exposure to a specific desired action.

This systematic approach ensures consistent outcomes and predictable customer engagement, irrespective of the campaign's specific implementation.

### 10. Launch our KPIs and measurement framework

In crowded markets, a private-label brand must start with a clear, disciplined set of KPIs and a solid measurement framework.

These metrics, both leading and lagging, anchor product, price, and messaging to reality.

By tracking them, you can spot early signals of potential performance issues and confirm whether past actions paid off, ensuring you stay on the right path from the outset.

Leading indicators keep you in the present, while lagging ones show the results that follow.

Keep a focused set, about three leading signals (such as early demand, engagement, or intent) and two or three lagging metrics (like revenue or repeat-purchase rate).

Track both at all times: the early signals reveal awareness, interest, and perceived value, and the outcomes confirm your ambitions later.

For example, consider a skincare line: each SKU can serve as both an early signal (e.g., social mentions, trial requests) and a confirmed outcome (e.g., repeat purchases).

Track these signals and outcomes monthly for at least two quarters, using a clear attribution model and reliable data sources.

This approach helps identify which SKUs generate the most interest and purchases, keeping you focused on the metrics that matter most even before the first sale.

By continuously monitoring these metrics, you can course-correct quickly and stay on the right path from the outset.

**Practical note:** document all data sources (ads, email, influencers, UGC) and test the model for a period to determine the difference in reported impact.

Channel benchmarks and product-specific targets should scale across platforms and reflect what each SKU can deliver.

Establish benchmarks that account for demand, seasonality, and margins, then set product-specific targets that acknowledge SKU economics and lifecycle.

**Real-world lens:** a beauty line may see higher CPMs on certain channels but better margin on bundle SKUs; targets should mirror that mix.

**Actionable step:** for every channel and SKU, set a 6-to-12-week target range and review quarterly. Cadence, dashboards, and governance set a rhythm for review.

Make concise dashboards on a weekly or monthly basis, assign owners, and set clear decision rights.

Regular, focused sessions with defined outcomes accelerate learning and enable rapid iterations.

**Takeaway:** appoint a KPI steward for each channel and SKU and schedule a monthly review with predefined decision criteria.

Compliance, accuracy, and ethical measurement must be trustworthy and transparent.

Maintain accuracy, avoid misrepresentation, and report clearly to stakeholders.

Ethics of measurement means documenting methodology, assumptions, and updating when sources change.

**Actionable guardrails:**

Publish a short data-methods note with every KPI set and conduct quarterly audits for consistency.

Use a compact set of leading and lagging indicators to guide early and late decisions.

Separate early signals from outcomes to drive timely optimization and robust validation.

Choose an attribution approach that fits your buying cycle and preserve your data across channels.

Set your channel-specific and product-specific targets that reflect your buy-and-hold season and demand, seasonality, and margins.

## 11. Takeaway

Before a product ever reaches a customer, the pre-launch phase sets the terms of engagement.

Its purpose is to cultivate trust through education, define clear activation plans, and keep the brand narrative cohesive across every touchpoint.

When executed well, this phase builds credibility, generates anticipation, and lays the groundwork for sustained sales.

### Educating the Audience

Authentic education lies at the heart of pre-launch momentum.

Avoid hype or unsubstantiated claims.

A well-planned content strategy should focus on:

- Developing a deep understanding of the target audience's needs and concerns
- Creating informative content that addresses those needs and delivers real value
- Ensuring messaging remains consistent across all channels

## Influencer Marketing and Partnerships

Leveraging trusted voices can amplify the educational message and extend reach, but it must be integrated thoughtfully to support the overall narrative and maintain brand integrity.

Influencers can amplify the message, but the real impact comes from those who genuinely believe the product aligns with their audience's goals.

Identify voices that are enthusiastic and authentic and evaluate their demographic fit and engagement rates.

Work closely with them to create content that feels natural and is willingly shared.

Establish clear, transparent guidelines to keep the material brand-consistent and spoiler-free, ensuring every piece of content is both compelling and compliant.

This thoughtful partnership strategy extends reach while preserving the integrity of the overall narrative.

Clear disclosures are essential for sustaining influencer trust in your brand and user-generated content (UGC). This requires:

- Declaring any potential conflicts of interest.
- Ensuring compliance with FDA/FTC guidance.

All these brands are born of education, transparency, and community spirit.

The focus on value, credibility, and consistently compelling storytelling has already begun, built on a needs-based audience map, a clear value proposition, and a simple checklist for anyone who wants to get involved.

Start with a transparent "value" proposition, select your influencers and target market, and build a straightforward UGC program with guidelines, incentives, and a disclosure checklist.

Measure everything—check off KPIs early and run real-time, data-driven experiments on content and channels.

Education, transparency, and consistency are the secret weapons that build trust and anticipation, mirroring shared values and telling the story of our common goals.

Measurement, iteration, and data-driven decisions optimize every activation by maintaining a clear funnel focus that helps identify and fix bottlenecks before launch.

## Section 2.

## Paid ads versus organic growth, credibility built through education, content strategy

To achieve widespread market presence for a private-label brand, you must blend paid promotion with organic growth, crafting credible communication that substantiates product claims with evidence.

The secret lies in understanding how these elements interlock: paid reach expands awareness, while organic momentum builds lasting loyalty.

By combining strategic advertising with authentic storytelling, you create a brand that penetrates the market and stands firm in consumers' minds.

When you align these tactics, the brand's reputation strengthens, and the business thrives, unchanged in its core values yet evolving to meet market demands.

This integrated approach is the key to becoming a recognized force in the industry.

## 1. Paid media versus organic growth strategy

Two engines power a growing private-label brand: paid media and organic growth.

They work together like pistons in a crankcase, each with its own rhythm and demands.

The key is to master the mix so that your product's budget, compliance, and market realities all fit together.

By understanding the cost-benefit ratio of paid media, its reach, scale, and the need for dedicated budgets that support testing and iteration, you can design a trade-off that lets both engines drive growth without stepping on each other's toes.

In short, paid media and organic growth are not competitors; they are complementary forces that, when balanced, propel a brand forward.

The initial outlay for content and community building is high, but once the foundation is laid, the cost per unit of reach drops dramatically.

Paid media accelerates scale, while organic growth rewards consistency and long-term value.

By shaping voice and discovery, you create a steady stream of engagement that doesn't rely on a fragile, ever-changing advertising stack.

Discipline in budgeting and a balanced mix of paid and earned tactics ensure that each engine supports the other, rather than competes, propelling the brand forward with sustainable momentum.

Organic growth hinges on credibility, content quality, and sustained engagement, producing lasting effects that build trust and reliability with the audience.

A blended strategy brings the best of both worlds together: advertising sparks immediate awareness and reaches the press-hungry, while organic tactics reinforce that message, deepening the connection to real-world experience.

By letting paid and earned channels complement rather than compete, brands create a seamless, sustainable momentum that keeps the audience coming back.

Brands like Patagonia have shown how a blend of paid and organic tactics can create lasting momentum.

By staying true to consistent values and delivering informative content, they use paid media to spark immediate awareness while letting organic growth deepen the connection over time.

The key is to start with clear trade-offs—cost, speed, and control—list your budget and targets, then invest in paid media for instant hits and follow up with organic initiatives that reinforce the message.

This balanced approach keeps the audience engaged and builds a sustainable partnership that grows stronger with each campaign.

Clearly define and document how the project will comply with its foundational requirements (e.g., regulatory standards, core user specifications).

Then, design and develop both primary channels (e.g., product development and service delivery) to intrinsically integrate and support these specified requirements.

## 2. Education-first marketing credibility

Credibility education is not built on bold promises, but on truth and unassailable stories.

It begins with an honest, verifiable story about how a product is made, detailing each ingredient, its role, and how it's sourced.

This transparent, authentic, and evidence-based storytelling allows consumers to confidently judge fit and risk, building lasting trust and a solid reputation.

Such an emphasis on truth and transparency should now have no more to hide than the glamour and glitz of a huge and expensive new product, becoming the chief ingredient of credibility rather than flashy packaging.

Sourcing, labeling, and permissible claims are the pillars that build consumer trust.

A complete ingredient list, nutritional data, and clear allergen warnings must be front-and-center, ensuring that every component is traceable to its origin and free from adulteration.

Claims should align with regulatory guidelines and the best available science and be backed by reputable third-party certifications such as Food Lab.org, NSF International, or ConsumerLab.com.

Adhering to Good Manufacturing Practices and demonstrating compliance with FDA/FTC standards reinforce credibility, turning transparency into a lasting reputation rather than mere packaging flair.

We show you how our testing practices are kept in line, share the methods used by experts, and certify that the rigor of our testing is flawless.

By publishing transparent ingredient lists, disclosing source-origin details, recording test results, and stamping them on the seal, we prove that our claims are evidence-based and verifiable.

This transparency builds trust, strengthens customer relationships, and provides actionable takeaways that let you see the full story behind every product.

Get your GMP certification and other third-party approvals to demonstrate that your brand lives by the same high standards.

Conduct independent testing, and ensure the results are clearly summarized and interpreted, considering practical applications and customer relevance.


### *3. Content formats that run the fastest*

In the web's crowded marketplace, attention is the first currency.

Brands win when they pair products with formats that move people, from awareness to action, across the channels used to reach customers.

This section identifies the content formats that consistently perform, with practical guidance you can apply immediately.

**Short-Form Video Snippets:**

15–60 second clips are built to grab attention, spell out benefits, and tease deeper content.

Their brevity suits feeds where scrolling is the norm, allowing you to spark curiosity and prompt quick actions.

For cosmetics and supplements, these clips can demonstrate a result, an application technique, or a before/after in a single glance, driving engagement, website visits, and conversions.

**Checklist:**

- Define three core benefits and present them as a single, eye-catching flash to prove the value.
- Produce three variations for testing, using crystal-clear appeal so the viewer's eye stays on the message.
- Include a strong call to action in both the text and the caption.
- Track quantity, click-throughs, and conversion rates to measure impact.
- Offer long-form educational content, guides, tutorials, webinars, or live/on-demand sessions, that provides deeper substance than mere breadcrumbs, giving buyers the knowledge they need before they buy.
- Cite credible sources and provide practical, actionable insights in a complete guide or live demonstration.
- Pick two key actions each quarter, combine them into a cohesive guide, and keep the tone consistent and engaging throughout.

- By delivering your message to those who are eager to listen and by weaving stories that are both authoritative and emotionally resonant, you'll build confidence in your arguments and create lasting impact. Use real customer stories, testimonials, and interactive campaigns to keep your audience engaged.
- Promote through targeted campaigns that nurture informed consideration, building trust and loyalty. Tell stories that show real outcomes, and keep the narrative consistent across pages, print, and interactive formats.
- Be persuasive without relying on vanity or force; instead, appeal to the heart and mind, acknowledging doubt and encouraging rational curiosity. Share what you see and hear, and let live-stream polls, quizzes, and community voices keep the conversation alive and relevant.
- Combine these tactics into a cohesive guide: choose two key actions each quarter, integrate them into a single narrative, and maintain a consistent, engaging tone throughout.

Keep your interactions concise, deliver immediate value, and make every step count toward a clear next action.

**Use a simple checklist:**

Set concrete objectives for each interaction, limit activities to 5–10 minutes, and keep results focused on the activity's purpose.

Respond promptly to comments and questions to maintain engagement.

Repurpose content across channels so a single asset fuels multiple touchpoints, a blog post can become a social series, an email sequence, and a video script.

Identify at least three new formats from one asset, adapt tone and length for each channel, and keep branding consistent.

Track performance per channel to inform future reuse and keep the conversation alive and relevant.

## Build a balanced mix:

Short clips for attention, long-form content for trust, stories for credibility, and interactive formats for data and engagement.

Plan to reuse as much of the material as possible for impact before it becomes too costly to rebuild.

Measure clear metrics for every format and adjust the mix quarterly to meet your needs.

## 4. Influencer compliance and disclosures

Foundation: Establishing a Baseline of Compliance and Trust in a Crowded Market

A private-label brand earns its seat at the table not by loud claims but by a solid foundation built on regulatory clarity and audience trust.

This opening section lays out the essentials of aligning with FTC rules, platform expectations, and the habits that keep a brand credible from day one.

Brands that neglect their reputations, often by adopting an "always with you" strategy, ultimately face consequences, underscoring the vital need for transparency. Therefore, the FTC Guidelines must be communicated to influencers in plain, truthful terms and made explicit.

The reason is simple: bias must be visible so that decisions remain honest and transparent.

The way out of the tangle: put up mandatory disclosure templates such as "This post is sponsored by [BrandName]. I received this free product from [BrandName] in exchange for this review." Keep a tiny library of templates for each format—video, caption, story, post—front and center.

This makes it easier to vet influencers for regulatory compliance and ensures that every creator you love can comply with the rules without hassle.

Before collaborating, carefully review the creator's past content for regulatory alignment.

Check that any material connections are consistently disclosed and that the posts reflect a clear pattern of transparency.

This diligence reduces risk, protects the brand's reputation, and builds audience trust.

Keep a simple scorecard that tracks disclosures, tone, and responsiveness to policy changes.

The post-approval workflow should involve a designated manager or team member who confirms compliance and brand fit before the content goes live.

By following these steps, every sponsored post stays compliant and credible.

Transparent sponsorship disclosures do more than just tick a compliance box; they build trust and credibility.

When audiences see clear, concise disclosures, they feel confident in the content and are more likely to stay loyal.

A simple, consistent disclosure system, ideally a short slide or statement that reveals material ties, keeps the process efficient and easy to apply across all formats.

Before any sponsored post goes live, a compliance check should confirm that the disclosure meets regulatory standards and that the content aligns with brand values.

This workflow not only protects the brand but also strengthens the relationship with the audience, ensuring that every post is both credible and compliant.

Treat transparency as a competitive edge, fortifying the audience's trust.

Brands that weave clear disclosure into every post leaving no room for surprise or error are the ones that resonate most with their audience.

By making disclosure rules crystal-clear and allowing viewers to see the practical side of the brand's actions as quickly as the intellectual one, you protect the brand and strengthen the relationship with the audience, ensuring every post is both credible and compliant.

## 5. Education by entertainment and storytelling

In a bustling store, a shopper confronts a rule-heavy claim on a product.

Rather than dry legal jargon, the brand offers a short, entertaining tale that clearly illustrates the rule and the practical steps a buyer can take.

The opening scene sets a fable-like tone, showing how storytelling turns abstract law into vivid, memorable guidance.

By linking education with engaging narrative, the lesson stays in the heart and motivates the shopper to apply what they've learned in real life.

The result is a clear, compelling message that keeps the rule alive and useful for everyone.

This approach works especially well for brands that sell physical products, where customers care about safety, claims, and real-world outcomes.

Take Maya, for example: she checks a supplement's label, verifies a third-party safety test, and reads how the claim feels in practice.

By turning regulatory jargon into concrete, actionable steps, the brand shows practical problem-solving from the customer's perspective, making the learning tangible and memorable.

## 6. Measurement, attribution, and data-driven optimization

Imagine launching a brand as if you were charting a course across unknown waters.

The instrument that keeps you afloat is measurement: the data you collect, the questions you ask, and the clarity you gain from the answers.

In this section, you'll discover how to lay a foundation that will guide every launch decision from the first ad to the landing page to the customer's journey and how that discipline scales with your brand.

It isn't a one-time task; it's a disciplined practice that keeps you on course every time you set off from your pad.

Conversion rates, website traffic and engagement metrics, and attribution hierarchies with weighting form the core of a disciplined launch strategy.

To ascribe sales accurately, map every touchpoint across offline and online channels and assign appropriate weights. First-click, last-click, and multi-touch attribution all play a role, but the foundation is data accuracy, trust in numbers begins with reliable data.

Prioritize governance and standardized tagging and tracking.

Build a data-management platform (DMP), conduct regular data audits, and establish clear data-governance policies. These practices give you the confidence to measure what matters and to explain the results to buyers and prospects.

Educate your audience through blogs, whitepapers, case studies, webinars, and workshops.

Leverage social-media channels to share that content and encourage dialogue.

Finally, integrate paid and organic signals so every channel contributes to a unified view of performance.

This disciplined, data-driven approach keeps your launch decisions on course and scales with your brand.

Paid advertising should not simply compete with organic discovery; it must amplify and support it.

By allocating budget to campaigns that reinforce the same signals driving SEO and content visibility, we can extend reach while keeping the organic foundation strong.

Regular monitoring of daily performance allows us to fine-tune tactics, and a quarterly optimization cycle ensures we stay responsive to shifting dynamics.

This disciplined, data-driven rhythm keeps every channel contributing to a unified view of performance, keeping launch decisions on course and scaling with the brand.

As you embed these practices, your private-label program becomes a reliable compass. The next chapters will translate the signals into launch experiments, planning tonight and real-world case studies that bring this framework to life.

## 7. Open house launches and live events

In the crowded tempo of product launches, a room becomes a stage where a brand's promise steps forward and invites touch, scent, and taste of possibility.

Open-house launches are more than gatherings; they are immersive experiences where exploration is hands-on, and the product speaks through the senses.

Whenever a passerby walks in, they are not simply spectators; they are participants who carry a tangible feeling of what the brand stands for and what they can bring into their lives.

The creation of such immersive experiences—*The Power of Open-House Launches*—has always excited me, because a great open-house opens a product's door to life through direct contact. You touch, smell, and taste the product, and at the same time the brand's promise comes alive in the room.

It's a lasting impression; a memory forged through direct contact.

When you touch, see, smell, and taste a product, the brand's promise comes alive in the room. In a beauty line, the first touch reveals the texture, the formula layers, and the finish, while the aroma lingers in the air—all in real time.

Authentic endorsements grow from these genuine experiences, and the credibility of the product rises as people share their true reactions.

This hands-on approach not only educates but also empowers both the brand and the consumer, turning a simple demo into a powerful, immersive encounter.

Such is education about formulation, usage, and ingredient transparency, deepening your understanding in its own right.

Mini classes create practical knowledge, care and maintenance workshops to remember, or on the other hand, guidance on the materials care that shows how long they are.

By the event, you see its power rise in its field; and the power you reach, in the midst of the event, through the clips and blogs you create, the web newsletters you create, the e-mails you send–are made for web channels, websites and print-out mailers.

Publishing as a way of spreading the life and power of your event, it keeps things exciting and keeps it up.

Measuring its effect–in the face of your actual-world measurements:

Go after the track leads, conversions, email signs, and purchase intent, etc., the gathering has captured, and analyzing these things reveals the things that were–and are–resonating to your heart, providing pointers to improvement, and enabling smarter resource planning ahead.

Quick start checklist:

–Define clear objectives and desired outcomes, design hands-on experiences with the product.

–Plan consent-based endorsements from credible voices.

–Build concise, practical education segments.

–Provide partners with product availability and cost.

–Make use of the content, create a website and newsletter that re-posts it.

–Set the KPIs and a measurement plan...

## 8. Crisis communication and reputation management

The crisis is not a question of if but when.

In those first hours the speed and clarity with which you respond determine the outcome long after the panic has broken through.

This section offers a practical blueprint: a crisis-response framework and a dedicated team designed to get in front, act fast, act consistently, and protect both operations and reputation.

The key elements of a robust framework, laid out in four pillars, are:

- **Roles and Responsibilities** – clearly define who does what to prevent confusion and duplication.
- **RACI/RAM (Responsibility Assignment Matrix)** – map tasks to the four roles: responsible, accountable, consulted, and informed.

With this structure you can move quickly, keep the team focused, and ensure that every decision is made with the right people at the right time.

- Align your plan with Regulators and Legal Counsel so that every decision meets legal standards and guidance, protecting you from risk from the first sign of a crisis.
- Build a focused crisis response team that includes a Crisis Manager, a Communications Specialist, and Subject-Matter Experts.

- Keep the team ready to move quickly from detection to recovery; the technical details are important, but the speed and clarity of the message are what drive recovery.
- Use pre-approved messaging templates for all channels, social media, news releases, internal communications, to ensure consistency, accuracy, and safety.
- These templates should be concise yet comprehensive, allowing you to respond swiftly while maintaining full compliance with regulatory expectations.

Use pre-approved messaging templates for all channels, social media, news releases, internal communications to ensure consistency, accuracy, and safety.

Create a crisis-ready bible for journalists, vetted for accuracy.

Build a set of ready-to-send press inquiry templates and short, firm FAQ responses that address the chief concerns of stakeholders, reduce rumor, and keep the Framework in the hands of the crisis team.

Develop a special escalation path that routes issues to the right party within 60 minutes and align it with regulators and legal counsel in a standing review process.

Test your messaging for accuracy, and work with the team to ensure fluency and speed of response are good for business.

You must fit your product type, regulatory landscape, and branding goals while addressing privacy, data protection, and supply-chain contingencies. Include a stakeholder engagement plan that respects both customers and partners.

Regular rehearsals sharpen your team's reflexes and keep templates fresh.

A clear RACI chart eliminates conflicting lines of command and ensures the right people see the right information.

Pre-approved messaging templates enable rapid, consistent communication.

Align the framework with legal and regulatory partners to strengthen your crisis response.

This official structure, supported by a dedicated team, is the best formula for swift, accurate escalation and effective business continuity.

## 9. Community building and social proof strategies

Trust is not a sticker you affix after the sale; it is the air that lives in a crowded market and breathes before a choice is made.

In that marketplace the strongest brands win because they give confidence that rests on real value, transparency, and a sense of community.

By inviting everyone into a shared space and by standing firmly on these principles, they build bonds that endure.

Brands build credibility by transparently communicating their value propositions, rather than obscuring their processes.

Clearly articulating the scientific basis and development methods behind products fosters trust.

An actionable approach involves systematically presenting the practical benefits and underlying rationale of offerings to stakeholders.

### COMMUNITY STORYTELLING DRIVES ALLIES TO REALITY

Cultivating customer storytelling, where authentic experiences define your brand narrative and a human connection is maintained, significantly boosts brand equity.

To achieve this, identify and empower your most engaged customers.

Implement accessible advocacy programs designed to encourage positive reviews and organic sharing of experiences.

Crucially, ensure that the incentives and the redemption processes within these programs are transparent, valuable, and genuinely resonate with your participants.

The importance of consistency in a brand's content is irresistible; it keeps the audience engaged and builds confidence in the brand.

Regular, predictable updates create a steady rhythm that lets people know exactly what to expect and where to find what they need.

This visibility and trust are the foundation of a strong reputation.

When it comes to moderation and ethical engagement, transparency is key.

Clearly outline the guidelines and be open about how they are applied.

This not only protects against misuse but also demonstrates integrity and responsibility.

By combining steady content delivery with honest, well-defined policies, you create an admirable mirror of your brand's values, one that customers can rely on and feel proud to support.

- Invite clients to share their stories, ensuring all necessary permissions are obtained for their demonstration.
- Establish a simple advocacy system with clear rewards and rules.
- Develop a basic content calendar and, when appropriate, adhere to a common publishing rhythm.
- Publish content.
- Enforce established regulations.

## 10. Brand case studies, The Ordinary, The Drunk Elephant

In the crowded world of skincare, the quiet shift has taken hold: consumers no longer buy just because a brand promises greatness; they buy when they understand why a product works and what it contains.

This is the opening chapter of a compelling story about two brands that have mastered the seductive power of education, transparency, and clarity—The Ordinary and Drunk Elephant.

They treat education as their core asset, proving that credibility comes from evidence-based claims and ingredient transparency, not from surface hype.

By sharing knowledge and building trust, they show how science, safety, and honesty can become the true drivers of consumer confidence.

Drunk Elephant builds credibility through an evidence-based approach that explains how each ingredient works and why its concentration matters.

By openly listing "suspicious" ingredients and inviting shoppers to compare their own formulations against a trusted standard, the brand moves beyond glossy claims and gives consumers the knowledge they need to make informed choices.

This transparency, coupled with a focus on science, safety and honesty, turns ingredient sourcing into a genuine trust-builder and keeps consumer confidence firmly rooted in facts rather than hype.

This approach is mirrored by leaders in the space: The Ordinary and Drunk Elephant both provide clear, single-voice guides that walk users through their skincare routines, offering practical, useful tips that feel personal yet universally applicable.

In this way, the brand's message remains consistent across all channels, reinforcing the idea that transparency and clarity are the cornerstones of lasting credibility.

This consistency underpins a clear brand identity and long-term loyalty.

**Regulatory Mindfulness in Marketing:** Align claims with FDA/FTC guidelines and label requirements. Both brands remain vigilant about marketing claims, steering clear of exaggerated benefits and grounding statements in solid evidence. Their approach meets regulatory expectations, emphasizing honesty and fostering trust with consumers who value compliance and truthful labeling.

**Paid Ads vs Organic Growth – Balancing for Sustainable Momentum:** Advertising still has a role, but organic growth driven by education and content is the foundation. By testing budgets and measuring customer acquisition cost (CAC) against lifetime value (LTV), these brands fine-tune investment, maintaining steady momentum while protecting trust and credibility.

**Key takeaways:**

- Ground claims in transparent ingredient information and verifiable evidence.
- Build trust through education-led content that informs rather than merely sells.
- Make your brand unmistakably stick on both sides of the channel and match your brand with regulatory guidelines to foster long-term trust.
- Balance paid and organic growth by testing, learning, and measuring ROI.
- Maintain a constant brand voice across channels to reinforce credibility.
- Align marketing with the regulatory codes to sustain long-term trust.

## 11. Takeaway

In the crowded marketplace, money buys trust, so a brand earns it not with a single splash of hype but by consistently teaching, informing, and delivering value.

The art lies in balancing paid ads that reach people now with earned educational content that builds credibility over time.

Too much pushy messaging feels intrusive, while too little reach makes education feel flat.

The goal is a deliberate equilibrium where paid amplification lifts stories of learning, allowing the brand to become a credible, ingredient-centered authority that lasts long enough to earn lasting trust.

This approach moves beyond puffery toward transparent discussions of what your product is and what it should be.

It means clear explanations, accessible education, and a commitment to helping your audience make informed choices.

Real-world examples are brands that openly discuss sourcing and formulation, back those claims with evidence, and build credibility that outlasts a single campaign.

To build a strong funnel, map awareness actions to purchase, then align ads, posts, and emails to those steps.

Measure progression continually to refine the path.

Awareness: Introduce your brand and products through targeted ads and social posts.

Consideration: Share educational content—blogs, short videos, and email sequences—so that every customer can access it, not just a select few.

Make the buying experience friction-free and reward value by caring for each step of the journey.

Use channel-specific formats to nurture the feed and keep the flow efficient.

Short-form video sparks interest and drives engagement, while blog posts provide deeper, richer insight and a shareable voice.

Email sequences warm leads, keep them informed, and help them make decisions.

By tailoring each medium to its strengths, you maintain a strong link between education and results, ensuring that every touchpoint feels purposeful and memorable.

By balancing paid ads with education and a clear funnel, you move beyond simple advertising and build lasting trust.

Keep the story transparent—share the ingredients, the journey, and the values—so every touchpoint feels authentic.

Use a three-stage funnel: Awareness, Consideration, Purchase.

Tailor each stage to the channel: short-form video, blog posts, and email sequences.

Measure progress, iterate, and let the data guide you toward loyalty and long-term growth.

# Chapter X

## Scaling and Managing Growth

### Section 1.
### *The KPIs, or "key performance indicators," were laid down*

By what means, then, is the brand scaled from visionary concept into the real world?

The answer lies in a disciplined framework of essential performance indicators that measure customer value, retention, and expansion effectiveness.

This framework turns the brand's vision into operational reality, giving clarity and precision to every decision.

It provides a systematic plan for diversification, market entry, and risk mitigation ensuring that every step taken is a deliberate move toward realizing the vision while safeguarding against failure.

### *1. Key performance indicators and analytics framework*

In the quiet hours before a new scale, a well-placed KPI can turn a sea of numbers into a clear compass.

It illuminates how we are acting, keeps us on course when the road gets hard, and helps us stay focused under pressure.

KPIs are not just metrics on a dashboard; they are quantifiable measures that reflect progress toward strategic objectives and serve as the single visible guide through which the plan sails.

By grounding our actions in practical KPIs, we can grow, sell to customers, and steer the business toward its goals.

This metric directs effort across marketing and sales, guiding campaigns, prioritizing channels, and aligning resources so every team contributes to the same outcome.

By setting a clear purpose and scope, we prevent drift and keep activities on track.

The core metrics to focus on are acquisition costs (or conversion rates), lifetime value of each channel, and retention rate.

These measures ensure that each team knows exactly what they need to achieve at every moment, keeping progress focused and measurable.

These metrics show how efficiently you attract, keep, and grow customers, guiding decisions on channel mix and product investment.

A balanced KPI set distinguishes leading indicators, such as website traffic and lead generation that forecast the future, from lagging indicators, like revenue and realized customer growth that confirm past performance.

Together they provide a timely, balanced view that helps you move ahead rather than merely follow history.

By setting realistic, ambitious targets you keep the team focused and motivated, ensuring progress remains measurable and sustainable.

Data are the best possible sources and system for data governance.

Define the sources, then lay out all the rules of data quality and integrity, and make sure that reliable data are available, so teams act with confidence rather than guesswork.

Tailored dashboards help marketing, operations and executives stay attuned to the day's news and stay focused on what matters.

Visual, real-time representations of KPI performance are so rapid that even the least vigilant can catch the pulse, while the broader strategic picture is preserved.

Analytics-driven expansion and retention insights should inform the growth of product lines.

By tracking satisfaction, usage patterns and retention, you know the opportunities for improving offerings and cutting churn are well within reach.

Linking outcomes to decisions closes the loop and keeps the team motivated and focused on measurable progress.

Finally, link the KPI results to concrete decisions, product-line investments, channel bets, and strategic pivots, so that each outcome is tied to a clear action.

By aligning a focused set of four to six core measures with the leader's top objectives, you give the data a purpose and let it tell a story that drives rapid, informed moves.

This data-centric approach turns numbers into actionable insights, making it easier for leadership to learn faster, steer the organization with clarity, and keep the team motivated toward measurable progress.

## 2. Customer lifetime value and retention strategies

In the early days of bringing a private-label product to market, the loudest voices shouted about trends, channels, and launches, but behind the noise lay a quieter truth: the decision to scale.

That decision is measured by CLV, the customer lifetime value.

CLV is not a single number but a prism that reflects the total dollar value a customer brings over time, guiding acquisition, retention, sales, and revenue planning.

It is the core metric for scale decisions, the yardstick by which we judge the worth of each customer not just today, but across the years to come.

CLV and its components are essential to building a profitable private-label brand.

### CLV Components

- **Value** – the average purchase value, the amount a customer spends on a product or service.
- **Duration** – the length of the customer's relationship, i.e., how long they stay with you.
- **Margin** – the profit earned on each purchase after costs.

### CLV Formula

- Basic form: **CLV = Average Purchase Value × Purchase Frequency × Customer Lifespan**.
- More comprehensive view: **CLV = average order value × purchase frequency × customer lifespan – costs** (including CAC and ongoing support).

In practice, a precise CLV emerges when all costs are included, making retention a true growth driver over time.

Retention is a most powerful engine of profitability, because it directly reduces CAC and increases revenues from the existing customer.

Even small improvements make a very big difference in a lifetime.

Take the effort to keep your people, the "in-the-room" approach to them, the targeted communications and the value-aligned offerings.

When you are in one of your "on-the-ground" touchpoints, you get a better welcome message, a thoughtful sample, and clear value messaging that will save you early drop-off and give you first-90-day retention.

When you are in one of your on-the-ground touchpoints, you can give the customer a well-structured welcome that includes a useful sample, crisp value messaging, and just the right amount of commercial tone.

This lets them see why they matter and helps them skip early burn-outs.

By offering the first thing they want—whether a point or a dollar—and then letting the rest unfold naturally, you lay the foundation for lasting affection.

Loyalty programs and subscription discounts reward loyalty by putting a premium on its attainment, and they are worth the price.

Examples such as Amazon Prime, Sephora Beauty Insider, and Dollar Shave Club show how loyalty builds CLV. Cohort analysis tracks customers' acquisition dates and informs retention tactics, ensuring that every touchpoint is optimized for early retention and first-90-day engagement.

In private-label environments, product purity, consistent quality, and transparent ingredients are crucial for building trust and encouraging repeat purchases.

This commitment to product integrity and honest communication is essential for long-term growth and reputational power.

Customer Lifetime Value (CLV) is a key metric that integrates customer value, duration, and margin to optimize the overall cost structure by informing decisions regarding customer acquisition cost (CAC) and loyalty expenses.

Effectively managing CLV requires proactively addressing customer churn, which is critical for maintaining customer loyalty and ensuring sustainable growth.

### 3. Product line expansion and SKU planning

In the crowded shelves of private-label brands, growth rarely announces itself outright; instead, it hides in the gaps between familiar products.

The goal is not to add more items, but to identify the right ones that fill those white spaces and give shoppers confidence.

White-Space Analysis serves as a practical compass, pointing out where a brand can expand without diluting its core identity.

By focusing on the gaps that matter, a company can turn invisible opportunities into tangible products that resonate with consumers and strengthen the brand's presence.

The process starts with a close look at the market, then at competitors, and most importantly at customers who need something they can't yet get.

From that view emerges a map of opportunities where your brand can innovate rather than simply copy.

It shows where to test, how to measure impact, and which gaps in the market and adjacent categories your private label can fill.

By targeting those unmet needs, you give your brand a clear, differentiated presence that strengthens its overall footprint.

By examining adjacent gaps and white-space opportunities, we can grow our brand in ways that feel natural to our existing portfolio.

The key is to understand our target audience, analyze customer data, monitor market shifts, and scrutinize competitors.

This deep knowledge lets us identify pockets where the brand can emerge defensively, aligning with core strengths and customer needs.

By focusing on profitable SKUs that resonate with buyers, we extend the brand beyond its current footprint and secure defensible growth.

Successful brands illustrate the approach: Kirkland Signature is growing not just because it knows what to do, but because it is doing it and becoming indispensable for customers.

Amazon Basics has entered the essential-goods realm with a clear value proposition and compelling appeal to shoppers.

Trader Joe's private labels have evolved from a bare core of basic goods into a distinctive, constantly reinvented line that resonates with buyers.

Each case shows how identifying gaps, adjacent spaces, and fit with customer needs drives sustainable growth.

**Actionable takeaways**: launch a few starter MVPs at least once every three weeks in any category, gather customer feedback, and refine the offering based on real results.

## 4. Geographic market expansion playbook

When a product leaves one city and enters another, it encounters new streets, laws, and expectations.

The challenge is to translate the original idea into a disciplined strategy that fits the local market.

A good geographic-market plan identifies where to compete, gauges growth potential, and assesses competition and distribution readiness.

By understanding local norms, consumer habits, and the regulatory environment, companies like Nike or Coca-Cola can align their channels, claims, and alliances with real-market needs.

The result is a clear framework that guides expansion into target regions while keeping the product's core identity intact.

Start by mapping where demand lies, where the rules are navigable, and how rivals operate.

Translate these insights into realistic timelines and measurable milestones, such as market-share or revenue targets, so the expansion stays on track.

Keep the plan flexible, reassessing it as market signals evolve.

A clear framework that balances demand, regulation, and competition will guide the channel, claim, and alliance strategy while preserving the product's core identity.

In market expansion, if a company does not proactively define its strategic path, it will find its path defined by market forces and competitors.

## 5. Funding options and investor readiness

In the crowded shelves of growth-stage private label brands, capital is drawn to clarity, credibility and a plan that can scale.

Investors look for a mature, scalable business with a clear path to expansion, a solid financial model, capable leadership, strong branding, regulatory alignment and tangible traction.

When a brand aligns its identity, messaging and materials to meet investor expectations, the hopeful pitch becomes a credible, investable proposition.

A disciplined, well-prepared brand signals readiness, and that readiness brings the investment and growth the firm needs to sail forward.

Real-world examples such as Kirkland Signature and Trader Joe's private labels illustrate the discipline and consistency that a credible, investable proposition demands.

Foundations must be solid and well understood:

- a clear, compelling business plan; a well-defined value proposition.
- a solid financial model with forward-looking P&L and cash-flow projections.
- competent management with a proven track record.
- a strong brand identity and messaging.
- regulatory alignment and compliance.
- and traction metrics that chart a clear growth path.

Capital-readiness criteria set guardrails before pitching: a minimum runway of 6–12 months of cash, a credible path to profitability, stable and predictable cash-flow patterns, and identified and mitigated risk thresholds.

This Investor Readiness Checklist ensures the brand signals readiness, attracting the investment and growth needed to move forward.

Then, explore crowdfunding, convertible notes, revenue-based financing, venture debt, accelerators, and strategic alliances.

Define valuation methods and structure funding around milestones to ensure capital release on completion.

Align milestones to unlock capital efficiently, mapping them to funding tranches for timely capital.

By following this comprehensive checklist and demonstrating readiness, growth-stage private-label brands increase their chances of securing funding and achieving their growth objectives.

## 6. Acquisition readiness and exit planning basics

Of those months following a sale, the private label brand is revealing itself–a pure clean set of systems, a clear value proposition, an all-encompassing roadmap that literally speaks directly to your buyers.

This section sketches the framework for acquisition readiness and the exit objective, then weaves the ideas into the practical path you can walk as you do your best thing for the year.

Consider all this as being the groundwork for a pure clean narrative that will resonate with the tastes of the kind of buyers who'll see you and the sort of growth and potential you can create.

### Acquisition Readiness Overview and Exit Objective Alignment

Acquisition readiness is the process by which a company shapes itself so that it will see a clean, investable opportunity for buyers.

It means meeting the criteria that buyers care about, clarifying what the business stands for, and presenting a product roadmap and a financial picture that support a sale-ready narrative.

To start, identify the elements you should have: a compelling value proposition, scalable product plans, and predictable financial performance.

Step by step, identify unit economics, ensure accurate forecast, present a compelling narrative about growth potential.

**Takeaway:** build a concise, buyer-focused story that links product plans with financial outcomes. define exit goals, the preferred buyers, the timeline for future progress.

To secure a strong exit, first define what you want: the price your strongest potential buyers will pay and the timeline you aim to close.

Identify who you will target—strategic buyers seeking market share and distribution synergies, or financial buyers focused on cash flow and margin expansion.

The Dollar Shave Club story illustrates how rapid growth, a compelling brand voice, and steady revenue can attract a strategic buyer at a premium.

Use that example as a real-world touchstone: map your exit goals to buyer archetypes and set a realistic target close date.

Keep your plan grounded in a clear map and a firm deadline so you stay on track.

**Summary**: detail your exit objectives, align them with the right buyer types, and commit to a specific closing window.

Your product roadmap and financials should be tightly aligned to showcase growth potential and profitability.

Present a clear picture of unit economics, margins, cash flow, and recurring revenue to signal financial hygiene and make the company more attractive to buyers.

Highlight how your brand and pricing position fit the valuation of a strategic acquirer, using examples like Beats by Dre, whose strong brand equity and favorable margins created a compelling acquisition story.

Emphasize that the timing of product milestones should be measured in dollars, not years, to demonstrate a focused, results-driven approach.

This combination of a solid roadmap, robust financials, and a strategic brand narrative will give you the power and appeal you need to secure the right buyer within your target window.

Tie your milestones to what buyer's value most—scalability, channel reach, and defensible positioning.

Short, clear proof of traction reduces perceived risk and strengthens the sale case.

Show a record that demonstrates how your model drives future value and let your market position and brand equity speak for themselves.

Keep the financials clean and predictable; the key is not just getting things right but maintaining consistent, trustworthy numbers that buyers can rely on.

This focused, results-driven approach will give you the power and appeal you need to secure the right buyer within your target window.

Prepare three years of historical records, forecast scenarios, and a transparent view of customer concentration and revenue recognition.

Build a robust financial hygiene story that makes due-diligence easier and gives buyers confidence in your numbers.

Clearly define your exit goals, buyer archetypes, and a realistic timeline, and document them in writing.

Plan your products around a sound financial forecast, build traction on all fronts, and strengthen your brand with concrete metrics.

Keep your auditor-ready financials clean and predictable so buyers can rely on consistent, trustworthy numbers that secure the right sale within your target window.


### 7. SKU rationalization and cannibalization controls

Every private-label launch must start with a clear product strategy, and the best chance of securing shelf space comes from a well-defined gate of differentiation.

These gates ensure that each new SKU meets the pillars of growth, profitability, and purpose, and that it does so without cannibalizing the existing line.

A successful entry requires a distinct value proposition, whether in performance, packaging, or sustainability that aligns with consumer need and the brand's strategic fit.

Key criteria for the gate include healthy margins, projected contribution, alignment with category goals, and solid proof points that demonstrate the product's unique appeal.

By keeping these gates in place, a brand can confidently introduce new items that drive future growth while preserving the integrity of its portfolio.

A portfolio that feels purposeful, not haphazard, is built on clear Rules for Launches and Retirements.

These rules must demonstrate growth potential while avoiding cannibalization, ensuring each new product adds distinct value.

By setting a differentiation strategy that highlights what makes each item unique, brands can maintain healthy margins and align every SKU with broader category goals.

This disciplined approach gives confidence that new launches will drive future growth without compromising the integrity of the portfolio.

Avoid chasing top-line growth that erodes margins through cannibalization.

By prioritizing contribution margin, you maximize the portfolio's profitability while staying aligned with Category Strategy and Regulatory Compliance.

SKU changes must stay in line with the category strategy, meet FDA/FTC requirements, and support sustainability goals.

Keeping these constraints front and center prevents drift and pre-serves competitiveness.

**Actionable takeaways:**
-define clear gates for every SKU launch.
-establish rules for when to retire or modify SKUs.
-adopt a quarterly lifecycle review with concrete criteria.
-monitor cannibalization across channels and adjust as needed.

Prioritize margins over revenue and maintain regulatory and sustain-ability standards.

## 8. Brand equity metrics and valuation signals

Brand equity lies at the heart of how customers perceive a brand, long before they buy.

It is the value held in their minds, shaped by awareness, quality sig-nals, the assurances a firm makes, and the promises it keeps.

To capture what matters most, I lay out a framework of seven key metrics: brand awareness, perceived quality, loyalty, trust through trans-parency, intellectual-property signals, market-based valuation indica-tors, and channel-legitimacy signals.

These dimensions guide the measurement of a brand's well-being and help us understand what a brand truly stands for.

By watching these metrics together, the business can spot gaps, set priorities, and steer its investments toward the most defensible areas.

Brand awareness and recall show where the brand holds the top-of-mind spot, while deeper measures reveal how far the brand pen-etrates consumers' minds.

A study that shows high ratings in packaging, clear quality claims, and favorable remarks about value demonstrates that the brand not only reaches the audience but also convinces them of its worth.

Thus, the company learns both how to be seen and how to be remembered, and it can measure the share of people who truly recognize and trust the brand.

A strong IP portfolio protects a brand's identity, keeps counterfeiters at bay, and backs price with a sturdy, profitable middle.

To reinforce this, clear product stories, notes, and safety standards must be published, highlighting patents, packaging patents, and infringement risks as key indicators of IP performance.

Keep a vigilant eye on channel legitimacy, selecting reputable retailers and dealers that uphold strong reputations.

A well-run partnership with top firms in these channels enhances credibility and drives growth.

Intellectual assets serve as our best watchdogs: they guard brand purity, prevent counterfeits, and help buyers sustain their own identity.

By judging their scores, we can identify the most valuable channels, those with the highest shares and gains and build lasting, profitable relationships with them.

Capture all seven dimensions of brand health to build a complete, holistic view.

Rely on simple, repeatable metrics, surveys, reviews, sales data to keep every decision grounded in the same evidence base.

Link each metric to a concrete action: adjust packaging, refine messaging, or strengthen distributor relationships.

By maintaining a disciplined, evidence-based perspective on these signals, a brand can chart a clearer path from awareness to lasting equity.

### 9. Partnerships and co-branding opportunities

A trio of partners can share customers, and all of a co-branded product must get their act together before they can achieve what they want.

To begin, define clear aims and follow the standard rules of co-branding.

Objectives might be to raise brand awareness, win sales, or enter new markets.

Use the SMART criteria: Specific, Measurable, Achievable, Relevant, and Time-bound.

For example, a co-branded exercise equipment could aim to increase cross-sell revenue by 15% within 12 months, capture the new market, and align all teams on the same dashboards.

Clear objectives align both parties toward the same end and enable honest progress checks.

Guardrails and legal boundaries set the boundaries that prevent confusion over ownership while facilitating joint advertising and product sharing.

All communications, decision-making, and conflict resolution must be agreed upon at the outset.

The most critical points are the intellectual-property (IP) ownership of trademarks, copyrights, and patents, the definition of licensing terms and usage rights, and the control of the final branding on the product.

By establishing these elements early, the co-branding effort can operate as a single, efficient unit while protecting each brand's interests.

Regulatory Compliance: You must comply strictly with the safety rules for your product, advertising, and labeling.

Build in checks for claims, disclosures, and those that must meet the requirements of your joint commercial interests.

Work closely with partners that share your values and the "real" audience, products that complement each other's worlds, not merely imitating each other.

The ultimate aim is to find a match that naturally fits you; and to find a match that truly lives up to your expectations and is not forced to conform to one. Most of all, best practices for commercial partnerships.

Thorough diligence in due course: Investigate your records, systems of quality, past successes with partners, and outcomes.

Develop a comprehensive agreement that outlines IP ownership, messaging guidelines, financial terms, governance, and exit conditions.

Start by setting SMART objectives and measuring progress against each one.

Build guardrails around IP, messaging, and regulatory compliance to avoid missteps.

Choose complementary brands that share your values for authentic connections.

Document every aspect of the partnership so that no detail slips through the cracks.

This disciplined approach turns a simple logo swap into a world-beating brand signal.

## 10. Risk management and scenario planning for growth

On a bright morning, a product idea lands on the desk, a private-label bottle, a label, a promise.

The question isn't just "will people buy this?" but "what risks stand between you and growth?"

This opening sets a growth-aware foundation.

It begins with clarity: identify what can go wrong, where it can happen, and how you will respond.

The goal is not to eliminate risk, but to illuminate it, quantify it, and bring actionable answers to every decision.

The real-world brands whose virtues so brilliantly flourished in the discipline of private-label leadership like Amazon Basics or Costco's Kirkland Signature, are in no wise less disciplined risk-makers than the private-label giants.

They do the thinking before they do the thinking.

So early on, try to make the category of risks that will most influence your margin and compliance:

- Regulatory risks: the changes in FDA/FTC rules, GMPs, labeling requirements and enforcement trends
- Legal risks: the likely lawsuits and liabilities
- Operational risks: day-to-day disruptions, supplier quality and production bottlenecks
- Financial risks: funding, revenue variability, and cost pressures.
- Capacity: do you have the capacity to meet the peaks?
- Quality: are processes consistent and reliable?
- Financial health: is the supplier financially stable enough to endure shocks?
- Resilience: how well can the supply base absorb disruptions and recover?

Treating Regulatory Risk as a Dynamic Factor

Regulatory risk isn't static; it shifts with policy updates and market enforcement. Treat it as an ongoing factor:

- Track FDA/FTC developments, GMP updates, and labeling changes.
- Monitor enforcement trends and adjust testing, documentation, and packaging accordingly.

Developing Scenario Templates for Growth

Define trigger metrics for growth strategies through structured scenario analysis.

- Base-case: likely outcome based on current trends and data.
- Best-case: optimistic scenario with favorable conditions.
- Worst-case: pessimistic scenario accounting for setbacks, such as the current oil-price collapse.

These templates let you stress strategies, budgets, and timelines before committing capital.

Defining Trigger Metrics for Pivots

Establish clear thresholds for activating contingency measures.

Implement predefined capital, reserve, and other contingency measures to mitigate crisis impacts. Proactively plan for capital and liquidity contingencies, establishing robust buffers to absorb sudden market shocks. Develop actionable response protocols to ensure effective resolution during periods of instability.

Use scenario insights to shape investment timing and product development milestones.

**Actionable takeaways:**

- Start with four risk categories and map your primary suppliers on capacity, quality, financial health, and resilience.
- Treat regulatory risk as a dynamic input; establish a 45–60-day monitoring cadence.
- Create base, best, and worst-case scenarios to stress-test plans and budgets.
- Define trigger metrics for pivots, maintain liquidity reserves, and keep flexible supplier arrangements.
- Build recall and remediation playbooks with traceability, timely notification, and clear corrective actions.

Embedding these practices lets you turn ambition into disciplined execution that withstands regulation, market shifts, and supply-chain shocks.

## 11. Takeaway

Growth isn't a lucky break; it's a disciplined, data-driven practice that keeps every decision aligned with clear goals.

In this section, I lay out a practical blueprint for sustainable expansion of physical products, a playbook you can use quarter after quarter.

Treat it as a framework that tracks core KPIs, CAC, LTV, gross margin, churn rate, repeat purchase rate across cohorts, so you can see patterns, refine tactics, and measure the impact of each decision.

Keep the focus tight, apply the system daily, and adjust as you learn what works and what doesn't.

The visible trends in these numbers show where to invest next and where to tighten up.

They are the engine of long-term growth, guiding programs that reward repeat purchases and keep churn low.

A practical approach is to lower churn, expand value, and extend offers so that each new product complements the old.

Real-world examples, brands that combine simple after-care and targeted re-engagement, demonstrate that thoughtful, data-driven tactics bring immediate, sustainable returns.

To achieve successful new market entry, adopt a structured approach.

Begin by thoroughly assessing market differences, localizing strategies, and identifying strategic partners.

Implement a careful, phased rollout that integrates local insights and partner validations to ensure market readiness before broad commitment.

- Define your core Key Performance Indicators (KPIs) and establish cohort-based targets for the next 90 days.
- Initiate a pilot program for a new product line to validate market acceptance and operational viability.
- Systematically map regulatory and localization requirements for your strategic objectives to create a comprehensive compliance framework.

## Section 2.

## *Growth and product line strategy, sequencing, expansion*

The best product in the market is built on a clear, systematic approach.

We start by arranging the items, judging their purpose, and establishing precise criteria for every decision.

Careful attention is paid to regulatory complexities, mapping out constraints and limits, and ensuring that all specifications meet the required standards.

This rigorous planning allows us to register the product for international expansion while respecting the laws of each country.

By focusing on data-driven checkpoints and covering every regulatory requirement, we create a robust system that guides each stage of the product's introduction and maximizes success across markets.

Essential to this growth is a firm commitment to sustainability, with transparent supply chains and rigorous tracking of environmental and social performance.

Strategic collaborations expand market reach while protecting brand integrity.

Thoughtful financial planning, strong operational practices, and continuous post-launch learning are also vital.

Combined, these elements form a platform for product success, clear portfolio direction, and lasting market trust.

## *1. Sequencing new product introductions and roadmap planning*

In the private-label world, a well-written plan is worth more than a shelf of slides.

A clear, concise roadmap becomes the standard contract for all product visions, setting direction, priorities, and how success will be measured over time.

The heart of the plan lies in a sequencing foundation, a phased approach that aligns product introductions with brand goals, regulatory readiness, and delivery capacity.

Key criteria for this sequencing are regulatory complexity, margin, and market gaps, ensuring each stage advances the portfolio effectively and sustainably.

The heart of the plan lies in a sequencing foundation, a phased approach that aligns product introductions with brand goals, regulatory readiness, and delivery capacity.

Key criteria for this sequencing are regulatory complexity, margin, and market gaps, ensuring each stage advances the portfolio effectively and sustainably.

By scoring your products against these factors, you reduce risk and position your lineup for success.

Real-world examples show that brands like Trader Joe's and Costco's Kirkland line illustrate how a disciplined, criteria-driven roster can maintain momentum in the marketplace.

When deciding which product types to pursue first, weigh the following:

- Regulatory complexity: prioritize higher-merit items that can secure approval and complete testing early.
- Margin: higher-margin products add a valuable profit buffer.
- Market gaps: offerings that address clear needs can capture significant share.

A practical illustration is a private-label skincare line that may face regulatory hurdles; scoring it against these criteria helps determine the optimal entry point and timing.

Launch a lower-margin staple first, then channel funds to higher-margin products once the initial launch is underway.

Set the high-margin milestones at the earliest regulated launch stage and build credibility by ensuring products are restocked quickly.

Map each high-margin item to its launch window so supplier capacity matches' demand.

As the staple gains traction, establish a ladder of regulatory milestones, safety, ingredient disclosure, claim compliance, and shelf-ready packaging, each with firm deadlines.

Align supplier capacity throughout the roadmap, ensuring every product line has a clear launch plan and regulatory schedule. Get closely with your suppliers to confirm they can meet demand for the planned launches and be ready to adjust the plan if capacity shifts.

Regular capacity reviews and contingency options, like alternative manufacturers or flexible packaging, keep the timetable realistic.

Build Metric-Driven Go/No-Go Gates: before moving to the next phase, require predefined targets such as pilot feedback, preliminary sales, and regulatory clearance.

Clear criteria ensure decisions are based on evidence, not guesswork.

This data-first discipline underpins a roadmap that can evolve while the brand stays firm.

**Key takeaways:** start from a phased, criteria-driven sequence that sticks to your brand's goals, regulatory readiness, and capacity.

For clarity and assurance, let gates drive decision making only.

Link each product to regulatory milestones and capacity, then employ data-driven gates to advance.

### 2. You have Limited Editions, drops and seasons!

At dawn, a faint whisper rolls through the streets, announcing the arrival of a new drop.

In the hours that follow, the limited editions vanish into eager hands, their scarcity sparking a rush of excitement.

Brands like Supreme and Nike have mastered the art of the drop, turning a single release into a moment of instant attention and lasting loyalty.

A drop is more than a product launch; it is a carefully timed event that creates urgency, exclusiveness, and a frenzy of engagement that keeps consumers coming back for the next limited-edition offering.

Clarifying Goals, Cadence, Limits, and Compliance When planning the limited edition or drop, clear the limits for the program.

Define objectives, which include buzz, sales, or brand awareness.

Establish the cadence, which would normally be one-time event or regular release.

Set the limits, which would normally be quantity, time, or customer segment.

To do this you would need to anticipate demand, so you could predict that demand would not be on a stretch and produce only one-time event (unless that was your plan).

When all is done, you need to synchronize the marketing and your production activities and make sure that on-time production and packaging are not to be faulted.

The timing and the markings of seasonal SKUs are the only things you can do.

- Ensure regulatory compliance: understand labeling, packaging, and advertising rules.
- Avoid unsupported claims: back marketing statements with evidence and substantiation.
- Storytelling and Brand Equity through Limited Editions: craft narratives and visuals that reinforce values and build loyalty.
- Create a compelling story that resonates with the target audience.
- Visual identity: maintain a consistent aesthetic across channels and product lines.

- Pricing and Margin Management across drops protect margins by defining price bands, promos, and replenishment thresholds.
- Conduct market research: gauge willingness to pay and compare competitors.
- Set prices to balance revenue goals with demand.
- Manage inventory: set replenishment thresholds to avoid stock-outs or overstocking.
- Forecast demand accurately, allocate stock efficiently, and monitor inventory to mitigate risks.

## 3. Cannibalization safeguards and portfolio management

Cannibalization is not a failure to grow; it is a signal that you need to sharpen your strategy.

As a private-label brand expands its product line, you must guard against the risk that new SKUs simply eat into the demand of existing ones.

The key is to set up clear, data-driven guardrails that protect profitability while still allowing bold expansion.

Define a clear moat: differentiate pricing and positioning so that each new product attracts new customers rather than cannibalizing the old ones.

By doing so, you keep your brand's growth on track and preserve the profit-raising edge you seek.

At a minimum, set margin thresholds that new launches must meet before they enter the mix.

In practice, this means pricing the premium variant at a higher margin while offering a lower-margin, budget-friendly option under a separate sub-brand.

The goal is to preserve the profitability of core sellers and capture attractive white space.

Cross-SKU and cross-channel monitoring is essential, watch the entire portfolio so you can spot shifts, pricing errors, or cannibalization early and act quickly.

If a launch falls short, recalibrate its price, adjust its feature set, or reposition its value proposition to keep the brand's growth on track and maintain that profit-raising edge you seek.

Put a simple dashboard in place that flags best-performers, laggards, and any cross-category movement.

In a real-world example, a private-label consumer goods line notices a new shampoo cannibalizing its best seller.

The response is clear: price-cut and feature-shift, then monitor the effect.

Build a disciplined, data-informed eye by following these steps: first, identify the top-performing items; second, detect cannibalization patterns across items and channels; third, adjust the product mix to protect the strongest performers.

This approach lets you learn dependencies, test hypotheses, and optimize the portfolio.

Sequence launches by substitution versus complement relations to minimize overlap, prioritize white-space opportunities, and avoid saturating core products.

Regular SKU rationalization keeps the portfolio lean, prune the low-performers, consolidate variants, and keep your brand firmly in front with a clear price architecture.

The result is reduced complexity, less cannibalization risk, and stronger profitability.

Lifecycle governance: disciplined gating for launches, launch new products, relegate them as stage planners, align with regulatory and supply constraints, and plan their endings or re-segmentation if needed.

Secure every addition against profitability and growth standards and avoid drifting product portfolios.

**Key actions:** define the value and minimum margin of every new product; monitor all items quarterly so that top performers stay; and analyze data to identify cannibalization patterns and adjust the mix accordingly.

This disciplined approach keeps the portfolio tight, protects against overlap, and ensures that every launch contributes to a clear, profitable future.

In the sequence of SKU rationalization, the portfolio gains clarity, aligning each launch with the enterprise's constraints and goals.

## 4. International expansion execution plan

Sometimes a private-label brand sees a distant shelf, blending disciplined hard work with energetic execution.

This section outlines the International Expansion Readiness and Execution Plan, the blueprint for moving from local success to a measured, profitable presence in new markets.

Before entering, a business must assess regulatory, supply, and market fit, mapping the requirements of each region, understanding its own rules of origin, and ensuring product labels, whether food, beverage, or other, meet the appropriate language, certification, and approval standards of the target country.

Beyond labeling, compliance with product safety standards and intellectual property protection is essential.

Start by mapping a regulatory heat-map for each target country, listing local packaging specifications, language requirements, certification thresholds, and pricing formats.

Use this map to build a clear, region-by-region playbook that guides the creation of a regulatory dossier and ensures every product meets the specific rules of each market.

This structured approach protects your brand, streamlines entry, and supports a profitable expansion strategy.

Map trademarks, formulations, and other IP through international filings and licenses. Register trademarks with the World Intellectual Property Organization (WIPO) and secure local distribution licenses to prevent unauthorized use and smooth market entry.

Prioritize IP filings early in the plan and align with distribution partners on licensing.

Planning translations, packaging, and pricing expansion requires thoughtful translations, packaging specifications, units, and pricing alignment.

Localize packaging, language, and currency to meet regional expectations, and adapt product labels to local preferences and regulatory demands.

Draft a packaging and labeling spec sheet per region, including language and currency requirements. Vet partners and suppliers carefully to ensure compliance and quality.

In regional compliance, quality, lead times, and IP protection, we must ensure that partners can meet local regulatory standards, maintain consistent quality, and safeguard intellectual property.

The key actions are:

- Establish a due-diligence checklist for suppliers and IP protection, including clear KPIs for international expansion.
- Set up a regional fulfillment center or warehouse close to target markets, taking into account tariff implications and carrier options.
- Develop a comprehensive regulatory compliance plan that covers antitrust, packaging, labeling, and translation requirements for each region.

By following these steps, we can secure reliable partners, protect our IP, and meet the needs of local regulators while supporting efficient market entry.

- Vet partners and suppliers to ensure compliance with regional rules and maintain quality. Establish regional fulfillment centers and warehouses to streamline logistics and make operations efficient and convenient for everyone involved.

## 5. Sustainability reporting and ESG messaging

In today's market, a product's value extends far beyond its basic function.

Consumers demand purpose, responsibility, and measurable impact, and they expect the company to prove it.

Sustainability must be more than a niche stance; it has to be a core belief that drives every decision.

By openly sharing details such as supplier names, locations, audit results, where a product comes from, and how it is made and audited, a company builds credibility with its customers, suppliers, and investors.

Publishing a current list of suppliers and their sites, along with audit findings and corrective action plans, enables informed assessments of sourcing risk and performance.

Defining clear standards and measuring them with measurable ESG metrics at the product level, such as carbon footprint, water use, waste, and supplier diversity, provides a concrete basis for improvement.

Life-cycle assessment tools help quantify impacts across sourcing, production, distribution, and end-of-life, guiding data-driven changes.

By collecting environmental and social data for each SKU, identifying hotspots, and tying metrics to specific product improvement targets, this comprehensive transparency turns sustainability into a growth strategy that earns trust and fuels long-term success, making the organization's vision a reality and encouraging leaders and workers alike to talk about it.

Sustainable packaging and materials are the next frontier in this journey.

Packaging design directly affects waste, emissions, and consumer perception.

Prioritize recyclability, compostability, and reduced plastic use.

Explore biodegradable materials, refillable formats, and minimal packaging to cut waste and encourage a circular approach.
- Replace traditional plastics with certified alternatives.
- Implement refillable or modular packaging where feasible.
- Design for end-of-life with clear disposal guidance.
- ESG Reporting Cadence and Standards Consistency matters for credibility.

Adopting established frameworks such as GRI and SASB helps create comparable, actionable disclosures. Commit to an annual ESG report that tracks progress, sets goals, and demonstrates accountability against standards.
- Choose a reporting framework and publish yearly.
- Align metrics to stakeholder priorities and industry norms.
- Include progress updates and future targets.

**Marketing Claims Aligned with Verification**

As a business, you must base your eco-claims on evidence.

Avoid greenwashing by securing third-party validation and bona fide certifications (e.g., ISO). Ensure every statement is backed by standardized, verifiable metrics and a continuous audit trail.

Let the facts guide your marketing, turning sustainability into a transparent, measurable growth strategy that builds lasting trust.

## 6. Strategic partnerships and alliances

On a quiet afternoon, a small private-label food brand realized that its next leap would hinge not only on what it made, but on who helped it reach shelves, kitchens, and households at scale.

Strategic partnerships became the true engine of growth, both scalable and compliant.

Alliances unlock new capabilities, accelerate product introductions, and protect brand and consumer standards.

When seeking partners, consider the standards they uphold and how they fit your category, ensuring that every collaboration drives success and compliance.

When selecting a partner, the first requirement is that they pass rigorous GMP and compliance checks, this guarantees consistency, protects brand reputation, and ensures that every product meets the highest safety and quality standards.

A strong alliance should extend your reach through co-branding and distribution, allowing you to tap into an established network while keeping your IP secure.

Treat the partnership as an investment: conduct thorough due diligence, outline clear roles and revenue shares in a formal letter of intent, and maintain control over your product's flavor and positioning.

By aligning with a partner that shares your commitment to excellence, you create a win-win relationship that delivers premium products to the market and strengthens both parties' reputations.

Real-world examples include private-label lines that co-brand with retailers or manufacturers who already command a large distribution network—so-called "branded lines." These partnerships can launch you rapidly by sheer scale while preserving your brand's integrity and keeping it fresh in consumers' minds.

Strategic partnerships for product-line sequencing let you stage introductions, cross-sell effectively, and maintain a coherent story for buyers.

A steady supply of high-quality materials from trusted manufacturers supports predictable cycles and lets you respond to shifting consumer preferences with speed.

Best practices for such partnerships include: conduct thorough due diligence on regulatory and compliance standards; define roles, responsibilities, and expectations clearly to prevent misunderstandings; and keep robust communication channels open.

Always monitor and keep an eye on your partner's performance; take actionable steps toward improved standards.

Start, if necessary, with some of the partners scorecard; make sure it looks like the GMP, compliance history and brand-values map.

## 7. Intellectual property strategy during growth

In the crowded marketplace a private-label brand's true worth rests on what customers cannot see but cannot live without: the name, the formula, and the packaging.

As a company scales across markets, guarding these assets becomes essential to quality and growth.

A thoughtful IP strategy is the backbone of expansion, ensuring that innovations and IP assets grow in value and support the firm's objectives.

Registering core trademarks early and keeping brand identifiers in order creates a protective moat that sustains future success.

Effective IP governance is critical for protecting an organization's proprietary assets, including its brand, unique formulas, and essential components.

Strategic management of intellectual property involves safeguarding core know-how as trade secrets while understanding the landscape of invention, patent protection, and the potential for reverse engineering.

Robust IP strategies are necessary to prevent unauthorized replication, ensure a distinctive market offering, and maintain competitive advantage.

Therefore, comprehensive IP governance frameworks must be established to secure these protections.

When operations cross borders, secure protection across regions with a clear governance system that respects each country's laws and regulatory frameworks.

Ensure that the entire IP strategy remains aligned with business objectives, not just legal compliance.

Manage third-party risks, vendors, partners, and licensing, through rigorous due diligence, audits, and well-drafted contracts.

Establish robust procedures for filing, renewal, monitoring, and enforcement to prevent disputes and maintain ownership.

This disciplined approach will elevate the value of third-party IP and keep your market offering distinctive and resilient.

Regularly scan for unauthorized uses of trademarks, patents, or design assets and pursue prompt enforcement when infringements arise.

A disciplined approach to surveillance signals that the brand stands on solid ground, aligning protection with marketing and truthful, compliant claims across markets.

The IP strategy should be broad-based and cross-border, matching regulatory rules such as those of the FDA and FTC, while keeping monitoring and enforcement plans up to date with industry standards.

This disciplined, proactive stance will safeguard ownership, elevate the value of third-party IP, and keep your market offering distinctive and resilient.

Align IP actions with regulatory requirements to protect claims and brands.

## 8. Growth financing and capital deployment

Growth financing is both a cash line and a strategic compass that steers a company toward a compelling product.

A well-planned program aligns the firm's cash needs with market demands, keeping capital as buoyant as the goods themselves.

By mapping out each milestone and directing funds to the right stage, a founder can launch products quickly, expand distribution, and train teams to sustain steady, potent growth.

The result is a business that not only reaches market faster but also maintains a resilient, scalable trajectory.

The best tactics lie at the intersection of ambition and discipline, balancing speed with capability.

A founder who steers capital through bootstrapping or selective external funding can launch products quickly, expand distribution, and train teams while avoiding excessive dilution.

External capital opens access to larger pools, enabling new regions, products, and talent, but the trade-off may involve equity, debt, or governance.

The result is a business that reaches market faster and sustains a resilient, scalable trajectory.

Each route has produced advantages in different contexts; the key is choosing the path that preserves the brand's long-term integrity while unlocking strategic opportunities.

Consider successful consumer brands that began with disciplined cash flow and later complemented that with targeted equity rounds to scale production and retail.

In setting a funding strategy, the costs and benefits of loan debt, equity finance, and convertible instruments must be weighed carefully.

A practical framework avoids unnecessary debt financing yet provides a solid structure for capital that does not require surrendering ownership.

Debt can be used to enhance capital at a reasonable interest rate, but only when it aligns with the brand's long-term goals.

Evaluate repayment schedules, interest rates, covenants, and the effect on cash flow and margins.

The goal is to align debt with the business's capacity to pay, ensuring that any borrowing enhances capital at a reasonable cost without compromising long-term goals.

Equity, including convertible notes, offers strategic value and potential upside, but it must be balanced against debt so that ownership and governance remain aligned with the company's vision.

By carefully weighing these instruments, you can secure the right mix of financing that supports growth while protecting your interests.

Precise language in negotiation terms is crucial to avoid unfavorable outcomes in funding discussions.

This attention to detail is fundamental across all financial instruments, including debts, equity, and convertible notes, and directly impacts margins, governance structures, and the alignment of current decisions with future strategic plans.

Developing clear term sheets is vital for establishing robust governance and safeguarding brand trajectory. Strategic decisions must define and align with key milestones, growth objectives, and future development plans.

## 9. Operational excellence improvement initiatives

The toil of running operations is the force that grows you and makes it possible.

In quiet tension, where idea and action seem to play the same note, the force of growth is *the* force. Establish the foundations early in your operation, look at the foundation of your machinery, packaging, and fulfillment, and then you will have the discipline and direction to carry your success.

These foundations become the backbone of your manufacturing, your packaging, and your fulfillment, holding up your promises forever.

Be certain that all your basic KPIs, on-time delivery, waste, margin, and defects, are on your side.

Standard operating procedures give consistency and quality everywhere, and every stage of operation is governed by clear, coherent, and well-chosen procedures.

Your governance is the sound law, the informed consensus, the power to move through crises, corrections, and to make the impossible possible.

**Real-world cue:**

-Leading brands codify core processes in SOPs and couple them with governance reviews to keep execution aligned with strategy.

**Key actions:**

- Define 4–6 KPIs for core operations (delivery timeliness, waste, margins, defects).
- Document baseline SOPs for critical workflows (manufacturing, packaging, fulfillment).
- Establish a governance framework with roles, responsibilities, and review cadence.
- Schedule quarterly performance reviews and compliance checks.

Instituting Cross-Functional SOPs and Quality Systems Cross-functional SOPs reduce variation, accelerate onboarding, and improve cross-team communication.

By standardizing processes across departments, you minimize errors and boost efficiency.

Invest in GMP-aligned quality systems to ensure products meet regulatory and brand standards, mitigating non-compliance risk while preserving customer trust.

**Key actions:**

- Map and standardize key processes across departments.
- Implement quality systems aligned with GMP principles where possible.
- Build vendor and supplier quality controls to quantify reliability and cost.
- Create a simple scorecard for cross-functional performance.
- Plan capacity and automate repetitive tasks with software.

Capacity planning with scenario modeling lets you anticipate swings and align operations with growth.

Analyze historical data and market signals to forecast demand, then adjust capacity accordingly.

Automating repeatable tasks reduces manual errors, speeds fulfillment, and frees teams for higher-value work.

**Key actions:**

-Build scenario-based capacity plans for 2–3 growth trajectories.
-Identify repeatable tasks suitable for automation and pilot solutions.
-Track automation impact on error rates and cycle times.
-Monitoring performance and driving continuous improvement.

The daily and weekly KPI dashboards illuminate trends and enable quick, data-driven decisions.

They track on-time delivery, waste, margin, defect rates, and standardize vendor and supplier scores to optimize the supply chain.

Launch simple charts with daily or weekly measures, review metrics frequently, and conduct regular supplier performance reviews.

These actions create continual improvement loops that foster growth.

Foundations are the base of your growth infrastructure, so gather everything you need, metrics, protocols, quality, capacity, automation, and continuous improvement, and align them across functions with GMP-aware quality systems.

Use scenario-planning and automation to free your teams up for more value.

Maintain discipline with regular monitoring and feedback loops.

## 10. Post-launch optimization and learning loops

By the time you have shipped your product, the real work of launch begins.

The launch is the start of a new cycle, learn, adapt, and shape the path to durable growth.

Let the book begin with a practical framework for a post-launch optimization foundation: disciplined learning loops, clear metrics, and rituals that keep PMF aligned with long-term business goals while responding constantly to market needs.

To move from a breakthrough to sustained momentum, teams build fast, repeatable learning loops that tie directly to PMF and growth targets.

The core is to translate data into action at a human pace, rapid, repeatable, and accountable.

### Key learning loops and metrics:

Sustaining profitability and brand value across channels is directly tied to effective customer retention and operational efficiency, such as maintaining product stock.

Businesses must assess the financial implications of customer churn and the value generated by a loyal customer base.

Key metrics are essential for this evaluation, including the Net Promoter Score (NPS), which measures customer loyalty by gauging their willingness to recommend a product or service.

Proactive monitoring of such metrics and continuous learning from customer feedback are crucial for fostering long-term relationships and maximizing customer lifetime value.

Continuous learning is essential for sustaining current endeavors and ensuring long-term success.

When introducing new products or services, it is crucial to adopt a strategy of low-risk, iterative testing.

Prioritize gathering comprehensive data from these initial evaluations, as this information is vital for informed decision-making and future development.

This proactive approach provides a stable foundation for innovation and adaptability, allowing you to build effectively on past efforts.

Profitability must keep pace with expansion, monitor COGS, freight, and discounts, and manage promotions thoughtfully to preserve margin while staying competitive.

Look first to your PMF-aligned metrics, CAC, LTV, retention, NPS, and review them monthly, then run quarterly reviews with action-oriented documentation.

Roll-out growth in stages, backed by category signals and readiness checks, and pursue incremental experiments to de-risk big moves.

Keep margins alive through vigilant cost control and pricing discipline, just as Lego, Nike, and Apple do.

Such a foundation will lay the foundations of rapid response to shifts in market conditions, customer needs, or growth prospects, if they are to succeed.

## 11. Takeaway

The growth of the material-product era hinges on a disciplined product-platform architecture that expands the portfolio, aligns with market demand, and keeps pace with customer ambition.

By threading market needs with organizational capability, we create a foundation for scalable, sustainable expansion.

When product decisions are grounded in who the customer is, what he wants, and how competitors stand, execution becomes precise.

A well-planned product-platform approach delivers clarity across teams, drives operational excellence, and sustains lasting momentum.

Together, we pursue the perfect product-platform fit with our own market needs, ensuring we remain one in the pursuit of excellence.

Create a product roadmap that aligns with the business strategy, channel-aware product line mapping allocates product lines by channel mix, margin, and fulfillment capability.

By grasping each channel's strengths and weaknesses, teams can shape the product mix to maximize revenue and profit.

Scored expansion introduces new products in a logical, cohesive order, prioritizing adjacent SKUs before broader diversification and guided by data-driven demand signals.

This approach reduces the risk of product failures, boosts customer loyalty and retention, and improves supply-chain efficiency.

To prevent misalignment and ensure successful launch sequences, establish cross-functional guardrails for launch sequencing.

Coordinate the packaging so the entire factory is ready to launch, meeting the regulations that the new, green SKUs must carry.

Regulatory readiness is essential; it eliminates costly delays and protects reputation.

By treating sustainable packaging as a growth lever, rather than merely a debt-free milestone plan, you can drive healthy, scalable growth while keeping costs in check.

Real-world benchmarks from brands like Ritual and The Ordinary show that prioritizing regulatory compliance and cost-effective product design leads to sustainable expansion.

In short, insist on high standards, deliver the most efficient new products, and let packaging become a strategic advantage that fuels long-term success.

Get your best practices, develop a tailored approach, and monitor progress to adjust strategies as needed.

Build growth on market insight, clear capability, and a well-orchestrated product roadmap.

Map your products by channel, margin, and fulfillment capacity, and use data signals to guide the sequence of new SKUs.

Establish cross-functional checks so launches remain coherent and regulatory readiness is prioritized.

Learn from real-world brands to fine-tune your path and keep the momentum going.

# Chapter XI

## Mindset, Resilience, and Leadership

### Section 1.

### *Common Legal & Financial Pitfalls: risk, contracts, IP, tax, cash flow considerations*

Private labels offer a highly profitable business model, but their success hinges on careful planning and a deep understanding of the legal, regulatory, and operational challenges they face.

This chapter outlines a practical framework that covers critical legal matters, from contract provisions and liability limits to intellectual property rights, and emphasizes the rigorous compliance required to meet quality standards.

It also addresses the financial discipline needed to manage cash flow, taxes, and risk-bearing insurance.

By mastering these elements, your brand can withstand market pressures and stand the test of time.

1. The common law and the financial and regulatory risk

In the crowded aisle of branded wares, private-label brands quietly shape consumer choice.

They are not merely products; they are commitments to value, consistency, and reliability.

This opening section maps the risks that private-label ventures face and offers guardrails for retailers and manufacturers to steer toward a durable, compliant enterprise.

Legal, regulatory, and financial dangers are intertwined: intellectual-property disputes, product liability, and compliance missteps can all bite if not managed.

Manufacturers who produce private-label lines may see their control of brand equity eroded as retailer strategies shift, threatening the very foundation of their business.

A well-drafted contract is essential for a successful private-label program.

It must clearly state who bears the costs, who owns the rights, and how disputes will be resolved.

The agreement should include robust provisions for intellectual-property protection, covering the products sold and the trademarks that define the brand.

To ensure this protection, manufacturers should conduct thorough pre-launch and periodic trademark searches to identify potential conflicts.

It is crucial to register core marks and key packaging elements.

Furthermore, establish a clear infringement response plan, with defined escalation paths to regulatory agencies for effective enforcement against any third-party infringements in online marketplaces or elsewhere.

Strong, transparent contracts—much like those that underpin Costco's Kirkland Signature or Walmart's Great Value—help safeguard brand equity while allowing retailers the flexibility to supply high-quality goods.

By diligently managing these steps, monitoring for infringement, and licensing thoughtfully, manufacturers can protect their intellectual property without alienating partners, thereby limiting liability and ensuring the long-term success of the private-label line.

Avoid making forbidden or misleading claims and ensure every label truthfully reflects the facts and current, verifiable data.

A healthy private-label operation requires disciplined cash-flow and tax planning: plan tax obligations, deductions, and credits while accounting for seasonal shifts in supply and demand and supplier payment terms.

Track cash flow carefully, adjust inventory against accounts receivable and payable, and maintain reserves at the right times.

Capitalize on the best bargains but always tax your receipts and deductions correctly.

This shrewd approach protects long-term survival and keeps the business compliant with regulatory agencies.

The payoff of real-world context is clear.

Clear contracts, vigilant enforcement of rules, disciplined compliance, solid cash flow are all not luxuries but foundations of durable private label programs.

## 2. Contract management pitfalls and supplier agreements

When you launch your own private label, the contract you sign with suppliers is more than a formal document, it's the foundation of your brand.

It defines how you'll operate, protects your reputation, keeps cash flowing, and ensures your products stay online.

A well-crafted agreement should translate your product vision into a clear, fail-proof plan.

It must cover every aspect of production, payment, and quality control, and it should leave no room for surprise.

Never allow suppliers to act on your behalf without explicit consent, give them the power you need, but keep the control firmly in your hands.

A good contract embodies your vision for what to make and how to make it, fitting neatly into an organized system that delivers predictable, cost-effective results.

To prevent scope creep and ensure every detail is crystal-clear, start by defining the product specifications: outline the required materials, dimensions, and performance standards.

Follow this with a comprehensive Bill of Materials that lists every component, its specifications, and any applicable certifications or compliance requirements.

Next, specify the packaging and labeling requirements, including regulatory compliance and certification needs.

Establish quality-acceptance criteria that set precise tolerances, testing requirements, and formal change-control processes.

Finally, detail the price, payment terms, and lead times so all parties know exactly what to expect and when.

This structured approach keeps the contract focused, the expectations aligned, and the project on schedule and within budget.

Ownership of Proprietary Ingredients: Clearly establish who owns proprietary ingredients and formulations.

Licensed Rights: Grant rights with defined use and any restrictions.

Improvements and Royalty Terms: Specify improvements, royalties, and payment structures.

Post-Termination IP Handling: Set guidelines for IP after termination, including restrictions and requirements.

Together, these elements form a contract that protects the brand, ensures regulatory alignment, and maintains smooth cash flow.

A robust agreement is not a burden but a foundation for scalable, compliant growth.

**Actionable takeaways:**

– Create a contract checklist covering scope, deliverables, specs, BOM, packaging, labeling, testing, and change control.

– Lock in pricing, payment terms, and lead times early; document remedies for delays. Define IP ownership, licensed use, improvements, royalties, and post-termination IP handling upfront.

– Ensure regulatory alignment and quality milestones are applied to reduce risk and to keep the name intact.

A real-world example of that: the Amazon Basics have shown you how precise their supplier contracts are, while maintaining the quality and the law.

## 3. Insufficient IP protection and gaps in trademark strategy

In the crowded shelves of today's retail, a private-label brand stands out as a subtle yet resilient shield.

It is like a muted coat on a white shelf, offering the secret to growth while guarding against counterfeiters and misaligned claims.

Early clarity about what can be protected is essential.

Private-label brands should map and protect:

- Names: brand names, product names, and slogans
- Marks: logos, trademarks, and service marks
- Packaging: trade dress, product design, and packaging materials
- Formulations: product formulas, recipes, and manufacturing processes

Real-world touchpoint: consider how successful private-labels like Trader Joe's or Kirkland Signature use distinct naming, packaging cues, and label design to reinforce their protection.

Differentiating trade dress and product formulas earns protection through different mechanisms.

Registering trademarks and trade dress secures exclusive rights to use the mark and the visual identity on products and packaging.

Confidentiality measures, non-disclosure agreements, internal process controls, and trade-secret protections, safeguard formulas and manufacturing know-how.

**A practical note:** keep a clear boundary between what is registered and what remains confidential to prevent inadvertent disclosure.

File for trademark protection in multiple jurisdictions where you intend to sell, especially those with strong e-commerce exposure.

Early registrations help secure your key assets as you move online and offline, reducing friction when you expand into new territories.

Proactive filings blunt counterfeit risk and smooth multi-market launches, ensuring your brand's identity is legally recognized before you cross into a new market.

Your strategy should fit your growth goals, integrate branding into a single, protected whole, and rely on IP law to guard against legal pitfalls and market-wide competition.

A proactive IP strategy keeps your brand protected as you expand into new markets.

Build a single, defensible portfolio of names, marks, packaging, and formulations, and maintain a clear risk register and renewal calendar.

Regular reviews guard against expiration and counterfeiting, ensuring your trademarks stay active and your brand's integrity remains intact.

By mapping and fortifying each asset early, you reduce disputes, close gaps, and support sustainable, multi-market growth.

Substantiate the claims and align them with your IP strategy of compliance, while keeping a timely renewal calendar and an ongoing infringement monitoring.

## 4. Financial management for bootstrapped startups, etc

In the early days of a bootstrapped venture, success rarely comes from a single breakthrough.

It grows from disciplined cash management, a clear view of receipts and disbursements, and a firm grip on burn rate.

Bootstrapped Finance: Disciplined Cash Planning for Sustainable Growth shows that the lifeblood of a self-funded startup is a steady cash-flow rhythm, weekly receipts, monthly outlays, and realistic forecasts that keep the lights on and the product moving forward.

By treating cash as a daily, real-world resource, founders can navigate the uncertainties of early growth without outside investors.

A cash-flow forecast must be a living tool, updated daily to reveal any impending shortfall or surplus.

Keep the numbers defensible by tying projections to solid revenue channels, ecommerce, wholesale, direct-to-consumer, or brick-and-mortar, and adjusting as real orders arrive.

Regular reconciliation with cloud-based bookkeeping keeps the muddle at bay and saves you surprises.

Focus the budget on margins and ROI: classify expenses by expected return and challenge every line that does not deliver.

This disciplined, margin-focused approach keeps the lights on and the product moving forward without external investors.

Make high-ROI actions the priority, especially packaging and marketing that convert at a predictable rate. Cut or defer low-ROI items to preserve capital for bets that move the business forward. Keep the spend lean and the returns clear.

Base everything on simple, verifiable bookkeeping.

Use cloud-based software to reconcile weekly, not monthly, so you can spot drifts early and avoid end-of-month surprises. A transparent record-keeping system is the foundation of financial clarity and the key to staying agile.

Clear, verifiable records build confidence with lenders, suppliers and regulatory bodies, and they create a transparent view of where the business stands.

Plan for Taxes and Regulatory Costs: Avoiding Unforeseen Expenses Taxes and regulatory costs can bite if you ignore them.

Set aside estimated quarterly taxes and track compliance expenses to stay ahead of obligations.

Proactively accounting for these costs prevents penalties and preserves working capital for growth activities such as product development or channel expansion.

Building Cash Reserves and Contingency Funds: Mitigating Risk and Ensuring Sustainability Aim for 3–6 months of operating expenses in reserve.

Contingency funds provide a cushion when demand dips or costs spike.

Build these reserves gradually, each month earmark a portion of revenue to a dedicated fund and revisit targets as the business grows and risks shift.

**Takeaways:** monitor cash flow monthly and forecast gaps using channel mix and seasonality; maintain a margins-focused budget, prioritize high-ROI items and trim low-ROI costs; keep bookkeeping simple, verifiable, and reconciled weekly; plan for taxes and regulatory costs to avoid penalties and last-minute cash shortages. Build 3–6 months of operating expenses in reserve to weather uncertainty and sustain growth.

## 5. Tax and accounting basics for product businesses

In every product-focused business the numbers tell a clear story: what sells, what costs, and what keeps the doors open when demand shifts.

A solid tax and accounting foundation is the backbone of growth and clarity, and choosing the right legal form is the first step toward that foundation.

The common options, sole proprietorship, partnership, LLC, and corporation, each have distinct profiles.

A sole proprietorship is simple and inexpensive for a single owner but offers no personal liability protection.

A partnership shares ownership, accountability, and tax transparency among all partners.

An LLC provides liability protection while allowing flexible tax treatment, and a corporation offers the strongest liability shield and potential for capital growth.

Selecting the firmest, most principled structure and pairing it with an appropriate tax strategy will give you the freedom to build, grow, and thrive with confidence.

Liability protection with flexible tax treatment is the hallmark of an LLC, while a corporation offers the strongest shield and easier access to outside capital.

The choice depends on your goals, risk tolerance, and growth pace.

Many early product-makers start as sole proprietorships or LLCs and evolve into corporations as they scale.

Set up a structure that clearly separates cost of goods sold from operating expenses and transparently tracks profit and loss.

This foundation gives you the freedom to build, grow, and thrive with confidence.

Inventory Valuation: FIFO, LIFO, or weighted average to do your reckoning with the same precision and certainty.

Sales Tax Obligations: keep your stores open as well as your customers, each store's rules and schedules are yours.

Cash Flow: always feel on top of the cash flow from sales and payments and keep that cash flow current.

Weekly Estimated Taxes and Deadlines: avoid paying your penalties as well as keep the transaction clean.

Weekly Accounts and Calendar Plans: always anticipate all coming tax duties and keep a running record of what you pay.

Plan for your Taxes: get to your quarterly tally with your yearly financial progress, and don't miss any of the money you've paid.

The quarterly deadlines fall on April 15, June 15, September 15, and January 15 of the following year.

Real-world examples from brands like Nike and Allbirds illustrate disciplined inventory and cost control, showing how a strong structure and integrated system let you move quickly without sacrificing compliance.

Use these stories as reminders that your accounting framework should align with your ambitions and support accurate forecasting of receipts.

Establish a channel-specific sales-tax plan and keep your cash-flow forecast tight, so you can stay on top of every payment and avoid surprises.

Mark your quarterly tax deadlines on the calendar and set realistic estimates for each period.

Keep your cash-flow forecast tight and use dashboards to track the results, so you can stay on top of every payment and avoid surprises.

Establish a channel-specific sales-tax plan and maintain a clear inventory-valuation system in your books.

By aligning your accounting framework with your ambitions, you'll support accurate forecasting and maintain order in your business operations.

## 6. Cash-flow mismanagement pitfalls and liquidity planning

Cash flow is the quiet engine that sustains every flourishing private-label brand.

When money moves smoothly, product ideas blossom, shelves stay stocked, and growth proceeds with confidence.

When cash flow falters, even the best brands can stall, and a few months of mismanagement can erase months of progress.

Cash-flow forecasting is the compass that guides you through the days when funds are tight, showing where gaps may appear and how to keep expenditures in check.

It helps you anticipate shortages before they become crises, ensuring that your brand continues to thrive without interruption.

Accurate forecasting supports stability, strengthens decision-making, and underpins long-term growth and strategic planning.

### Proactive Cash Flow Planning

To stay ahead of shortages and surpluses, project cash flow over a 12-week window, accounting for seasonality and delays.

- **Analyzing Historical Data:** Review past sales, expenses, and cash-flow patterns to identify recurring trends and anomalies.
- **Identifying Cash Flow Drivers:** Map the factors that move cash—payment terms, inventory turns, lead times, and upcharges for rush orders.
- **Creating a Cash Flow Calendar:** Build a rolling 12-week plan that marks projected inflows and outflows, with buffers for known seasonality.

### Strategies for Managing Cash Flow

Several tactics help maintain liquidity without sacrificing growth.

Negotiate Favorable Supplier Terms: Seek longer payment terms or early-payment discounts to improve working capital without hurting supplier relationships.

Extend Payment Terms: When possible, stretch terms with customers, but balance this with expectations for service, reliability, and timely collections.

Inventory Planning: Align stock levels with demand forecasts and supplier lead times to avoid tying up capital in excess stock.

Building Contingency Reserves: Having a reserve protects the business from shocks and keeps operations running.

Set Aside 3–6 Months of Expenses: Keep funds in a readily accessible savings account to cover unexpected costs, price shifts, or supply interruptions.

Support Business Continuity: In revenue shortfalls, reserves sustain critical activities and keep teams focused.

Revenue Recognition Timing Plan: Recognize revenue when control transfers to the customer, and for subscription-based or service components, spread recognition across the service period to reflect the true flow of cash.

Real-World Examples and Takeaways: The private-label programs of Kirkland Signature and Amazon Basics demonstrate disciplined cash-flow practices, clear supplier terms, careful inventory management, and deliberate revenue timing.

**Actionable Takeaways**: Build a 12-week cash-flow calendar now, including seasonality and delays; identify your top three cash-flow drivers and map their impact on inflows and outflows.

Maintain cash reserves sufficient to cover several months of operating expenses. Establish clear and consistent revenue recognition policies that accurately reflect the delivery of goods or services.

Adhering to these principles will enhance financial liquidity, reduce operational risks, and foster sustainable business growth.

## 7. Compliance budgets and cost control

In the early days of private-label brands, the scale of risk seems almost invisible, and the cost to your reputation is hard to see.

Yet the true cost, regulation, quality, and legal, depends on having a well-developed compliance budget.

A good budget creates an orderly framework that protects your name and makes it difficult for problems to spiral out of control.

Start with the basics and build from there; without a budget you can never truly begin or finish. Always begin with the smallest, most essential measures and let them grow into a robust protection plan.

FDA/FTC compliance: covering these rules and regulations and doing them.

The GMP audits: regular assessments to verify manufacturing practices and sure quality.

Legal fees: to hear the counsel who can get you through any regulatory mirages and keep you on solid footing.

"Forecasting" Costs Your forecast is two-fold: your recurring costs and your one-time setup costs.

Recurring: labeling and packaging audits, vendor audits, third-party inspections and certifications.

One-time setup: preliminary GMP audits, FDA/FTC compliance consultations, and legal guidance for regulatory pathways.

An estimated realistic forecast helps you avoid abrupt funding gaps and keeps your stake intact.

Make sure your budgetary structure is on the line:

- Labeling and packaging, plus suppliers' audits, second-party inspections, and certifications.
- Transparent claims and compliance control keep daily operations smooth and risk-aware.
- Milestone-based funding is essential: audits, tests, and regulatory approvals are your allies, and real-time checks on spend against budget give you clear visibility into what remains to be spent.

- Dashboards that show daily spend versus budget, flag overruns and variances, and reveal daily differences are your best ally.
- Regular reporting—monthly or quarterly—keeps everyone in the loop and helps you stay ahead of mistakes that slip under the radar.
- A total cost-control system that balances claims, compliance, and real-time data is the tool you need to keep the budget on track and the project moving forward.
- A budget that matches risk protects your brand from costly missteps. Prioritize FDA, FTC, and GMP compliance, audits, and legal counsel while avoiding unmerited recurring bills.

Use milestone-based funding to see exactly how much to spend at each stage.

Build a dashboard and routine reports to keep financial and regulatory clarity intact.

Real-world brands win when budgeting is a vital capability, not just an afterthought.

## 8. Insurance considerations and risk transfer

Insurance for a startup's first product is the foundation of its protection.

The general liability coverage you secure will guard against claims of bodily injury, property damage, and other third-party liabilities that arise in the day-to-day operation of your business.

Think of it as a guardrail that keeps the founders' nerves steady and the company's reputation intact.

When you launch a private label, you'll often find yourself in the middle of the business, facing risks from bodily injury, damage to goods on the premises, theft, fire, and other ordinary calamities.

Having solid insurance coverage ensures you can defend yourself and your product without hesitation or doubt.

Beyond coverage for judgments, it serves as a vital fund-raising resource for legal defense and settlement costs at every juncture, keeping cash flowing when disputes arise.

For a private-label brand, this protection is invaluable when addressing problems caused by a non-commercial producer's mistake, a labeling error, or a failure to keep goods in good condition.

In sectors such as cosmetics and supplements, the stakes are even higher; the regulatory environment is tougher and the potential for costly lawsuits is greater.

Having solid insurance coverage ensures you can defend yourself and your product without hesitation or doubt, and it keeps you from being caught off-guard by an unforeseen lawsuit or settlement expense.

All-Risk coverage is designed to simplify the defense and the cause of a claim.

It protects you against a wide range of liabilities, from errors in design and professional negligence to omissions in service or product delivery.

When a customer experiences a reaction or a labeling inaccuracy, the coverage handles the investigation, legal defense, and any resulting expenses.

Supply-chain protection is also essential, as it safeguards the vital lifeline that delivers your product to the market.

Business-interruption coverage helps cover lost profits when a claim disrupts operations. Together, these policies give you comprehensive protection against the many ways a product can fail to meet expectations and the financial fallout that can follow.

Disruptions of the factory line, shipments, or delays in another line of business (the "factory) often eat up the capital of profits and expenses in recovery.

I always stress to you how, when an alliance or partnership with one of your rivals is dissolved, and your firm is suddenly out of business, how the contract-risk transfer that is the basis of our insurance scheme should serve to bring the indemnity provisions of a contract to their best condition, insuring that the policy will stand strong, even when the link in the chain falters.

In this way, if the contracts of both parties are treated so as to be adapted to the stipulations of the terms at issue, the policy will hold together and stand firm.

In a connected commerce environment, the dangers of cyber threats and data breaches are real.

Protecting customer data, payment systems, and e-commerce platforms is essential, and a layered program, starting with general liability, then product liability, and finally broader cyber coverage, provides a robust shield.

For cosmetics and supplements, focus on accurate labeling, defect coverage, and recall readiness to safeguard both the product and the brand.

Likewise, cover all supply-chain risks and IP protection to maintain revenue and reputation.

This comprehensive approach ensures that, even when a partnership dissolves or a supply link falters, the indemnity provisions of your contracts remain strong, and the policy holds firm.

## 9. Fraud risks, and the vendor-verification gaps

Fraud risk in physical goods is not a product defect that appears at the point of sale; it starts the moment trust is opened with a vendor.

The first line of defense is a rigorous verification of the supplier's authenticity.

Look for certificates, licenses, and Good Manufacturing Practice (GMP) compliance, and confirm claims with third-party test results from accredited laboratories.

By insisting on these credentials and a transparent supply chain, you establish credibility that protects the brand and the buyer alike.

This disciplined approach is the only reliable standard for ensuring that every item that leaves the vendor's door is truly what it claims to be.

- Certificates of compliance
- Test results
- Communications with vendors

Use of contract protections: contracts safeguard what matters most, intellectual property and accurate representations.

Core protections include:

- Warranties
- Termination rights
- Hold-harmless clauses

Establishing ongoing vendor verification: vendors must continue to meet standards over time.

Key mechanisms:

- Scheduled audits
- Refreshed certifications
- Periodic lab retests

Guarding against payment fraud: financial risk demands a multilayered approach.

Strategies include multiple payment methods, thorough vendor verification, and real-time fraud alerts to detect and stop unauthorized transactions before losses mount.

**Takeaways:** build the baseline, then scale, begin with verified legitimacy and a strong qualification checklist.

Require objective proof: licenses, GMP, and independent lab results should be non-negotiable.

Keep a living record of certifications, test results, and communications, your audit trail must be up-to-date and accessible.

Use contracts and controls to protect your IP: include warranties, termination rights, and hold-harmless clauses that safeguard both parties.

Regularly audit, re-certify, and retest to stay ahead of fraud and maintain supply-chain integrity.

Keep the financial side in check by monitoring payment lines and real-time alerts, so you can act swiftly if anything goes wrong.

This disciplined approach builds trust, ensures compliance, and keeps your business resilient.

## 10. Recall and crisis cost planning

When a fault appears in a product, a clock starts ticking.

Recall is more than a press-release or a refund window; it is a holistic crisis that touches supply chains, brand trust, and the bottom line.

This frame lays out the practical map of the sure-fire route out of risk into a controlled reaction and cost clarity.

Knowing recall costs demands our resources, especially in supply-chain logistics and transportation.

We must fix or repair the defect, identify the root cause, and implement corrective actions at every stage of the process while navigating legal and regulatory requirements.

The focus is on turning a crisis into an opportunity to strengthen resilience and protect brand esteem.

- List the costs that must be paid before a crisis arrives; assign owners and timelines.

- Find a simple, itemized cost model that can be updated in real time at a recall.
- Pre-commit to recall plans in contracts: embed recall protocols and cost-sharing terms with suppliers and distributors to reduce delays and disputes.
- This creates a clear framework for who covers which costs, how recalls are triggered, and how information flows between parties.

**Actionable takeaways:** make recall triggers, notification timelines, and shared financial responsibilities part of key agreements; run table-top drills with suppliers to validate response speed and cost allocation.

IP and regulatory claims risk assessment: recall scenarios expose the company to product liability, potential IP infringements, and regulatory non-compliance risks.

It helps us plan ahead, since foresight is a sure sign of good business, and foresight of what might happen in a crisis shows us how we should respond.

A quarterly risk review, with a careful focus on IP and regulatory exposures, should make us more aware of potential liabilities during a crisis.

Remember, whenever a crisis arises, we should have a standard communications playbook ready for rapid action.

Financial reserve planning is critical to cover the cost of logistics, refunds, remediation, and business continuity.

This proactive approach ensures we can respond swiftly and manage the financial impact of any recall or regulatory event.

Take advantage of early deductions and credits, aligning tax timing with cash flow to avoid after-tax repercussions.

Work closely with your tax advisers to identify eligible deductions and credits and incorporate them into your program promptly.

Review expense schedules and chart expected tax outcomes, ensuring communications remain fluid and clear, don't be coy or evasive, or you'll lose track of the correct information.

By staying proactive and transparent, you'll feel secure knowing you've managed the financial impact effectively.

## 11. Takeaway

A successful private-label brand is built on a foundation of integrity, uncompromising quality, and proactive protection.

This involves diligently safeguarding intellectual property from its inception and establishing robust processes for legal, regulatory, and contractual compliance.

Sustained growth and resilience are achieved through continuous validation, transparent data, and intelligent financial management, ensuring the brand's enduring reputation and market position.

This integrated approach creates a lasting mark of excellence, prepared for any scrutiny or change.

## Section 2.
## Mind-set, resilience and leadership

To become a truly private label brand that doesn't just survive the markets, but thrive through the complexities of market regulators, a special blend of discipline and adaptability is required; consistent progress is desirable and actively pursued.

It is more than mere ambition; it is the anchor that maintains the brand where it stays, through market shifts, regulatory change and unexpected stumbling blocks—an anchor that not only establishes a steady rhythm for its growth, but one with which it is its greatest bond.

Conscious and explicit practice and continual personal communication reinforce the strength of both individuals and teams in their ability to handle strategic crises and sustain and renew even crisis-ridden product launches.

## 1. Staying consistent amid setbacks and uncertainty

In competitive markets, the sustainability of a private label hinges on consistent quality and reliable performance, rather than short-term appeal.

This disciplined consistency provides a stable anchor.

While external factors like supply chain volatility or regulatory adjustments can alter business costs, a product's established reliability ensures steady growth despite such challenges.

This foundational resilience stems from a brand's unwavering identity, a product's lasting value, and a strategy capable of converting market changes into ongoing progress.

In practice, brands like Kirkland Signature and Amazon Basics demonstrate how standardized processes and rigorous quality checks sustain performance across a wide range of products.

To achieve this, define and track each micro-goal, breaking large targets into manageable steps that keep the team moving forward.

Avoid vague "launch soon" statements; instead, focus on completing the first ten product tests within a week to establish a rhythm that carries through the entire development cycle.

Regulatory compliance is not a one-off checklist but a continuous pulse.

By setting a routine around regulatory milestones, regular reviews, updates, and documentation, the brand ensures that compliance becomes part of the everyday workflow, not a separate event.

This persistent rhythm builds confidence, turning each small success into a building block for long-term resilience.

Create routines around FDA/FTC checks, GMP milestones, and other applicable regulatory requirements.

Make regular appointments with regulatory experts, set reminders for important deadlines, and designate time to follow up on every infraction, don't let anything slip.

This persistent rhythm keeps things in order and spurs you toward the small victories that build long-term resilience.

The Power of Reflective Practice grows when you set aside time each week to journal, seek mentor feedback, and learn from colleagues.

By reflecting on what went well and what needs improvement, you turn each small success into a building block for a more meaningful, compliant workflow.

You are building and nurturing networks of peers who, like a quiet compass, guide you through the private-label landscape.

These connections become the nourishment that keeps you moving when the path grows dark.

Transparent communication, sharing plans, risks, and progress, acts as the light in the fog, turning uncertainty into a clear route.

By openly discussing what works and what needs improvement, you turn each small success into a building block for a more resilient, compliant workflow.

The more you collaborate, the more you avoid pitfalls and stay focused on the journey ahead.

## 2. Managing burnout and workload balance

In the competitive landscape of physical product development, resilience is a fundamental discipline influencing every decision, from specifications of size, weight, and price to supplier management and crisis response.

It serves as a foundational element that provides strategic direction, enabling sustained growth and maintaining operational continuity even under significant pressure.

Beyond merely surviving regulatory cycles, a resilient operation enhances organizational effectiveness by maintaining team focus and keeping product development on schedule.

Effective leadership, characterized by a comprehensive understanding of specifications and potential vulnerabilities, directs engineering efforts and sustains team performance under pressure, transforming operational challenges into actionable insights and maintaining process momentum.

In real life, private-label ecosystems such as Trader Joe's and Kirkland demonstrate how implementing routine, repeatable decision-making and strict standards builds resilience, enabling scale while keeping brand promises intact.

They teach us that resilience should be tangible in daily practice, not just a concept.

A solid Personal Resilience Plan, built around sleep, nutrition, and recovery, keeps the team focused and the product on track.

- **Sleep**: Target 7-9 hours a night to recharge body and mind, especially under stress and burnout.
- **Nutrition**: Eat a balanced diet rich in whole foods, fresh fruits, vegetables, and plenty of water to sustain energy and well-being.
- **Recovery**: Incorporate regular rest and mental recuperation to turn strain into information and maintain momentum throughout the process.

Recovery routines: Build time for relaxation and stress reduction through exercise, deep breathing, or gentle stretching. These practices facilitate mental disengagement from work, promote a balanced perspective, and encourage the release of stress and unproductive thoughts.

Set boundaries for your work: Keep outside tasks from creeping in and prioritize the most important duties. Delegate to experts and drop the unessential.

Communicate effectively with the team, investors, customers, and shareholders, focus on the work that matters most.

Ensure compliance by making sure outsiders understand and follow all applicable rules, FDA, FTC, labeling claims, and the like.

Create a clear regulatory schedule or map it out and block the calendar-time window for focused work hours.

Start a no-surprise policy with everyone and run regular check-ins and monthly reviews.

Communicate progress openly, giving everyone a visible clock that shows where you are.

Reveal your survival plan, a sleep schedule, nutrition scheme, and a prescribed routine, to avoid confusion and misunderstandings.

Finally, build a vendor scorecard, keep a regulatory milestone-and-deadline cycle, and run your meetings on a weekly cadence to keep everything on track.

### 3. Building a resilient leadership mindset

On a late afternoon in a bustling laboratory, a private-label team faces a final regulatory review that could extend for weeks.

The pressure is substantial, but subsequent actions will be guided by resilient leadership rather than apprehension.

Resiliency is not a transient emotional state, but a deliberate and sustained strategic approach.

Product success is contingent upon long-term endurance and viability.

A growth mindset drives progress, enabling a resilient leader to manage setbacks constructively, maintain operational momentum, and guide the team toward practical achievements.

When regulators weigh in, a growth-minded leader sees a chance to refine the product and tighten compliance, not a blow to status.

Apple's disciplined, iterative approach to launching devices and features shows how feedback loops can produce clearer requirements and faster learning.

Treat every criticism as data, not a verdict.

Actively solicit feedback from regulators, customers and suppliers, document lessons learned, and track changes in the next cycle.

Celebrate small refinements that improve compliance and performance and keep the team's momentum moving forward through uncertainty.

Develop a clear set of criteria for risk assessment, map out the key stakeholders, and draft robust contingency plans for potential setbacks.

Build emotional resilience as you navigate audits and approvals, ensuring that the process remains realistic and grounded in the realities of your organization.

Celebrate small wins that enhance compliance and performance and keep the team's momentum moving forward through uncertainty.

Build emotional resilience as you navigate audits and approvals, ensuring that the process remains realistic and grounded in the realities of your organization.

Celebrate small wins that enhance compliance and performance and keep the team's momentum moving forward through uncertainty.

Create an environment where individuals can freely express themselves and share ideas, raising concerns when they feel heard.

This blend of clarity, safety, and accountability significantly improves the operational environment, fostering credibility even when facing difficulties.

Routines for Recovery, Reflection, and Continuous Learning maintain vigilance during complex regulated product launches, cultivating a robust and adaptable team capable of performing effectively in dynamic and evolving environments.

## 4. To create a team culture around trust and quality

In a world where a single defect can ripple through the supply chain, the simplest commitment a company can make is to keep its first steps clean and to set practical standards for every link in the chain.

Leadership must act with honesty, consistency, and accountability, showing workers what good looks like in practice.

By rewarding openness with trust, sweat, and tears, and by being transparent to staff, suppliers, and customers, a culture of safety for reporting problems can be built.

This requires clear contracts, regular audits, training, and the psychological safety that only the right practices can bring.

People are best when they can speak up without fear of punishment.

Provide safe channels for defects, near-misses, and improvement ideas, plus protections for those who raise concerns.

Regular, non-punitive problem-solving is what people do.

Establish Cross-Functional Quality Circles with Clear KPIs Set up cross-functional teams focused on product areas, with KPI dashboards that cover specifications, packaging accuracy and compliance metrics.

Get regular reviews of gaps and guide concrete, shared actions.

Implement Transparent Vendor Audits and Third-Party Testing Documented supplier evaluations and third-party testing ensure accountability across the network.

Verify GMP compliance, labeling accuracy, and traceability to reduce risk.

Invest in GMP and Labeling Training for Teams Continues GMP, and labeling training reduces mislabeling and regulatory drift.

Keep on regular refreshers and hands-on practice so that front-line teams stay confident in the standards.

**Actionable takeaways**: publish core values and expectations across the organization and supply base; establish safe reporting channels with protections for reporters; launch cross-functional quality circles with

KPI dashboards; audit suppliers transparently and require third-party testing; and plan regular GMP and labeling training for all teams.

## 5. Decision frameworks for product companies

Successful product launches hinge on the choices you make long before the first unit hits the shelf.

In launching a private-label brand, every decision must be informed, data-driven, and tightly tied to what the brand stands for and the value it promises customers.

This section lays out the practical pillars you can rely on as you build a launch plan that sticks.

Your brand's purpose is the compass for every decision, it isn't a slogan on a wall, but the reason the brand exists and the standard by which all choices are judged.

When you design packaging, select suppliers, or define features, test each one against the brand's values, mission, and vision to ensure consistency and integrity throughout the launch.

For instance, Patagonia's sourcing choices tell a clear story of environmental responsibility, while Apple's product simplicity and Nike's deep consumer insights guide where each brand invests in performance and experience.

In short, every decision should align with what the brand stands for and the promises it makes to customers.

Structured decision-processes turn the evaluation of options into a repeatable, disciplined exercise, ensuring you choose the right product at the right time and avoid costly missteps.

This consistency is especially vital when private-label launches become tighter, as a coherent, repeatable pattern shows exactly what to expect and how to make concessions without losing sight of the brand's core values.

Key Principles for Effective Decision-Making – Customer-first decisions that deliver real value.

Data-driven choices grounded in evidence, not gut feeling.

Consistency with the brand's purpose and values.

A clear, repeatable process for evaluating options and making decisions.

Benefits of this approach include product-market fit by centering customer needs and value, reduced risk through evidence-based trade-offs, and increased efficiency by standardizing how decisions are made.

**Takeaways:** tie every decision to the brand's purpose and the value offered to customers, use a structured, repeatable process to evaluate options and document reasoning, and build a decision cadence that keeps teams moving while guarding against bias.

## 6. The iterative test and learning loops

Following the public introduction of a product idea, establishing effective feedback mechanisms is crucial.

Decision-making necessitates a candid assessment, overcoming any internal or external hesitations.

Transparency and iterative experimentation are fundamental to this process.

All mistakes must be objectively appraised, acknowledging their inevitability in the development cycle.

Rather than being viewed as failures, mistakes should be treated as valuable data points for learning and improvement.

This approach establishes a consistent and effective cycle of iterative refinement.

Teams grow more resilient, and ideas mature faster when each iteration feeds new information into the next.

Adopt an iterative testing rhythm as the core of your culture, letting short feedback loops steer decisions and drive quick adjustments.

Founders who embrace this approach validate assumptions with real data, testing how customers react to packaging, claims and messaging before launching anything.

Measure results with clear metrics, accuracy of claims, conversion rates, retention, while staying within regulatory bounds, and use those numbers to inform the next cycle.

Clear metrics keep you focused on customer needs while staying within industry regulations.

Capture every insight, translate it into repeatable playbooks, and record the results so you can iterate and build lasting momentum.

Foster a culture of safety and continuous learning, like that seen at Trader Joe's and Costco, by implementing rigorous testing, setting clear expectations, and establishing a steady cadence of improvement driven by these metrics and continuous insights.

Use these data-driven lessons to guide each new cycle and keep the momentum going.

Track compliance-aware, actionable metrics aligned with regulations. Turn learning into repeatable processes and practical playbooks.

## 7. Leadership communication and stakeholder management

When you announce a private-label line, the loudest voice in the room isn't always the one you expect.

The real power lies in how clearly you communicate with the people who matter most, those who shape decisions, set quality, and determine price.

Early clarity in these conversations lights the way for the project, making it solid and focused.

Stakeholder mapping becomes a practical tool to organize the groups of interest, to see who cares, where they stand, and what they expect.

By putting each stakeholder in its proper place, you can win the will of the team and keep everyone accountable.

The outcome is smoother communications, stronger trust, and productive collaboration with suppliers, internal teams, customers, and regulators.

### Steps for Stakeholder Mapping and Prioritization

1. **Identify Stakeholders** – Include internal teams, customers, suppliers, partners, and regulatory bodies that affect or are affected by the launch.
2. **Assess Interest and Influence** – Use a stakeholder matrix to plot each stakeholder's level of interest against their influence.
3. **Prioritize Stakeholders** – Create tiers that highlight those with high interest and high influence as the top focus.
4. **Tailor Communication Strategies** – Craft tier-specific messages and touchpoints that address each group's unique needs and concerns.

### Benefits of Stakeholder Mapping and Prioritization

Improved communication: understanding what matters to each group allows messages that land with clarity.

Increased Efficiency: Concentrating effort on critical parties reduces wasted time and resources.

Enhanced Trust and Collaboration: Meaningful, timely engagement strengthens confidence and cooperative momentum.

### Practical Case – Private-Label Launch

Consider a private-label initiative, such as a product line developed in collaboration with a major retailer.

Key stakeholders typically include product development teams, category managers, quality and compliance leads, key suppliers, and regulatory contacts.

Analyzing stakeholder influence and their potential to impede or facilitate project progression enables the team to schedule reviews, align on specifications, and secure approvals without delays.

**Actionable Takeaways:**

- Build a simple stakeholder matrix for interest vs. influence.
- Group stakeholders into three tiers and assign a brief, tailored message for each.
- Schedule regular touchpoints with high-priority groups to maintain alignment.

**Key takeaway:** clear, targeted communication with the right people speeds the journey from idea to market.

## 8. Hiring, training, and building capabilities

Private label brands rarely stall at their first stirrings.

Demand grows, channels multiply, and the standards of production, quality, and character must rise in tandem.

The result is people who understand not just what to do, but why it matters.

This section outlines the hiring and training framework that supports scalable brands, with concrete roles, purposeful onboarding, and a culture of continuous learning that fuels sustainable progress.

Clear responsibilities for compliance and operations—regulatory affairs, QA, sourcing, and marketing—are essential at the heart of every scalable brand, ensuring adherence to FDA, FTC, and industry standards while maintaining brand integrity.

Quality Assurance (QA): establish and maintain quality control processes that guarantee the safety and efficacy of the product.

Sourcing: secure reliable suppliers and negotiate favorable terms that sustain supply and consistency.

Marketing: design and execute strategies that responsibly promote the brand and its products.

Onboarding New Hires with Purpose and Values: new hires join a team with a clear purpose and shared standards, illuminated by the mission, vision, and the standards that guide every decision.

Clear Communication: provide a comprehensive understanding of the brand's mission, vision, and values.

Expectation Setting: outline roles, responsibilities, and performance standards.

Training and Support: essential training and resources to enable success in their roles, including investment in GMP and regulatory training.

A solid foundation in GMP and regulatory literacy protects the brand and drives smooth performance.

The core principles demand strict quality control and assurance, while the regulatory requirements require the team to be familiar with relevant laws and industry norms.

Testing and compliance must be understood by everyone, ensuring that protocols and procedures are followed consistently.

An environment of continuous learning, structured induction, weekly training sessions, and ongoing development, keeps the team at the cutting edge of knowledge.

Equally important is leadership succession and talent building, which secures the future of the business by cultivating the best leaders and fostering a culture of excellence.

Identifying future leaders means spotting high-potential employees and nurturing them through structured development programs that build mastery and readiness.

Leadership development initiatives should cover a broad spectrum of capabilities, preparing the next generation for the challenges ahead.

Succession planning must ensure smooth, orderly transitions as the brand grows, keeping the organization stable while fostering a culture of continuous learning.

Together, these elements create a pipeline of tomorrow's leaders and secure the business's long-term success.

### 9. Ethics, purpose, and mission alignment!

In a world where every claim can be checked and every product scrutinized, the question for the brand founder is not what you sell, but what you stand for.

When the tie between purpose, ethics, and mission is never broken, trust grows, people prosper, and growth follows naturally.

A brand that is clear on all sides, what is good for you, for the world, and for every human being, becomes a responsible being that draws everyone into making responsible choices.

The building blocks of such a brand are ethics, purpose, and mission coherence, which steer product choice, branding, partnerships, and the way people become what they should be.

I need to take the leading role in every good decision that goes into any product and packaging, and it must be transparent about everything.

The products must have their uses clearly defined, and the ethics that guide their selection and packaging must also be public.

We cannot have sourcing and supply chains without being honest about them, sharing their origin and ethics in our business.

Transparency is the way of the organization, guiding all its behavior and building a shared norms system.

This helps regulators and customers, which is my goal, and it builds a common norm of accountability across the organization.

By openly revealing the ethics of the source and the suppliers, we create a brand that people can trust and feel proud of.

Third-party verification is essential for purpose-driven growth, ensuring that we meet all requirements and maintain the integrity of our brand.

## 10. My resilience playbook: routines and rituals

In those early days of bringing a private-label brand to life, the line between inspiration and fatigue blurs.

The disciplined set of daily and weekly practices becomes a steady heartbeat that preserves energy, focus, and well-being.

It's not a flourish of flair; it's a practical framework that supports execution, compliance, and clear branding.

Take a pause each day before the decisions pile up.

Set aside a few minutes for quiet reflection, a short walk, or a brief journal entry.

These moments of self-scrutiny help you see how today's choices fit into tomorrow's priorities and your long-term vision.

By keeping this rhythm, you maintain the rhythm of the brand and the rhythm of your own well-being.

Building on these moments of reflection, operationalize your focus to slow impulses, sharpen priorities, and ensure every choice moves toward defined targets.

**Steps to implement:**

List the top three of the day.

Ask: Which of the options best protects the brand's standards and regulatory commitments?

Capture a one-line aim for the day and revisit it at dusk.

### Timeboxing and Focused Work Blocks

Deep work sessions tied to launch milestones are a foundation for progress.

Timebox critical tasks, minimize interruptions, and track what moves your product from concept to shelf. Use calendars, project boards, and status dashboards to keep momentum visible.

### Practical setup:

- 2–3 deep work blocks per day, 60–90 minutes each.

Clear boundaries: no non-urgent emails during blocks.

- End-of-block review: note what moved forward, what needs attention tomorrow.
- Structured Weekly Reflection Rituals: a routine that grounds learning, celebrates wins, acknowledges losses, and recalibrates priorities.
- Core elements: evaluate progress toward goals, identify improvement areas without blame, adjust strategies for the coming week, and celebrate tangible successes, no matter the size.
- Crisis Response Drills and Playbooks: prepare for supply delays, regulatory queries, and quality concerns with drills and written playbooks. Regular rehearsals shorten response times and reduce impact when real issues arise.

How to start: identify three credible crisis scenarios, create simple, action-ready playbooks with roles, contacts, and first steps, and schedule quarterly drills to test readiness and refine processes.

### Wellbeing Integration for Sustainable Leadership

- **Sleep:** aim for 7-9 hours to support cognitive function.
- **Movement:** regular activity sustains energy and resilience.
- **Boundaries:** clear lines between work and personal time prevent burnout.

Embedding these routines daily and weekly helps founders maintain energy, sharpen decision-making, and keep momentum steady as a private-label brand moves from concept to market.

### Key takeaways:

- A daily decision pause reduces impulsive moves and aligns choices with goals.
- Timeboxing unlocks steady progress on critical launch tasks.
- A weekly reflection ritual turns experience into sharper plans.
- Crisis drills create ready-to-run responses, minimizing disruption.
- Prioritizing sleep, movement, and boundaries sustains leadership over the long run.

## 11. Conclusion and final reflections

The journey of a brand, from its nascent days to sustained success, hinges on a founder's perspective: how they perceive constraints, embrace opportunities, and empower people.

This forward-thinking mindset transforms challenges into catalysts for growth and uncertainty into unwavering resolve.

It is the enduring engine that drives innovation and sustains momentum, irrespective of market shifts or logistical hurdles.

Ultimately, a founder's vision for limits and possibilities dictates whether they stall or stride, shaping not just a product, but a legacy.

To build such a legacy, founders must forge strong, clear partnerships and cultivate a capable team network.

They must balance daring branding with rigorous regulatory discipline, always operating with integrity and an adaptive spirit.

### 12. Resource list: tools, templates, and references for private label founders

Private-label brands operate within a framework of regulations designed to protect health, ensure honest advertising, and foster fair competition.

This section outlines key regulatory areas and suggests types of external resources, tools, and templates that can support compliance, quality, and trust as brands scale.

Food Safety Modernization Act (FSMA): Resources for developing food safety plans and recall processes.

Ingredient Disclosure: Guidance on accurate labeling, including allergens and GMOs.

Good Manufacturing Practices (GMPs): Tools for monitoring processing, packaging, and storage to ensure consistent product quality.

Supplier Management: Templates for approved supplier programs, audits, and documentation.

Recall Readiness: Protocols and traceability systems for protecting consumers and brands.

Quality Control: Frameworks for robust QC processes to confirm safety and efficacy standards.

FDA Compliance Resources: Access official FDA guidance, check-lists, and templates for food safety plans, ingredient declarations, GMPs, supplier qualification, and recall plans.

FTC Compliance Resources

GMP Compliance Resources

By leveraging these resources, private labels can reduce enforcement risk, uphold consumer trust, and lay a solid foundation for growth and resilience.

The world of private label manufacturing, supplements, and cosmetics is filled with specialized terminology and regulatory language. This glossary was created to help entrepreneurs, brand owners, and formulators navigate industry jargon with confidence. From production methods to compliance standards, these terms form the foundation of successful product development and brand management.

**Active Ingredient:** The main ingredient responsible for a product's therapeutic, nutritional, or cosmetic effect.

**Batch Record (BR):** Documentation outlining the entire production process for a specific batch, including ingredients, personnel, and equipment used.

**Bioavailability:** The rate and extent to which a nutrient or active compound is absorbed and utilized by the body.

**cGMP (Current Good Manufacturing Practices):** Regulatory standards set by the FDA to ensure supplements and cosmetics are consistently produced under quality-controlled conditions.

**Certificate of Analysis (COA):** A document provided by a manufacturer or testing lab confirming a product meets its quality specifications.

**Contract Manufacturer (CM):** A third-party company that produces products on behalf of another brand under private label or white label agreements.

**DSHEA (Dietary Supplement Health and Education Act of 1994):** The U.S. law defining dietary supplements, setting labeling rules, and clarifying their distinction from drugs.

**FDA (Food and Drug Administration):** The U.S. agency that regulates food, dietary supplements, drugs, and cosmetics for safety and labeling accuracy.

**Formulation:** The precise combination of ingredients that make up a cosmetic or supplement product.

**GMP (Good Manufacturing Practices):** A quality system that ensures products are produced and controlled consistently according to set standards.

**INCI (International Nomenclature of Cosmetic Ingredients):** The standardized naming system used globally to identify cosmetic ingredients.

**Label Claims:** Statements made on product packaging that describe benefits or functions and must be substantiated by evidence.

**Lot Number:** A unique identifier assigned to a specific batch for tracking and recall purposes.

**MOQ (Minimum Order Quantity):** The smallest quantity of units a manufacturer will produce or sell in a production run.

**Private Label:** A product manufactured by one company and sold under another company's brand name.

**Quality Assurance (QA):** The process of ensuring consistent quality through documented systems, training, and audits.

**Quality Control (QC):** The physical and analytical testing performed to verify that a product meets quality standards.

**Stability Testing:** A scientific test that determines how a product maintains quality and performance over time under various storage conditions.

**Turnkey Manufacturing:** A full-service model where a manufacturer manages all stages of production — from formulation and testing to packaging and fulfillment.

**White Label:** A pre-made product that can be rebranded and sold by multiple companies with minimal customization.

# About the Author

Lorand Fabian is the founder of **Ingredientsage**, an educational platform dedicated to demystifying the worlds of **supplements, cosmetics, manufacturing, and ingredient science**. With years of hands-on experience as a **private label manufacturer**, Lorand has helped countless wellness brands turn ideas into market-ready products—while empowering founders with the knowledge to build smarter, cleaner, and more resilient companies.

Through Ingredientsage, Lorand creates **industry-level educational content** designed for two audiences:

1. **Professionals, brand owners, and entrepreneurs** seeking actionable insights on formulation, manufacturing, regulations, sourcing, and product strategy.
2. **Consumers** who want transparent, science-backed explanations of ingredients, wellness trends, and product quality—presented in an accessible, easy-to-understand format.

As the host of **The Ingredientsage Podcast**, Lorand provides deep dives into ingredient science, private label manufacturing, product development, and consumer safety. Each episode follows his signature style: cutting through industry jargon to reveal what really matters behind labels, certifications, active ingredients, and quality standards.

Listen here:
**Spotify:** https://open.spotify.com/search/ingredientsage
**Apple Podcasts:** https://podcasts.apple.com/us/podcast/ingredientsage

In addition to the podcast, Lorand publishes regular articles and deep-dive guides on the **Ingredientsage Blog**, offering educational resources for brand builders, formulators, and curious consumers:

**Blog:** https://ingredientsage.com/blog

Lorand is also active across social media, where he shares daily educational content—ranging from ingredient breakdowns and regulatory insights to prod-

uct formulation tips and brand-building strategy.
Follow his work here:

- **Instagram:** https://instagram.com/ingredientsage
- **TikTok:** https://tiktok.com/@ingredientsage
- **YouTube:** https://youtube.com/@ingredientsage
- **LinkedIn:** https://www.linkedin.com/company/ingredientsage

For readers inspired to launch or expand their own wellness brand, Ingredientsage also provides **private label manufacturing services**. Whether you need supplements, skincare, or wellness formulations, Lorand and his team can quote and manufacture products tailored to your goals.
To request a quote, simply fill out the form on the website:

**https://ingredientsage.com**

Driven by the belief that **clarity creates empowerment**, Lorand dedicates his work to bringing transparency to an often-opaque industry. His mission is simple but powerful: **to educate, elevate, and protect both the founder and the consumer—one ingredient at a time.**

www.ingramcontent.com/pod-product-compliance
Lightning Source LLC
Chambersburg PA
CBHW060402130626
46555CB00005B/1971